Programming in FORTRAN

CHAPMAN AND HALL COMPUTING SERIES

COMPUTER OPERATING SYSTEMS
For micros, minis and mainframes
2nd edition
David Barron

MICROCOMPUTER GRAPICS
Michael Batty

THE PICK OPERATING SYSTEM
Malcolm Bull

PROGRAMMING IN FORTRAN
3rd edition
V.J. Calderbank

EXPERT SYSTEMS
Principles and case studies
2nd edition
Edited by Richard Forsyth

MACHINE LEARNING
Principles and techniques
Edited by Richard Forsyth

EXPERT SYSTEMS
Knowledge, uncertainty and decision
Ian Graham and Peter Llewelyn Jones

COMPUTER GRAPHICS AND APPLICATIONS
Dennis Harris

ARTIFICIAL INTELLIGENCE AND HUMAN
LEARNING
Intelligent computer-aided instruction
Edited by John Self

ARTIFICIAL INTELLIGENCE
Principles and applications
Edited by Masoud Yazdani

Programming in FORTRAN

Third edition

V. J. Calderbank
Information Technology Division, UKAEA
Culham Laboratory

CHAPMAN AND HALL

LONDON · NEW YORK · TOKYO · MELBOURNE · MADRAS

UK   Chapman and Hall, 11 New Fetter Lane,
London EC4P 4EE

USA   Chapman and Hall, 29 West 35th Street,
New York NY10001

JAPAN   Chapman and Hall Japan, Thomson Publishing Japan,
Hirakawacho Nemoto Building, 7F, 1-7-11 Hirakawa-cho,
Chiyoda-ku, Tokyo 102

AUSTRALIA   Chapman and Hall Australia, Thomas Nelson Australia,
480 La Trobe Street, PO Box 4725, Melbourne 3000

INDIA   Chapman and Hall India, R. Sheshadri, 32 Second Main
Road, CIT East, Madras 600 035

First edition 1969
Second edition 1983
Third edition 1989
Reprinted 1990

© 1969, 1983, 1989 V. J. Calderbank

Typeset in 10/12 Times by
Colset Private Ltd, Singapore
Printed in Great Britain by
T. J. Press Ltd, Padstow, Cornwall

ISBN 0 412 30500 3 (HB)
0 412 30510 0 (PB)

British Library Cataloguing in Publication Data

Calderbank, Valerie J. (Valerie Joyce), *1944–*
   Programming for FORTRAN. — 3rd ed.
   1. Computer systems. Programming languages
   : FORTRAN 77 language
I. Title II. Calderbank, Valerie J.
   (Valerie Joyce), *1944–*. Course on
   programming on FORTRAN
   005.13'3

Library of Congress Cataloging in Publication Data

Calderbank, Valerie Joyce.
   Programming in FORTRAN / V.J. Calderbank. — 3rd ed.
     p. cm.
   Rev.ed.of: A course on programming in FORTRAN. 2nd ed,
   rev. to incorporate FORTRAN 77. c1983.
     Includes index.
     ISBN 0–412–30500–3. ISBN 0–412–30510–0 (pbk.)
     1. FORTRAN (Computer program language) I. Calderbank,
   Valerie Joyce. Course on programming in FORTRAN. II. Title.
   QA76.73.F25C35 1989
   005.13'3—dc19   88–25964
                                           CIP

Contents

Preface   ix

1 Fundamentals   1

  1.1   Basic computer concepts   1
  1.2   Algorithms   3
  1.3   Structured design   6
  1.4   The FORTRAN language   8
  1.5   Layout of FORTRAN programs   10
  1.6   The PROGRAM and END statements   13
  1.7   Statement classification   14
  1.8   Variables and constants   15
  1.9   Internal representation   19
  1.10 Summary   22
Exercises 1   22

2 Construction of a simple FORTRAN program   24

  2.1   Sequences   24
  2.2   Simple input and output statements   24
  2.3   Arithmetic expressions   29
  2.4   Arithmetic assignment statements   33
  2.5   The STOP statement   36
  2.6   Compiling and running your program   36
  2.7   Intrinsic functions   37
  2.8   Summary   39
Exercises 2   40

3 Selections and other control statements   43

  3.1   Introduction   43
  3.2   The block-IF statement   43
  3.3   Logical expressions   47
  3.4   The logical IF statement   51

3.5   The GOTO statement   51
3.6   The arithmetic IF statement   54
3.7   The computed GOTO statement   55
3.8   The assigned GOTO statement   56
3.9   Summary   56
Exercises 3   57

4 Repetitions and arrays   59

4.1   Introduction   59
4.2   The DO statement   60
4.3   The CONTINUE statement   64
4.4   Conditional loops   65
4.5   Nested loops   66
4.6   Arrays and subscripts   69
4.7   Dimensioning arrays   70
4.8   The DIMENSION statement   76
4.9   A sorting program   76
4.10 Summary   77
Exercises 4   78

5 Types   80

5.1   Introduction   80
5.2   Type statements   80
5.3   Character type   82
5.4   Double precision type   90
5.5   Complex type   92
5.6   Logical type   93
5.7   The IMPLICIT statement   95
5.8   The PARAMETER statement   96
5.9   The DATA statement   97
5.10 Mixed mode arithmetic   99
5.11 Binary, octal and hexadecimal types   101
5.12 Summary   101
Exercises 5   102

6 Formatted I/O   104

6.1   Introduction   104
6.2   The FORMAT statement   108
6.3   The I/O list   109
6.4   Repetition factors   113
6.5   The implied DO statement   115

6.6   Format specifications   116
6.7   Scale factors   127
6.8   Run-time format statements   128
6.9   STOP and PAUSE   129
6.10 Summary   130
Exercises 6   131

7 Files   133

7.1   Introduction   133
7.2   Control information specifiers REC, ERR, END and IOSTAT   134
7.3   OPEN and CLOSE   136
7.4   INQUIRE   139
7.5   Internal files   142
7.6   The ENDFILE statement   145
7.7   BACKSPACE and REWIND   145
7.8   Summary   148
Exercises 7   149

8 Functions and subroutines   151

8.1   Introduction   151
8.2   The main program and the PROGRAM statement   152
8.3   Statement ordering   153
8.4   Intrinsic functions and the INTRINSIC statement   154
8.5   The statement function   155
8.6   The FUNCTION subprogram and RETURN   157
8.7   The SUBROUTINE subprogram and the CALL statement   161
8.8   The EXTERNAL statement   165
8.9   Adjustable dimensions   167
8.10 Multiple entry and return points   170
8.11 Summary   173
Exercises 8   174

9 The organization of store   176

9.1   Introduction   176
9.2   Blank COMMON   178
9.3   Named COMMON   182
9.4   The BLOCK DATA subprogram   184
9.5   The SAVE statement   185
9.6   The EQUIVALENCE statement   187
9.7   Summary   189
Exercises 9   190

Conclusion   192

Appendix A: Intrinsic functions   194

Appendix B: Common character codes   198

Solutions to exercises   200

Index   231

Preface

During the eighteen years since this book was first published the success of FORTRAN as a programming language has continued unabated. The language was first standardized in 1966 by the American National Standards Institute (ANSI) and this definition of the language was, by and large, the subject of the first edition of the book. In 1977 the ANSI committee published a revised standard definition of the language which became known as ANSI 77 FORTRAN or simply FORTRAN 77 (see ANSI X3.9, 1978 for a description of this). The second edition of this book was published at a time when there was widespread interest in this language, but compilers for it were not universally available. This edition therefore acted as a transition book and described both FORTRAN 66 and FORTRAN 77 side by side. There is now no doubt that almost all FORTRAN programmers today program in FORTRAN 77, and interest in the old standard has largely died out. In fact, the FORTRAN community is now looking forward to the finalization of the ANSI standard for FORTRAN 8x which should appear in the next year. Many new facilities are being added to the 8x standard and many features of the old FORTRAN will be deprecated or become obsolete.

It is with all this in mind that this third edition has been written. First, it seeks to teach FORTRAN 77 from scratch without reference to FORTRAN 66, and therefore topics are introduced in a somewhat different order from the way they were handled in the second edition. Second, it tries to push into the background features of FORTRAN 77 which are undesirable, partly with the intention of encouraging better programming techniques and partly with an eye to the new 8x standard. Third, it tries to encourage the use of structured programming techniques in the hope of fostering improved software standards, particularly among the increasing army of D.I.Y. programmers who are not computer professionals, but who nevertheless spend many man-days programming personal computers or scientific workstations. It is for my readers to determine whether I have succeeded in my aims.

I have many people to thank for help in the production of various editions of this book. My special thanks must always go to Professor E. J. Burge, Head of the Physics Department of Chelsea College, London, for giving me the courage to write the first edition. Special thanks also to my family for enabling me to spend the hours which are inevitably necessary in the production of a book of this kind. Thanks, of course, must go to the numerous scientific colleagues, university lecturers, students and critics who have contributed to what I hope is a FORTRAN text which has gradually improved over the years. Last, but not least, I must thank my publishers (Chapman and Hall) for their continuing confidence in me and for the many hours of work which they have put into all three editions.

V. J. Calderbank
Information Technology Division
Culham Laboratory
1988

1

Fundamentals

1.1 Basic computer concepts

The purpose of this book is to teach the reader to program a computer in the FORTRAN programming language. It is not intended to discuss the way in which a modern computer is constructed or operated. However, some knowledge of the way a computer works is required before any attempt can be made to program it, and therefore a brief introduction is given here.

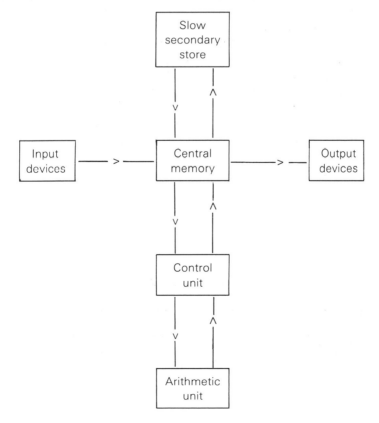

FIG. 1.1 A schematic diagram of a typical computer system

Computer architecture can vary greatly in detailed design but the basic principle of most systems may be represented by the diagram in Fig. 1.1. Instructions or data are entered into the computer via an *input device* and stored in the central *memory*. The basic unit of memory is the *binary digit* (or bit). For convenience, bits are grouped together in larger units called *bytes* (typically 8 bits) and *words* (which are different sizes on different computers but may typically be 8, 16, 32, 48 or 64 bits). Note that a computer word is a collection of binary digits and as such is very different from a natural language word which is a collection of characters. Natural language words may be stored in computer words, however, using a numerical code to represent each character.

The position of a word or byte in computer memory is known as its *address*. To clarify this with an everyday analogy, think of a computer's memory as a chest of drawers where each drawer is divided into, say, 16 compartments across its width. This is shown in the diagram of Fig. 1.2. Imagine that each drawer is equivalent to a computer word and each compartment is equivalent to a computer bit; then this chest of drawers represents a 16 bit word memory (each of which may contain two 8 bit bytes).

If we number the drawers from 0 to 5 starting from the top, then the third drawer down is at address 2, the fourth at address 3 and so on (this numbering is chosen because computer memory is often addressed from 0 upwards). Within the drawer, the compartments themselves are numbered from 0 to 15, starting from the right. This is equivalent to bit 0, bit 1 and so on in the computer word.

Let us suppose that any compartment in this drawer is allowed to contain either one item or nothing at all. Then this is analogous to a computer bit

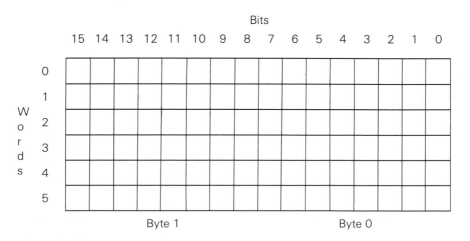

FIG. 1.2 A schematic representation of computer memory

which can hold the value 1 or 0 (often represented electronically by a current being on or off).

All information, whether instructions or data, is held in the computer's memory in this way. Groups of binary digits can represent larger numbers, or characters held in a coded numerical form. For example, one bit can only hold the value 0 or 1, but two bits can represent 00, 01, 10 or 11 (this will be described more fully when internal representation is discussed later).

Once data has been entered and stored in the computer's memory, it may be required to perform calculations on it. To do this, the data must be moved from memory locations, along a data highway or *high-speed bus* to the *arithmetic unit* which contains one or more accumulators or high-speed working *registers*. Very fast computations may be carried out in these registers and the results returned to memory along the bus. Computers vary in the number of bits of information that can be carried along the bus in one operation and in the number that can be held in the registers, e.g. there may be an 8 bit bus and 16 bit registers; this basic architecture obviously affects the speed of the machine.

Instructions to move data and perform calculations on it are held in the memory in the form of a *program* and it is the *control unit* which controls and interprets these instructions. It is able to access instructions stored sequentially in the memory, decode them and initiate the appropriate action. The arithmetic unit, control unit, registers and central memory together form the *central processor unit (CPU)*. To this are connected *input/output* devices such as *visual display units, teletypes and lineprinters*, and storage devices (such as magnetic tapes, discs and drums) known as *secondary store* or backing store. All of these devices are collectively known as *peripherals*.

A typical modern scientific computer installation will provide a variety of peripherals such as on-line terminals (teletypes and visual display units) for both input and output, magnetic tapes, discs, drums, cassettes and cartridges for storing programs and data, and output devices such as lineprinters and graph plotters.

1.2 Algorithms

The CPU of any computer contains logic circuits which can themselves perform simple basic instructions such as addition, subtraction, multiplication, division and so on. Thus a circuit may take as its input two 16 bit numbers, say, and produce, by means of logic gates, one output which is the sum of these two. More complex operations are performed by breaking them down into logical sequences of these basic operations. So just as it is possible to build a palace from a few basic ingredients such as bricks and mortar, so it is possible to solve enormously complex problems using the basic instruction set of a computer. But just as the architect has to provide instructions and blueprints from which the palace can be built, so must the programmer provide instructions and diagrams from which a program can be written to solve a particular problem. In computing and mathematics, a prescription for solving a problem is generally called an *algorithm* whether or not it ultimately will become a computer program.

There are many everyday examples of algorithms; a recipe for making a cake is a set of instructions which when obeyed in sequence result in a cake. Thus the recipe is an algorithm for performing this task. Another example may be a list of directions to reach your home from your place of work, e.g. turn left at the main exit, drive straight on for 2 miles, at the next T junction turn right and so on. You may give these written instructions to any number of colleagues, and if they are clear and unambiguous then they should all ultimately arrive at your home. On the other hand, if they are ambiguous or incorrect then your colleagues will lose their way or perhaps spend hours driving around in circles. So it is with algorithms for computer programs. A computer will obey, in a moronic way, the exact instructions that it is given. This may result in the wrong answer or in the CPU looping for perhaps hours.

Let us consider algorithms in a little more detail by returning to the analogy of a chest of drawers introduced in the previous section. Suppose that the first drawer contains one knife, the second drawer contains one fork and the third drawer contains one spoon in each compartment, then the instructions to lay one place setting on a table may be as follows:

Open drawer 0
Take a knife from compartment 0
Close drawer 0
Open drawer 1
Take a fork from compartment 0
Close drawer 1
Open drawer 2
Take a spoon from compartment 0
Close drawer 2
Go to the table
Lay one knife, one fork and one spoon on the table

This algorithm may be repeated three more times to lay four place settings but each time taking the knives, forks and spoons from a different compartment, i.e. 1, 2 and 3.

So this is an algorithm, but not one which can be directly converted into a computer program. Consider now a more numerical algorithm to add two numbers and print the result. This might read as follows:

Read the first number
Read the second number
Add the two numbers together
Print the result

This is obviously a simple but limited task that a computer could perform and we shall see later how this becomes a FORTRAN program. It consists of a sequence of four basic instructions and that is all. A slightly more powerful algorithm might sum the squares of N numbers and print the result as follows:

Read N
Set the 'sum so far' to zero
Repeat the following N times:
     Read a number
     Square it
     Add the result to the 'sum so far'

This algorithm spells out, in an English-like language, the primitive steps which have to be performed to sum the squares of N numbers. It consists of two basic constructs – elementary operations or commands which must be obeyed in sequence (e.g. Square it, Add the result to the 'sum so far'), and repetitions which require a group of instructions to be performed repeatedly, usually not for evermore, but until some condition becomes true (in this case, until they have been obeyed N times).

It can be seen from this that algorithms can be written in a type of English regardless of whether they are to be subsequently written as actual programs for a machine to obey or not. Here we must make one of the first important statements about how to write a computer program. Spend a long time designing your algorithm before you make any attempt to program it. There is a widely held view that the sooner you actually start programming, the longer the program will take to develop.

Many programs do not work because the algorithms do not work in the first place, just as your colleagues will get lost if you give them wrong directions. Only when you are sure that your design is right should you tackle the separate problem of coding this in a computer language for input to a computer.

So, to summarize, a computer is able to produce a solution to a particular problem only if it is presented with a series of simple instructions which will, when obeyed in a specific order, produce the desired result. This sequence of instructions is referred to as a program; programs are collectively termed *computer software* in contrast to the actual physical devices which collectively form the *hardware*. The instructions which form a program are loaded into the computer's memory in an encoded form and the control unit works sequentially through the instructions, decoding and obeying them. In so doing, it may use data stored at other locations in memory.

1.3 Structured design

The algorithms in the preceding section illustrate the use of two important elements in program design – sequences of elementary operations and repetitions. A third important construct for writing algorithms is the selection. Suppose we wish to calculate the income tax payable on a number of salaries in the range £1 to £20 000. Suppose tax is to be calculated at a rate of 25% on the first £750, 30% on the next £5000 and 45% on the remainder. Let us suppose that the calculation is to end when a salary is found which is not in the above range.

We shall approach the design of this algorithm using *top–down design*. That is, first of all we state the overall aim of the program which may be represented by:

Calculate and print income taxes

We now break this down a bit further by defining the process 'calculate and print income taxes'; this is a repetition of 'calculate tax' and 'print tax' which in turn are defined as follows:

Read salary
If the salary is between £1 and £20 000 then
    Calculate tax
    Print tax
else
    ∗∗∗Error – invalid salary
end if

The process 'calculate tax' may be further broken down into its basic tasks as follows:

Calculate tax at 25% on the first £750
If the salary is greater than £750 then
    Calculate tax at 30% on the next £5000
    If the salary is greater than £5750 then
        Calculate tax on the remainder at 45%
    end if
end if

This example provides several illustrations of the selection which is of the form 'If this is true then do the following' and may or may not have an alternative clause 'else do the following'. The end of each 'if' clause is marked by a corresponding 'end if' for clarity.

These then are the basic logical elements which may be combined to form an algorithm – *sequences*, *selections* and *repetitions* (also called *loops* or *iterations*). Using these and top–down analysis, large and complicated programs may be broken down into small manageable tasks, each of which may be designed, coded and tested out as a separate component of the whole structure. Always remember that a large problem is simply a collection of smaller problems and should be treated as such. Isolate, solve and test each component of the problem separately before assembling the whole.

A useful additional aid to design is to represent the algorithm in a diagrammatic form known as a *Structure Diagram*. In such a diagram, sequences of basic instructions (e.g. Read a number, Square it) are represented by rectangular boxes; selections (or alternatives) are represented by a circle in a rectangular box; repetitions are represented by an asterisk in a rectangular box as follows:

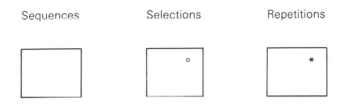

Sequences   Selections   Repetitions

Using such a diagrammatic representation, the earlier algorithm to sum the squares of N numbers might be defined as shown in Fig. 1.3. More examples will be given throughout this book and the student is advised either to draw structure diagrams or to write structural specifications for all of the programming exercises. As an exercise, try drawing a structure diagram for the algorithm to calculate taxes given at the beginning of this section. There is no scope here to discuss good program design at any greater length but the interested reader is recommended to study the book *Principles of Program Design* by Michael Jackson to learn more about the subject.

Note that it is good practice to design algorithms at the outset to handle possible failure conditions which may result from reading erroneous data for example. Only too often this aspect of programming is ignored at the early stages and patched in as an afterthought later. Such programs are often badly structured and incomplete in their handling of errors. The whole area of error treatment is known as *exception handling* and some computer languages provide special features for dealing with errors. Whilst FORTRAN only does this to a limited extent, it is still good practice to design algorithms which include the explicit handling of error conditions and subsequently these can be converted into suitable FORTRAN statements. It can be seen in Fig. 1.3 that the process 'Read number' breaks down into the selection 'Read valid number' or 'Error' which automatically detects and processes an error as soon as an attempt is made to read a data item which is something other than a valid number.

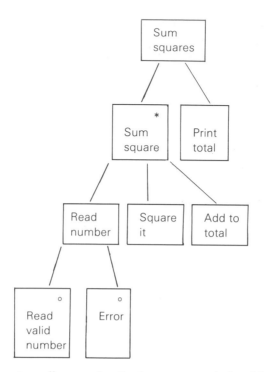

FIG. 1.3 A structure diagram for the 'sum squares' algorithm

1.4 The FORTRAN language

Once an algorithm has been designed and the corresponding structural spe-cification written and verified, the quite separate problem of producing the program which corresponds to this must be addressed, i.e. a sequence of instructions must be written in a language which the computer can under-stand. Any computer is constructed in such a way that it can fundamentally understand only one language – the *machine language* of that computer. Since programming in this basic machine language is a tedious and error-prone process, a multitude of so-called *high-level* languages have been designed to ease the programmer's task. A program written in such a language cannot be directly understood by the computer – it must be translated from the high-level language into the machine language of the computer. This task is performed by a program resident in the computer and known as the *compiler* (or *translator*). The compiler takes a *source* program in the high-level language and produces a logically equivalent *object* program in the machine code. This process is known as compiling the program. Once compiled, the resulting sequence of machine code instructions is stored in an encoded form in computer memory waiting to be decoded and obeyed.

This is known as *running* or *executing* the program. From this it can be appreciated that any program written in a high-level language cannot be run on a computer which does not have a compiler for that particular language or version of that language.

This book describes the grammatical rules for writing programs in FORTRAN. The FORTRAN project was started in the early 1950s and it produced a high-level language for scientific use on IBM computers (the name FORTRAN in fact stands for FORmula TRANslation). It was designed at a time when programs and data were read into computers on punched cards and this early influence is still present in the language today. Since that time it has become one of the world's most widely used scientific languages and almost all computer manufacturers provide a compiler for it. This in itself presents a problem, for although the language is in widespread use, there was for some time no universally recognized definition of it. The version of FORTRAN recognized by one compiler could be quite different from that recognized by another. To remedy this, the American National Standards Institute (ANSI) produced a definition of FORTRAN in 1966 and all manufacturers were encouraged to provide compilers which conformed to this standard. The result of this, it was argued, would be an improvement in program portability, i.e. a FORTRAN program written for one computer to the *ANSI 66* standard should run with little or no modification on any other computer with an ANSI FORTRAN compiler. However, so many FORTRAN compilers produced by manufacturers provided enhancements to the ANSI definition of the language that many programmers still produced non-portable programs.

In 1977, the ANSI committee produced an upgraded definition of the language widely known as *ANSI 77 FORTRAN* or *FORTRAN 77*. This incorporated many of the widely used enhancements to FORTRAN provided by manufacturers but by no means all. The second edition of this book described both the ANSI 66 and ANSI 77 definitions of FORTRAN side by side and was intended to aid programmers in converting from one standard to the other. This edition teaches FORTRAN 77 as a new language in its own right since it is now the most widely used version of FORTRAN. So whenever the term FORTRAN is used in this book it should be taken to mean ANSI 77 FORTRAN.

There are many advantages to using FORTRAN 77 (as opposed to earlier versions of the language) since it provides better building blocks to enable correct, well-structured programs to be written; it has a more powerful input and output system which on the one hand enables beginners to write more simple programs, and on the other hand provides more power to the advanced programmer; and it provides extra features such as character handling which are essential in text processing applications and were not available before. For this reason, FORTRAN can no longer be described as a purely scientific language and may be used in commercial and systems programming applications. Examples in this book therefore will try to cater for all types of user although, on balance, may still tend to favour the scientist, engineer or mathematician.

The following is a small FORTRAN program to sum two integer numbers and it illustrates many points about the language:

```
      PROGRAM SUM2
*
* A FORTRAN program to sum two numbers
*
      READ *,NUM1,NUM2
      NUM3 = NUM1 + NUM2
      PRINT *,NUM3,' is the sum of ',NUM1,' and ',NUM2
      STOP
      END
```

We must now describe some of the basic concepts of the FORTRAN language so that this simple program may be understood fully, thus enabling you to write similar simple programs yourself.

1.5 Layout of FORTRAN programs

The first thing to notice about the above example program is the way it is typed and laid out. Historically, FORTRAN is a card-oriented language and this early influence is still apparent in the language today. The statements of FORTRAN programs are typed on 80 character lines, one statement per line. Each character position on the line is called a column; this derives from early nomenclature when FORTRAN statements were typed on 80-column punched cards. Columns are numbered from left to right starting with column 1.

Lines are divided into four distinct regions – columns 1 to 5, column 6, columns 7 to 72, and columns 73 to 80. FORTRAN statements may be typed in region 3, i.e. columns 7 to 72 only, but may be positioned anywhere within that region. In general, spaces or blanks are ignored in FORTRAN statements and may be used to improve readability.

Region 1 is reserved for labels. Any FORTRAN statement may be labelled with a numeric label of 1 to 5 decimal digits which may be positioned anywhere within columns 1 to 5 of the line.

Region 4, i.e. columns 73 to 80 of the line, are ignored by the compiler and may be used for any purpose. In the heyday of punched cards this region was often used to number the statements of the program in order, so that if a deck of cards were dropped the program could be re-assembled easily in correct order. You may still use this region to number your statements or for any other comment if you wish. More often than not this region is not used.

Region 2 (i.e. column 6) is used to indicate continuation lines. Long statements, which will not fit onto one line, may be typed across several lines by specifying a continuation character in column 6 on every line except the first.

```
****************************************************************************
*                                                                          *
*                        PROGRAM SUMSQR                                    *
*                                                                          *
*  A program to sum the squares of N numbers where N lies between 1 and 1000 *
*                                                                          *
****************************************************************************
        PROGRAM SUMSQR                                             010
        PRINT *,'Enter N:                                          020
        READ *,N                                                  030
        IF ((N .GT. 0) .AND. (N .LE. 1000)) THEN                  040
           ISUM=0                                                 050
           DO 10, I = 1,N                                         060
              READ (*,ERR = 20)NUM                                070
   10         ISUM = ISUM + NUM**2                                080
           PRINT *,'The sum of the squares of ',N,                090
      1             ' numbers is',ISUM                            100
        ELSE                                                      110
              PRINT *,'***Error - invalid value of N ',N          120
        END IF                                                    130
        STOP                                                      140
   20   PRINT *,'***Error - attempt to read invalid number ',NUM  150
        STOP                                                      160
        END                                                       170
```

FIG. 1.4 A FORTRAN program to sum the squares of N numbers

Many of these features of FORTRAN are not shown in the simple example on page 10, but further illustration can be found in Figs 1.4 and 1.5. Figure 1.4 is the FORTRAN program corresponding to the structure diagram given in Fig. 1.3; Fig. 1.5 is the FORTRAN program corresponding to the structural specification of the income tax program given in section 1.3.

An example of a long statement can be seen in Fig. 1.4 at lines 90 and 100. These two lines form one FORTRAN **PRINT** statement; the second line is marked by the use of the continuation character 1 in column 6. A continuation character may be any character except space or zero. Popular conventions adopted for continuation lines include using the numbers 1, 2, 3, etc. for each successive continuation line of the statement; alternatively, a character such as a $, which is not used for anything else in a FORTRAN program and therefore stands out from the rest of the text, may be used. Whatever the convention adopted, the standard definition of FORTRAN does not allow more than 19 continuation lines for any one statement (although in practice, compilers may produce errors for less than that number). Statements may be split at any reasonable point and do not have to extend up to column 72 before they are continued. Columns 1 to 5 of a continuation line must be blank. Note also that the first line of the statement may only have a space or zero in column 6.

Comment lines may appear anywhere in a FORTRAN program and are totally ignored by the compiler. They are indicated by an asterisk (*) or a C in column 1 and the whole of the rest of the line (columns 2 to 80) may be used for explanatory comment. A comment line may contain any character which is capable of representation in the computer and not just those characters

```
*******************************************************************************
*                                                                             *
*                          PROGRAM INCTAX                                     *
*                                                                             *
* A program to calculate the income tax payable on a set of salaries at a     *
* rate of 25% on the first £750, 30% on the next £5000 and 45% on the         *
* remainder. The program first reads the number of salaries.                  *
*                                                                             *
*******************************************************************************
        PROGRAM INCTAX                                                      010
        PRINT *,'Enter the number of salaries:'                            020
        READ *,N                                                          030
        DO 10, I = 1,N                                                     040
           PRINT *,'Enter salary:'                                        050
           READ *,SALARY                                                   060
           IF ((SALARY .GE. 1.0) .AND. (SALARY .LE. 20000.0)) THEN         070
              IF (SALARY .LE. 750.0)THEN                                  080
                 TAX = SALARY / 4.0                                       090
              ELSE                                                         100
                 TAX = 750.0 / 4.0                                        110
                 REM = SALARY - 750.0                                     120
                 IF (REM .LE. 5000.0)THEN                                 130
                    TAX = TAX + (REM * 0.3)                               140
                 ELSE                                                      150
                    TAX = TAX + (5000.0 * 0.3)                            160
                    REM = REM - 5000.0                                    170
                    TAX = TAX + (0.45 * REM)                              180
                 END IF                                                    190
              END IF                                                       200
              PRINT *,'The tax payable on salary ',SALARY,' is ',TAX      210
           ELSE                                                            220
              PRINT *,'***Error - invalid salary ',SALARY                 230
           END IF                                                          240
     10 CONTINUE                                                           250
        STOP                                                               260
        END                                                               270
```

FIG. 1.5 A FORTRAN program to calculate income taxes

which form the FORTRAN character set. Lines which are completely blank from columns 1 to 72 (or 80) are also accepted as valid comment lines by some compilers but are not standard. The liberal use of the comment facility improves program readability and is to be encouraged. More hints on writing good FORTRAN programs are given throughout the book and in the Conclusion.

So let us look in a little more detail at the layout of the program in Fig. 1.4. The first 7 lines are comments which mark the start of the program, give its name and describe its function briefly. The comment lines begin with an asterisk in column 1 and, in this example, extend across the full 80 column width of the line. They are completely ignored by the compiler and do not in any way form part of the compiled machine code program.

The program proper starts with the **PROGRAM** statement at line 10 and the text of the program ends with the **END** statement at line 170. Note that, because these are FORTRAN statements, they must not begin before column 7 and must not extend beyond column 72. The statements are numbered in column 73 onwards so that they may be easily referenced from this text. This numbering is optional.

Note that the statements at line 80 and line 150 are labelled with the integer numbers 10 and 20 which may be placed anywhere in columns 1 to 5. The use of these will be explained later.

Since FORTRAN is a language, like any other language it must have an alphabet in which it can be written and typed. This consists of:

1. The decimal digits 0 to 9
2. The upper case letters A to Z
3. The arithmetic operators $+ - * /$
4. Left and right parentheses ( )
5. Equals $=$
6. Comma , and decimal point .
7. Apostrophe ' and colon :
8. The currency symbol $ (sometimes £)
9. Space or blank

(In this book the terms space and blank are used synonymously.)

The decimal digits and letters together are known as the alphanumeric characters.

All other characters are collectively known as the non-alphanumeric characters.

Note that although the currency symbol $ forms part of the character set, rules are not given in the standard about how it should be used.

All FORTRAN program statements must be written in upper case. This is an unfortunate restriction to the language which now lags behind most computer technology almost all of which caters for both upper and lower case letters. The exceptions to this strictly upper case rule are that comments may be written in both upper and lower case as may character strings, which will be described later, but which here are used in statements 20, 50, 210 and 230 of Fig. 1.5 to print messages on the output device.

These rules for the layout of lines apply only to FORTRAN statements in programs. They do not apply to the layout of data for the program. As we shall see later, this is under the control of the programmer who has all 80 columns available for this purpose.

1.6 The PROGRAM and END statements

From the FORTRAN program examples given in the previous section, it can be seen that they all consist of a sequence of FORTRAN statements commencing with a **PROGRAM** statement and ending with an **END** statement. The **PROGRAM** statement is of the form

PROGRAM *name*

where *name* may be any valid FORTRAN symbolic name. FORTRAN symbolic names are invented by the programmer and are used for a variety of purposes within a program – one purpose being the name of the program itself. Symbolic names may be made up of any sequence of capital letters and decimal digits but must begin with a letter. They may not contain any character other than a letter or a digit and there may not be more than six characters in all. This limitation of six characters to a name is another unfortunate restriction of FORTRAN and makes it more difficult for programmers to write readable programs. Some compilers remove this restriction and allow longer names to be used but, since this is not a standard feature, programs which take advantage of this are liable to be non-portable (i.e. they will not necessarily compile and run on all machines).

The following are all examples of valid program names:

SUMSQR
INCTAX
ROOT1
P2D2

but the following are not:

2DCODE	(does not begin with a letter)
INCOMETAX	(contains more than six characters)
SUM_SQUARES	(contains more than six characters and a character which is neither a letter nor a digit)
Roots	(contains lower case letters)

The **PROGRAM** statement is an entirely optional statement – it need not be present at all. This is largely for historical reasons since it did not form part of the ANSI 66 standard and one of the aims of FORTRAN 77 is that it should be upwards compatible, i.e. valid FORTRAN 66 programs should also be valid FORTRAN 77 programs.

The **END** statement marks the textual end of the program and as such is always physically the last statement. It simply consists of the word **END** typed anywhere in columns 7 to 72 of the line.

1.7 Statement classification

The **PROGRAM** and **END** statements are examples of non-executable statements. All statements in FORTRAN may be broadly classified into two types – executable and non-executable and it is very important to understand the difference between these two.

Executable statements are translated by the compiler directly into equivalent machine code instructions. In other words, if you were to obtain a printed listing of the machine code program produced by the compiler you would find groups of machine code instructions which corresponded directly to all the executable statements in the FORTRAN source program. These instructions are of course directly obeyed by the control unit and actually cause the computer to do something.

Non-executable statements on the other hand, do not form part of the machine code program. They exist mainly to provide the compiler with information it requires to translate the program into machine code or to provide help to users of the program. These statements do not exist when the program is actually executed. The **PROGRAM** statement is an example of this. Comments are also non-executable statements; these are completely ignored by the compiler and exist only as a program documentation aid.

Execution of a program always commences at the first executable FORTRAN statement, i.e. at the statement immediately following the **PROGRAM** statement in this case. Therefore in Figs 1.4 and 1.5, execution of the programs actually starts at line 20 in both cases.

1.8 Variables and constants

In section 1.2 we described an algorithm to lay a table from the contents of a chest of drawers. We likened a chest of drawers to a computer memory which was addressed numerically from 0 upwards.

In high-level programming languages such as FORTRAN one never addresses locations in memory by referring directly to numerical addresses. To do this would be tedious and error prone. Instead FORTRAN allows the programmer to invent symbolic names for locations in memory and the compiler allocates memory locations to each name, keeping a record (in a dictionary or symbol table) of which symbolic names refer to which memory locations.

Returning to our chest of drawers analogy, let us suppose that the drawers are painted in the following colours from the top down:

```
0    WHITE
1    RED
2    BLUE
3    GREEN
4    PINK
5    BLACK
```

Then the algorithm to lay the table could equally well be written:

```
Open the WHITE drawer
Take a knife from compartment 0
Close the WHITE drawer
Open the RED drawer
Take a fork from compartment 0
Close the RED drawer
```

Open the BLUE drawer
Take a spoon from compartment 0
Close the BLUE drawer
Go to the table
Lay one knife, one fork and one spoon on the table

Here the names WHITE, RED and BLUE are being used as symbolic names to address the drawers rather than the numerical addresses based on the positions of the drawers in the chest. WHITE is address 0, RED is address 1 and BLUE is address 2.

In a similar way, FORTRAN symbolic names may be used to refer to distinct locations in computer memory. The rules for forming symbolic names have already been given in section 1.6 when the **PROGRAM** statement was described, i.e. a name must begin with a capital letter and may be optionally followed by up to five more capital letters or digits. The FORTRAN compiler will allocate addresses to each symbolic name and substitute these whenever the names are used in the program.

So in our FORTRAN program to sum two numbers, we wish to read the numbers into the computer memory locations with the symbolic names **NUM1** and **NUM2**. We then wish to add the contents of these two locations together and put the result in the location whose symbolic name is **NUM3** (note that we do not know where in the computer memory these locations are; they need not necessarily be together).

Now, suppose that as part of a FORTRAN program we wish to evaluate the expression $y = 4x + 1$. Then an algorithm to do this might read as follows:

Read the value of x into the named location X
Multiply the contents of location X by 4
Add 1 to the contents of location X
Move the final result to location Y

In this algorithm we refer not only to named locations which are variables (i.e. memory locations in the computer whose contents are liable to change such as X and Y) but also to constants (4 and 1). These two basic components – constants and variables, form the elementary ingredients of many FORTRAN statements.

All computers work, in principle, by obeying the instructions of a program stored at a particular address in memory. These instructions operate on data stored (either as variables or constants) in other locations in memory. Many different types of data may be stored in a computer's memory and each may require a different unit of store, e.g. a word, several words, a bit or a byte.

FORTRAN allows six basic data types – integer, real, double precision, complex, character and logical. A more detailed discussion of types is given in Chapter 5 but for simplicity we shall consider only the numeric types, real and integer, at this stage.

FORTRAN numeric constants or variables may be either integer numbers (which have an exact value) or real numbers (which have a fractional part). Integer constants are represented within FORTRAN statements as a sequence of decimal digits without a decimal point and may be preceded optionally by a + or − sign, e.g. 50, −25 and +3 are all valid FORTRAN constants. Unsigned constants are assumed to be positive.

Neither decimal points nor commas are permitted in integer constants. Spaces within constants are allowed and are ignored by the compiler. Leading zeros may be specified, e.g. 059 and 59 are both valid and have the same value as do 75 43 and 7543.

The following are all examples of valid integer constants:

237   −82   +1   000   0028   −0   +0

but these are not:

23.0   (decimal point not allowed)
−3,500   (comma not allowed)

There are numerous examples of the use of integer constants in Fig. 1.4, e.g. statement 40 uses the integer constants 0 and 1000, statement 50 uses the integer constant 0 and so on.

A real constant in a FORTRAN program consists of an integer part followed by a decimal point followed by a fractional part, in that order. The constant may be preceded by an optional sign. Both the integer and fractional parts are sequences of decimal digits either of which may be omitted but not both. Examples of valid real constants are:

2.163   +0.   −.59   +28.   −101.35

A real constant may be followed by an optional exponent which is the letter E (or e) followed by a signed or unsigned integer constant. The exponent represents the power of 10 by which the real constant mantissa is to be multiplied. For example 25.63E1 represents the number 256.3 (i.e. the number is multiplied by 10 which effectively moves the decimal point one position to the right). The mantissa is 25.63 and the exponent is E1. Similarly 25.63E − 1 represents the number 2.563 (i.e. the number is divided by 10 which effectively moves the decimal point one position to the left).

Valid real constants with exponents are

−59.e − 2   (representing the value −0.59)
.002163E3   (representing the value 2.163)
+0.00028E + 5   (representing the value 28.0)
−10135E − 2   (representing the value −101.35)

The following are not valid:

2,163.2   (commas not allowed)
59   (no decimal point so this is an integer constant)
.59e2.5   (exponent not an integer)
E10   (exponent alone not allowed, this must be written 1E10)

Note that, as for integer constants, spaces and leading zeros may be included in both the mantissa and the exponent.

An integer constant followed by an exponent is also a valid real constant.

A real constant represented in any way is known as a floating point constant. Real constants are not used at all in the entirely integer program of Fig. 1.4. However the income tax program of Fig. 1.5 requires the use of real constants frequently (e.g. 1.0, 20000.0, 0.45, 0.3, etc).

Symbolic names may be used to address locations which hold integer or real numbers and the name has an associated type which defines the type of information it is to represent. The type of a variable name is given implicitly by the initial letter of its name. If the first letter is I, J, K, L, M or N then the name identifies an integer type, i.e. the corresponding storage location in computer memory will be used to store an integer quantity. Variable names beginning with any other letter refer to real quantities.

Examples of correct real variable names in FORTRAN are

B24AC   DERIV   ALPHA   XEQ16   FNX1   FNX2   XFN

and examples of correct integer variable names are

INDEX   NOVAR   M4   K6X29Z

Incorrect variable names are

2X139	(does not begin with a letter)
PRODUCT	(contains more than six characters)
MK3/1	(contains a character other than a letter or a digit)

Note that every character and its position is significant. Thus **FNX1**, **FNX2** and **XFN** are all quite distinct variables referring to different locations in the computer.

It is good practice when writing programs to invent names of variables which describe the quantities they represent. Thus we could write down the equation for electrical power by letting the variable A represent watts, B represent volts and C represent amps. Then the expression

A = B ∗ C

is true but not very meaningful to someone reading the program (∗ here represents multiplication). It would be far more comprehensible if we chose the names WATTS, VOLTS and AMPS to represent the relevant quantities and then wrote

WATTS = VOLTS ∗ AMPS

In fact, a good habit to cultivate when writing a program is to try the 'telephone test', i.e. imagine that you are reading it out over the telephone to someone else. How meaningful and how logically clear do you think it sounds? There is almost always room for improvement in any program.

The programmer is given complete freedom to invent suitable names of variables but is warned that some compilers will not allow names which are reserved by the system for some particular purpose (e.g. system functions such as **SQRT** or **SIN**, FORTRAN keywords such as **DO, IF, END**, etc.). These restrictions are non-standard, however.

It is worth pointing out here that it is possible (but not essential) to declare any variable to be of any type (whatever its initial letter) by using a special type declaration statement. In fact, it is good programming practice always to declare all variables in type declaration statements. But since it is better to introduce facilities gradually when teaching, the use of this facility will be deferred until Chapter 5.

Now that some basic language elements have been introduced, we can proceed in the next chapter to describe how these may be used to form statements. Before doing so, we shall end this chapter with a section to describe binary arithmetic and the internal representation of numbers in the computer. Whilst it is not absolutely essential to understand this when writing simple programs, if any serious numerical work is to be done some knowledge of this is required and so a section is included for the interested student.

1.9 Internal representation

An integer constant in a FORTRAN program is written as a decimal number, i.e. it uses a number system based on powers of 10. In this system the number 365 means 5 times 1, plus 6 times 10, plus 3 times 100 (i.e. 10 squared).

Decimal numbers are converted by the FORTRAN compiler to a binary representation which is the form in which they are stored in the computer memory. In this system, each digit in the number may be only 0 or 1 and represents a power of 2 instead of a power of 10 (where the rightmost bit is 2 to the power of 0, i.e. 1). In this representation, the number 101 represents 1 times 1 (or 2 to the power 0), plus 0 times 2 (or 2 to the power 1), plus 1 times 4 (or 2 to the power 2), i.e. it is the decimal number 5.

A few decimal numbers with the corresponding binary representations are

5	101	$(1*2^2 + 0*2^1 + 1*2^0 = 5)$
32	100000	$(1*2^5 = 32)$
10	1010	$(1*2^3 + 0*2^2 + 1*2^1 + 0*2^0 = 10)$

To convert a number from decimal to binary it is necessary to repeatedly divide by powers of 2, e.g. the number 77 becomes

$$77 = 64 (2^6) + 8 (2^3) + 4 (2^2) + 1 (2^0) = 1001101$$

Each bit in a computer word represents a binary digit and can hold the value 0 or 1. The rightmost bit represents 2 to the power 0 and so on up to 2 to the power 15, for example, on a machine with a word length of 16 bits. It follows from this that the maximum-sized integer which can be held in a computer is dependent on the word length of that computer and this varies from one machine to another. It is given by the value which is obtained when all the bits, except the leftmost bit, are set to 1. The leftmost bit of the word is reserved usually for the sign bit which is zero if the number is positive and 1 otherwise. Thus in a 16 bit word machine, the maximum-sized positive integer that may be stored is represented by a leftmost bit of zero and all other bits 1 (i.e. 32 767). Most computers use the twos-complement system for negative numbers, i.e. the binary representation of a positive number is changed so that all bits set to 1 become 0, and all bits set to 0 become 1; this gives the corresponding negative number. Thus, the maximum-sized negative number is represented by a leftmost bit of 1 and all other bits zero (i.e. −32 768). Note that a word with all bits set to 1 usually represents −1.

The internal representation should not, however, concern the FORTRAN programmer unduly. Decimal numbers are used throughout FORTRAN programs. But note that integers are held exactly in the computer (up to the maximum allowed value that is) and that a large constant such as 1512357 may be valid on some machines but not on others.

A real constant has one numeric storage location allocated to it, as does an integer constant, but internally the bits have a different significance. Part of the word is used to store the mantissa (e.g. on a 32 bit machine this may be 24 bits), and part of the word to store the exponent (e.g. 8 bits). The leftmost bit of the exponent may be used to represent its sign. It follows from this that there is an upper limit on the size of the mantissa and of the exponent in a real constant and this is machine-dependent.

A large integer constant (e.g. 1512357) could be written as the real constant 1.512357E6 and stored in the computer in that form. So it can be seen that integer numbers which exceed the storage capacity of a particular machine can be converted to real numbers and stored in that form. FORTRAN allows the programmer to specify more decimal digits in the fractional part than are capable of representation in the computer. Truncation to the nearest value will take place. Computers often hold real constants in normalized form, i.e. an integer part of zero with the exponent adjusted accordingly (0.1512357E7). The precision for a real value is seven decimal digits on a 32 bit word length machine (if a greater precision than this is required then the type Double Precision should be used – see Chapter 5).

Note that most computers are designed so that there is no distinction between +0 and −0, and so never write a program which relies on this distinction.

The important lessons to be learned from this discussion are that integer and real numbers have entirely different representations within the computer and must be considered completely different types; there is an upper limit to the magnitude of all numeric constants and this is different for different machines. Real numbers are held to a limited accuracy which depends on the word length of the computer memory and varies from one machine to another. This latter point can cause confusion to a beginner since a number written in the program as 10.3, say, may be held as 10.29999 in the computer and an operation to divide 10.3 by 3.0 and then multiply the result by 3.0 will not necessarily give the answer 10.3.

Effects of this type can result in unexpected errors in programs and will be discussed in other chapters in this book.

Another effect of this method of representation in a computer is that numbers which look very similar have remarkably different representations in the computer. For example, on a hypothetical 16 bit machine with a 4 bit exponent and a 12 bit mantissa, the numbers 4, 4.0 and −4 are held as follows:

| 0 | 0 | 0 | 0 | 0 | 0 | 0 | 0 | 0 | 0 | 0 | 0 | 0 | 1 | 0 | 0 |

| 0 | 0 | 1 | 1 | 1 | 0 | 0 | 0 | 0 | 0 | 0 | 0 | 0 | 0 | 0 | 0 |

| 1 | 1 | 1 | 1 | 1 | 1 | 1 | 1 | 1 | 1 | 1 | 1 | 1 | 1 | 0 | 0 |

whereas the number 20047 and the word NO are both held as follows:

| 0 | 1 | 0 | 0 | 1 | 1 | 1 | 0 | 0 | 1 | 0 | 0 | 1 | 1 | 1 | 1 |

Here we see that the characters N and O which form the word NO are held as numbers within an 8 bit byte. Thus byte 0 (which is the rightmost 8 bits, i.e. 01001111) contains the letter O which happens to be represented by the number 79, and byte 1 (which is the leftmost 8 bits, i.e. 01001110) contains the letter N which is represented by the number 78 (check that you agree with these binary representations). There are two widely used internationally recognized standard codes for representing characters in a numerical form within a computer. One is the ASCII code (the American Standard Code for Information Interchange) and the other is the EBCDIC code (Extended Binary Coded Decimal Interchange Code). A computer is either an ASCII machine or an EBCDIC machine in basic design and if information is to pass from one type of machine to the other then a code conversion is necessary. The representation of characters within a computer will be discussed more fully when the character type is described in Chapter 5.

It should be noted carefully how negative numbers are held. Thus, in the third example on the previous page, the fact that bit 15 is 1 indicates that the number is negative (bit 15 is 2 to the power 15 which is 32 768). The rest of the word represents the number 32 764. Therefore the number represented is −32 768 + 32 764 which is −4.

Note that when you add the binary representations of −4 and 4 together you get the answer 0. Check this for yourself assuming that 0 + 0 is 0, 1 + 0 is 1 and 1 + 1 is 0 with 1 carried to the next binary position.

1.10 Summary

- FORTRAN statements are written in upper case on 80 character lines.
- Statements are positioned in columns 7 to 72.
- Column 6 is the continuation column.
- Columns 1 to 5 are for labels.
- Columns 73 to 80 can be used for anything and are treated as comments.
- Programs commence with the **PROGRAM** statement and end with the **END** statement.
- Comment lines can contain any characters and have an * or C in column 1.
- Symbolic names in FORTRAN statements must begin with a capital letter and can be followed by up to five more capital letters or digits.
- Symbolic names may be used as program names or as names of variables. Names beginning with the letters I, J, K, L, M or N must represent integers. All other names represent real numbers.
- Statements may also contain integer or real constants.
- Constants are represented as decimal numbers in FORTRAN programs but are converted to an internal binary representation.

Exercises 1

1. Which of the following are correct representations of:
   (a) integer constants; (b) real constants; and (c) neither?
   Give reasons for (c).

2225	.137	2E − 7	− 25	1.562
E − 10	− 97612	101.2E + 2.	− .137	10000
0	+ 0162.2E − 02	005326	+ 258.	3.6E − 22	2,360

2. Which of the following are correct names for:
   (a) integer variables; (b) real variables; and (c) neither?
   Give reasons for (c).

PI	2X13	NUMBER	M63 − 2	BSQUARED	AMPS
FRED	I123	ZETA	X + Y	ITER	K(2)
Q	IP	COUNTS	INC*	NUMBER1	L3.6
POWER	L1369P	JIM'S			

3. Write the decimal equivalent of the following binary numbers:

   011   101   111001   11111111

   and the binary representation of the following decimal numbers:

   32   129   10   27

4. Design an algorithm for a program which reads in an integer *M* followed by a list of *N* integers and counts all the occurrences of *M* in the list. Print out the number of occurrences and the position in the list of each occurrence. Either draw a structure diagram or write out the structural specification.

5. Design an algorithm which reads *a*, *b* and *c* (the lengths in metres of the sides of a triangle), computes the area of this triangle and then determines the number of one-litre tins of paint required to paint this area with one coat of paint (assuming that one litre of paint can cover 10 square metres). Note that the area of a triangle is given by

   $$s * (s − a)*(s − b)*(s − c)^{\frac{1}{2}}$$

   where $s = 0.5*(a + b + c)$.

2

Construction of a simple FORTRAN program

2.1 Sequences

In section 1.3 it was explained how algorithms for computer programs could be broken down into structural components of which the simplest is a sequence of basic operations. The simple program to sum two numbers is such a sequence and consists of a statement to read the data (i.e. the numbers to be summed), a statement to compute the sum and a statement to print the result. In this chapter we shall describe in more detail the FORTRAN statements to perform these operations.

2.2 Simple input and output statements

Almost all computer programs are written in a general form to operate on data read into memory each time the program is executed. For example, it is possible to write a program to sum the squares of the first 100 integer numbers but if you wish to sum the squares of the first 500 integer numbers at some other time, then the program would have to be changed and recompiled before it could do this. It is far better, therefore, to write a program to sum the squares of N integer numbers and then read in a value for N as data for the program followed by the N integer numbers to be summed. Then if you wish to sum a different set of numbers, you may do so by running the program again with new data without actually changing the program itself at all. But to do this the program must be equipped with some mechanism by which it can read in the data and print out the results. This is the function of the **INPUT/OUTPUT** (or I/O) statements. Two simple statements in FORTRAN – the **READ** and the **PRINT** statements – are all that are required to perform simple input/output operations. These statements are used in the program to sum two numbers and their use is also illustrated in Fig. 1.4 at lines 20, 30, 70, 90, 120 and 150, and in Fig. 1.5 at lines 20, 30, 50, 60, 210 and 230.

The simple **READ** statement in FORTRAN consists of the word **READ** followed by a definition of the input device from which the data are to be read, together with the type of that data. Actual physical devices are never referred to as such within a FORTRAN program. Instead, logical unit numbers are used and the correspondence between the logical unit number and an actual physical device is defined outside the program. Exactly how this is done depends on the computer that you are using but the principle is the same on all machines. Thus in a program one never makes a statement of the form 'read a number from the on-line terminal' but rather makes the statement 'read a number from unit 1'. Outside the program one makes a statement of the form 'when this program is run let unit 1 be the on-line terminal'.

A FORTRAN program is capable of reading or writing data from a number of different logical units (sometimes called channels or streams). For example, it may read some from the on-line terminal and some from magnetic tape or disc; similarly, data may be written to the on-line terminal, the printer or magnetic tape or disc. On most computers a default device is provided. This means that if a unit number is not used in an input or output statement then it will be assumed that you wish to use the default device which is usually the on-line terminal. Thus the simplest forms of the **READ** and **PRINT** statements do not require a unit number to be specified but assume the default device.

All the examples and exercises in the first five chapters of this book will assume that the default device is used and that this device is the on-line terminal.

It is also necessary in a **READ** or **PRINT** statement to specify the types of the data which are to be read or written (i.e. whether they are integer, real or character values, for example), but in the simplest I/O statements this type of information is defined by the types of the FORTRAN variables into which the data values are to be read. This is known as *list-directed I/O*. Thus the simplest form of the **READ** statement is

READ *,*list*

where *list* is a list of FORTRAN variables which specify the named locations into which the data are to be read from the input device. The * specifies that this is a list-directed read, i.e. the types of data which will be read are defined by the types of the corresponding FORTRAN variables in the list. Since no unit number is given in this statement then it is assumed that the data will be read from the default device.

Consider the statement

READ *, SALARY

which is used at line 60 in Fig. 1.5. Since **SALARY** begins with the letter S it is a real variable by definition and therefore this statement will read a real number from the default input unit into the location named **SALARY**, i.e. one could type a number such as 13176.35 on the on-line terminal in response to this statement.

However, it may be required to read more than one number in a **READ** statement. Thus in the program to sum two numbers, the statement

READ *,NUM1,NUM2

will read two integer numbers into the named locations **NUM1** and **NUM2**, e.g. the numbers 107 and 232 could be typed in response to this statement. However, the question arises here as to how the two numbers are separated. If, for example, you typed 107232 on the keyboard followed by the end-of-line symbol (usually the '**RETURN**' key) then the number 107232 will be read into **NUM1** and nothing will be read into **NUM2**. Therefore it is necessary to separate the two numbers by some kind of separator character which is most commonly one or more spaces but can also be a comma. Therefore the line should be keyed in as 107 232 (followed by '**RETURN**') for the input to be correctly read. Note that it follows from this that, in data, spaces must not be used within a number, i.e. if the line 1 07 232 is keyed in, then this would result in the value 1 being read into **NUM1**, the value 07 being read into **NUM2** and the rest of the line being ignored.

In the above discussion, we have frequently referred to a *line*, i.e. a sequence of characters keyed in and terminated by the end-of-line character which is usually '**RETURN**'. FORTRAN expects that all of the data required for one **READ** statement be keyed in on one line. Thus the statement

READ *, NUM1,NUM2

expects two integers on the same line but the statements

READ *,NUM1
READ *,NUM2

expect two integers on two lines (typed one per line). Thus data for the first statement might be

107   232

but data for the second statements might be

107
232

This is an important feature of the FORTRAN I/O system which should be well understood and never forgotten. Many errors in programs are caused by forgetting this simple fact.

So, to summarize, the data on the incoming unit may be thought of as a number of lines or *records* of information. The length of a record may be different on different devices. For example, at the on-line terminal a record may be a line of characters of maximum length 80. Each time a **READ** statement is encountered a new record is read from the input device. If list-directed I/O is used, data may be typed on that record according to the rules required for a constant of the corresponding type in the I/O list. So, for example, a real number may be read into **SALARY** from an input record of the form

8740.0

and three real numbers may be read into A, B and C from an input record of the form

12.5   17.6   30.5

by the statement:

READ *,A,B,C

Different types of information may be mixed on one record provided that the types of the variables in the I/O list correspond in order and type. Thus if you wish to read in an integer I, real values P and Q, and an integer L from one record followed by another record containing two integers M and N and two reals X and Y then the following read statements are required:

READ *,I,P,Q,L
READ *,M,N,X,Y

Typical data records may be as follows:

```
12   -0.362  225.13  -76
802  -10     312.5   -98.4
```

So it should be possible for you now to understand most of the **READ** statements in the program examples of Chapter 1 (except for the statement at line 70 in Fig. 1.4, in which an extra clause **ERR** = 20 causes a jump to label 20 if an error occurs on input; a full explanation of this is given in section 7.2). But what of the statements to print the results? The simple **PRINT** statement is of the form

PRINT *,list

where *list* is as defined for the **READ** statement. This will print the contents of the named locations in the I/O list onto the default output device which again is often the on-line terminal. Thus the information read in by the above two statements will be printed out by the following two statements:

PRINT *,I,P,Q,L
PRINT *,M,N,X,Y

The exact layout or format of the data on the output device will depend on the convention adopted for list-directed I/O on your particular computer. It may well be different from the way in which it is laid out on the input record and you will have no control over this as long as you are using simple list-directed I/O. As in the case of the **READ** statement, each **PRINT** statement will start a new output record. Thus the first four values will be printed on one line of the terminal and the second four on the next line. If you wished all eight numbers to appear on one line then a statement of the form:

PRINT *,I,P,Q,L,M,N,X,Y

would be required.

Numbers alone on the output are not usually very meaningful. It is better to provide some descriptive information as well, for example,

The Current is 100.24 amps

is more meaningful than the number 100.24 alone. To do this it is necessary to mix character information and numerical information in the output. FORTRAN allows strings of characters to be enclosed in apostrophes and these strings may be printed out by including them in the **PRINT** statement list. For example,

PRINT *,'The Current is'

will print the record

The Current is

onto the default device. Note that a character string may contain any characters which are capable of representation in your computer – this does not restrict them to the FORTRAN character set only; in particular, upper and lower case letters may be used.

Now if you wish numerical information to be printed out also, then you may do this simply by including the named variable in the output list at the appropriate point. For example,

PRINT *,'The Current is ',AMPS,' amps'

will produce the record above if the named location **AMPS** contains 100.24. Thus, in our simple program to sum two numbers, we print the result with the statement

PRINT *,NUM3,' is the sum of ',NUM1,' and ',NUM2

If the two numbers read in were 107 and 232 then this statement would cause the line

339 is the sum of 107 and 232

to be output to the terminal.

In section 1.8 we introduced integer and real constants and here we have introduced another type of constant – the character constant. This is any sequence of characters enclosed between apostrophes. It is sometimes called a string. Any valid character may be included in a character constant, i.e. upper or lower case letters, the numbers 0 to 9 or any of the special characters such as £ , + − etc. Note the importance of including spaces in the character string to get the layout you require.

Another very popular use of character strings is to provide prompts for data to be input at the on-line terminal. For example,

PRINT *,'Enter your age:'
READ *,MYAGE

will output the prompt

Enter your age:

at the on-line terminal and will then wait for you to type your age on the next line.

It can be seen that the first executable statements of the program in Figs 1.4 and 1.5 are both statements of this form.

2.3 Arithmetic expressions

In the previous section we have described how numbers may be read and printed, and we are now close to understanding the simple program to sum two numbers introduced in Chapter 1. However, having read the two numbers into the computer's memory we must know how to add these together to produce the result in the location **NUM3**. To do this we must learn to write arithmetic expressions and arithmetic assignment statements and these will be discussed in the next two sections.

The variables and constants introduced in Chapter 1 can be combined together with operators to construct FORTRAN arithmetic expressions. The simplest form of arithmetic expression is a single variable or constant, e.g. **SUM** or 4.0 are valid FORTRAN expressions.

A variable or constant used in an expression is usually called an operand and it can be combined with another operand by one of the five arithmetic operators

+   Addition
−   Subtraction
*   Multiplication
/   Division
**   Exponentiation

Each of these operators operates on two operands and is placed between them, e.g. **SUM** + 4.0. Thus two integer numbers can be added together by the expression **NUM1** + **NUM2** as seen in our simple program example. But what does this expression cause the machine to do? The answer is that it takes the contents of the location named **NUM1** and transmits that value along the data bus to the accumulator. Then it takes the contents of the memory location named **NUM2** along the data bus to the accumulator and adds it to the value already there. Thus the result of **NUM1** + **NUM2** is now in the accumulator. More complicated expressions work in exactly the same way but more operations are involved. When we describe the arithmetic assignment statement in the next section we shall see how this result is taken from the accumulator and placed back in memory, but for the moment let us consider expressions in more detail.

We shall consider at this stage the operands already introduced – that is, real and integer variables and constants. Expressions of the following form can now be written:

X + Y
VOLTS∗AMPS
THETA/3.14159
CHI∗∗2
4.0∗A∗C
NOFUN/2

One important difference between these FORTRAN expressions and mathematical equations is that all operators must be explicitly stated. Whereas in mathematics AC means A times C, in FORTRAN this must always be written as **A∗C**. If the multiplication operation were not stated explicitly AC would be indistinguishable from the FORTRAN variable named **AC**.

Another important rule which applies to arithmetic expressions in FORTRAN is that no two operators can be juxtaposed. This means that an expression of the form NOFUN/ −2 is not allowed, since the operators / and − are next to each other. In a case such as this the operators must be separated by the use of parentheses and the expression written in the form NOFUN/(−2).

It is generally good practice to ensure that all operands in the same expression are of the same type, e.g. either all integer constants and variables or all real constants and variables. Thus expressions of the form

4.0∗A∗C

should be written in preference to the form

4∗A∗C

Whilst both forms are valid in FORTRAN, unexpected results can sometimes occur when operands of different types are mixed in expressions. The rules for performing such mixed mode arithmetic will be discussed in Chapter 5. However, the programmer is warned that it is generally considered bad programming practice to use mixed mode arithmetic and is advised to avoid it. Mixed expressions will not be used in the examples in this book, except in the special case when a real number is raised to an integer power.

The minus operator alone may be used to operate on one operand only and is placed before it to negate its value, e.g. −4.0. This means 'take the constant 4.0 to the accumulator and negate it'. So an expression of the form

−NUM3 + 10

means 'take the contents of the location **NUM3** to the accumulator, negate the value in the accumulator and then add 10 to it'. A minus sign used in this way is known as the unary minus operator. A unary plus may also be used but is unnecessary since a plus is assumed by default (i.e. the expression **+NUM3** + 10 is valid but is exactly the same as **NUM3** + 10).

Note that ∗∗ is treated as a single symbol representing the operation 'to raise to a power'.

The examples of arithmetic expressions given so far in this chapter have been of a simple kind. When longer and more complicated expressions are used, care must be taken to ensure that no ambiguity is introduced into the meaning of the expression. For example, does the expression

$X - Y + Z$

mean 'subtract Y from X and add Z to the result' or does it mean 'add Y to Z and subtract this result from X' (these would produce the entirely different results $+17$ and -23 for $X = 2$, $Y = 5$ and $Z = 20$)? Similarly does

VOLTS∗AMPS∗∗2

mean 'multiply VOLTS by AMPS and square the result' or does it mean 'square AMPS and multiply the result by VOLTS'? This ambiguity is resolved both in mathematical and FORTRAN expressions by the use of parentheses. Thus $X - Y + Z$ is written as $(X - Y) + Z$ or $X - (Y + Z)$ according to which is intended. Similarly, **VOLTS∗AMPS∗∗2** is written as either **(VOLTS∗AMPS)∗∗2** or **VOLTS∗(AMPS∗∗2)**, the former meaning 'multiply VOLTS by AMPS and square the result' and the latter meaning 'square AMPS and multiply the result by VOLTS'.

However, if algebraic brackets are not used in an arithmetic expression the FORTRAN operators are given an implicit priority which determines the order in which the operations will be performed. This hierarchy of operators is:

All exponentiations are performed first.
All multiplications and divisions are performed second.
All additions and subtractions are performed last.

A unary minus operation is performed after exponentation but before any multiplication, division, addition or subtraction.

Thus **VOLTS∗AMPS∗∗2** is equivalent to **VOLTS∗(AMPS∗∗2)** – that is, the exponentiation, which is of greater priority than the multiplication, is performed first. Similarly,

P/Q∗∗2 + X/Y + Z∗∗2

is identical in meaning to

(P/(Q∗∗2)) + (X/Y) + (Z∗∗2)

It can be seen, however, that multiply and divide have the same priority and add and subtract have the same priority. This raises the question of how an expression which consists entirely of operators of the same priority is evaluated. The answer is that the expression is evaluated in order from left to right. Under this scheme $X - Y + Z$ is equivalent to $(X - Y) + Z$. Similarly,

X/Y*Z + P*Q/R*S/T

is equivalent to

((X/Y)*Z) + ((((P*Q)/R)*S)/T)

or in mathematical notation

$$\frac{xz}{y} + \frac{pqs}{rt}$$

An important exception to this left-to-right rule occurs when an expression consists entirely of exponentiations. In this case the operations are performed from right to left. That is, **I**J**K** means 'raise J to the power K and raise I to this resulting power', i.e. it is equivalent to **I**(J**K)**.

Exponentiation operators may be used to raise an entity of any type to an integer power. In fact, it is more efficient to write an expression such as

A**4

which is evaluated by repeated multiplication (**A*A*A*A**) than the expression

A**4.0

which is evaluated by taking the exponential of four times the logarithm of A.

It is important to remember that the presence of parentheses overrides the natural order of priority. The use of parentheses in complicated arithmetic expressions, even when they are not absolutely necessary, is often advisable not only for the sake of clarity but also as a precaution to ensure that the expression is actually evaluated in the way you intend.

Parentheses used in this way in arithmetic expressions denote only grouping. They do not imply multiplication. The presence of an operator is essential always. Therefore $(X + Y)(P + Q)$ must be written as **(X + Y)*(P + Q)**.

Any arithmetic expression is evaluated in the computer to produce a numeric result which is integer or real, e.g. the expression

I + 5

will be interpreted as follows:

Take the contents of the location whose address is given by the symbolic name I.
Add the contents of the constant location 5.

This yields an integer result depending on the contents of the location I when the expression is evaluated, e.g. 7 if I contains 2.

It can be seen from this discussion, that in Fig. 1.4 at line 80, the expression

ISUM + NUM**2

is an entirely integer expression which squares the current value of **NUM** and adds it to the current value of **ISUM**. It is done this way because of the implied operator precedence.

Similarly, in Fig. 1.5 many examples of real expressions can be seen. For example, the expression

TAX + (REM*0.3)

multiplies the remaining salary **REM** by 0.3 and then adds this to the current value of **TAX**. This expression could equally well have been written

TAX + REM*0.3

because of the implied operator precedence.

2.4 Arithmetic assignment statements

An arithmetic expression alone is not a valid FORTRAN statement itself but forms a component of several FORTRAN statements – one of these being the arithmetic assignment statement.

The result of the evaluation of an expression may be assigned to another location in memory by means of the arithmetic assignment statement which is of the general form

VARIABLE = EXPRESSION

This means, take from the accumulator the result of evaluating the expression on the right-hand side and store it in the memory location named on the left-hand side (this may be a variable name or the name of other entities in FORTRAN such as array elements which will be described later).

There is an important difference between the arithmetic assignment statement and the very similar algebraic equation. In FORTRAN the statement **X = Y + Z** is an instruction to the computer to 'take to an accumulator the contents of the storage location named Y, add to this the contents of the storage location named Z and put the result in the storage location named X'. By this definition the following statement can be written quite legitimately:

X = X + 1.0

This would be nonsense as an algebraic equation, but as an assignment in FORTRAN it means 'take the present contents of the storage location X, add 1.0 to this number and put the answer back in location X, overwriting anything which is already present in this location'. Thus if X is 5.0 when this statement is encountered its value will be changed to 6.0, and whenever X is used again at a later stage in the program it will have the value 6.0 unless it is changed by another statement. It is always important to have in mind this basic difference between FORTRAN and mathematical notation.

As an example, what are the final values in locations X, Y and Z at the end of execution of the following sequence of statements?

```
X = 5.0
Y = 3.0
X = X + 10.0
Y = Y + X - 5.0
Z = Y * X
```

(Answer: $X = 15.0$, $Y = 13.0$, $Z = 195.0$).

We can now understand how the statement

NUM3 = NUM1 + NUM2

in our simple program to sum two numbers, can add the contents of the memory locations **NUM1** and **NUM2** and put the result back in the memory location **NUM3**.

Note that a FORTRAN program must always set all named locations to an initial value before being used on the right-hand side of an assignment (even if the value is zero). It must never be assumed that the computer will do this for you (although some computers do set all of memory to zero before a program is executed, this is not a universal rule on which you can rely), e.g.

```
SUM1 = 0.0
SUM2 = 0.0
SUM1 = SUM1 + 10.0
SUM2 = SUM2 + 20.0
```

would result in values of 10.0 for **SUM1** and 20.0 for **SUM2**, whereas the statements

```
SUM1 = SUM1 + 10.0
SUM2 = SUM2 + 20.0
```

alone would not necessarily do so because **SUM1** and **SUM2** have not been initialized to zero.

It should be apparent now that it is illegal to write a statement of the form

A − B = P2 + Q**2**

The left-hand side of an assignment statement cannot be an expression since this does not define a named location in memory.

If the expression on the right-hand side is a real expression with a real result then it is safer to assign this to a real variable on the left-hand side. Similarly, an integer expression should be assigned to an integer variable. On the other hand, mixed assignment is allowed and automatic type conversion will take place before the assignment. This is alright if you are sure you know what you are doing, e.g.

```
X = 5.0
Y = 10.5
Z = 2.0
I = (X + Y)/Z
```

would result in the value 7 being assigned to I (a straight truncation takes place). This could give unexpected results in some cases, e.g.

```
X = 3.0
Y = 1.0
I = (Y/X)*X
```

One might expect the value 1 to be assigned to I but remember that real numbers are held to a limited accuracy. Thus the result of dividing 1.0 by 3.0 and then multiplying by 3.0 may well be 0.999999 which when truncated and assigned to an integer yields the perhaps unexpected value zero.

Because of these pitfalls it is generally considered safer programming practice to avoid mixing types in either expressions or assignment statements. It will be seen later that functions can be used to do explicit type conversions in a program.

The reader may gain more familiarity with FORTRAN assignment statements and expressions by doing Exercises 2, number 1.

Note that because of the way an assignment statement works, it is not as easy to exchange the values of two memory locations as it might seem at first sight, i.e.

```
X = Y
Y = X
```

will not give the required result. If X is initially 5.0 and Y is 9.0, say, then the first assignment statement sets location X to 9.0. The second statement sets location Y equal to the contents of location X which is now 9.0. Thus at the end of execution of these two statements X and Y are both 9.0.

A temporary location must be used as working space to achieve the required result, i.e.

```
TEMP = X
   X = Y
   Y = TEMP
```

will set X to 9.0 and Y to 5.0.

Finally, in any computer program beware of accidental division by zero which will not be detected by the compiler and which will result in a program error, e.g. a programmer is unlikely to write $A = B/0.0$ but may write $A = B/C$ when at some earlier point in the execution of the program C assumes the value zero.

2.5 The STOP statement

We have now described all of the statements used in our simple program to sum two numbers. In the first two chapters of this book, we have seen how algorithms may be designed to solve problems using sequences of basic operations, selections and repetitions. We have seen how FORTRAN programs consist of sequences of FORTRAN statements enclosed between **PROGRAM** and **END** statements. We have used simple list-directed I/O to input data from the keyboard and output results to the on-line terminal. We have shown how operations may be performed on data by means of arithmetic assignment statements.

Execution of a FORTRAN program begins at the first executable statement and proceeds to execute each statement in sequence until a **STOP** statement is encountered. This consists of the word **STOP** placed anywhere in columns 7 to 72 (lines 140 and 160 of Fig. 1.4 and line 260 of Fig. 1.5).

The **STOP** statement causes the execution of the program to be terminated as soon as it is obeyed. This is very different from the **END** statement which signifies the textual end of the program, i.e. there must be no more FORTRAN statements following it. The **STOP** statement indicates the logical end of the execution of a program and there may be more than one such statement in a program; this may or may not be the textual end of the program as well.

If a **STOP** statement is not included anywhere in the program then execution will be terminated when the **END** statement is encountered although this is not to be encouraged since it is a logically different statement.

2.6 Compiling and running your program

You should now completely understand the simple program to sum two numbers, and your next step is to find out how to compile and run this program on your own computer. Since this is a different procedure for every machine, it is not possible in this book to tell you how to do this in detail. However, the same processes are involved on all computers and we can discuss these in general terms.

First, you must type the program into the computer; the usual way of doing this is to use your system editor to type the text of the program on the keyboard into a named file on a floppy disc or fixed hard disc. Care must be taken to follow the correct layout for a FORTRAN program.

Once this is done, you must compile the program using whatever command your system provides (this may typically be called F77, FORTRAN, FTN77, or **COMPILE** etc.); the command will require you to specify the name of the file in which the program is stored. It will then proceed to try to compile the program but at this stage various *syntax errors* may be found. These indicate that the compiler has found one or more statements which do not follow the grammatically correct rule for a valid FORTRAN statement. Syntax errors may simply be caused by a typing error (for example, if you accidentally type PROGTAM instead of PROGRAM) or you may have actually forgotten the correct format for a particular statement. Whatever the cause, you must use your editor to correct the syntax errors and then recompile the program. You must repeat this process until the program is correctly compiled.

Once you have a syntactically correct program, the compiler should produce a compiled object program in a different file from the original source and this is the program you must run. Before you can do this, it may be necessary to *link* the object program together with other object files such as the FORTRAN library routines, for example. Errors will be caused at this stage if any essential routines are missing. To do this you use your system Job Control Language; this is also used to assign the default device (the on line terminal) to the program and then execute it.

When your program runs, more errors may occur. These are called runtime or *execution errors*. These may be caused by invalid data, loops within a program, attempts to divide by zero and so on. Whatever the cause, these must be detected and corrected until the program runs correctly and produces the required results. This whole process of correcting and running programs repeatedly until they work is called *debugging*.

Once the program is running successfully, it will stop when it reaches the statement **READ *,NUM1,NUM2** and expect you to type in the two numbers to be added. Once you have done this it will proceed to print the sum and stop when it reaches the **STOP** statement.

When you have successfully run this simple program on your machine, you may gain more practical experience by writing the programs specified in Exercises 2.

You will be well advised not to proceed further with this book until you have successfully executed these simple programs on your machine.

2.7 Intrinsic functions

In mathematics, expressions may contain not only simple operands (such as x or y) but also references to functions such as sine and cosine. These standard functions are used so frequently in mathematics (and therefore frequently required by programmers) that FORTRAN provides a set of such functions as an integral part of the system. They are known as intrinsic functions and they may be called in a FORTRAN program by giving the name of the function followed by its arguments enclosed in parentheses. There may be one or more arguments in the form of FORTRAN expressions which provide the data for which the function is to be evaluated.

Thus if a programmer wishes to calculate the square root, sine or cosine of the variable X then the expression **SQRT(X)**, **SIN(X)** or **COS(X)** will invoke the intrinsic function which will return the required value. **SQRT, SIN** and **COS** are the function names and X is the argument. Since an argument may be any expression, the square root of

$$b^2 - 4ac$$

can be found by simply writing **SQRT(B**2 − 4.0*A*C)**.

The concept of functions in FORTRAN is discussed more fully in Chapter 8. It is briefly introduced at this early stage so that beginners may use intrinsic functions without necessarily understanding the way they work. Frequently available functions include:

SQRT	finds the square root of a real argument
SIN	finds the sine of an angle in radians
COS	finds the cosine of an angle in radians
TAN	finds the tangent of an angle in radians
ASIN	finds the arcsin in radians
ACOS	finds the arccos in radians
ATAN	finds the arctan in radians
LOG10	finds the logarithm to the base 10
EXP	finds the exponential
LOG	finds the natural logarithm
INT	converts a real argument to an integer
REAL	converts an integer argument to real
NINT	converts a real argument to the nearest integer

The following are examples of mathematical expressions and their FORTRAN equivalents:

$$V = \sqrt{\frac{E}{\rho}}$$ **V = SQRT(E/RHO)**

$$y = a \sin\frac{2\pi}{\lambda}(vt - x)$$ **Y = A*SIN(2.0*PI/RLMBDA*(V*T − X))**

$$l = \sqrt{[(x_1 - x_2)^2 + (y_1 - y_2)^2]}$$ **RL = SQRT((X1 − X2)**2 + (Y1 − Y2)**2)**

$$E = mc^2$$ **ENERGY = AMASS*C*C**

Note that it is required that the variables corresponding to λ and l be real in the FORTRAN expressions. If the variables LAMBDA and L were used then they would be typed as integers since L lies in the range I to N.

By preceding them with the letter R, they become real variables and the use of mixed mode arithmetic is avoided.

Thus the equation

$$M = \frac{PV}{RT}$$

may be written

RM = P*V/(R*T)

Alternatively, the functions **REAL** and **INT** may be used to convert the type, e.g.

$$n = 10 \log_{10} \frac{P_2}{P_1}$$

may be written

N = INT(10.0*LOG10(P2/P1))

and

$$f = \frac{1}{2L} \sqrt{\frac{T}{M}}$$

may be written

F = (1.0/(2.0*REAL(L)))*SQRT(T/REAL(M))

Note that the function **NINT** is a useful function and may help avoid the unexpected results from the inaccuracies described in previous sections, i.e.

I = (X/Y)*Y

may yield the value zero as does the expression

I = INT((X/Y)*Y)

but the result 1 will be obtained from

I = NINT((X/Y)*Y)

since **NINT** rounds the result to the nearest integer.

Similarly, the arithmetic mean of a sum of five integer numbers **(ISUM)** may be found by

AMEAN = REAL(ISUM)/5.0

and would yield a value of 14.4 for **AMEAN** if **ISUM** were 72 unlike the statement

MEAN = ISUM/5

which would yield the value 14.

Many more intrinsic functions are provided and a complete list of these is given in Appendix A. The programmer is warned that any invented symbolic names used in a program must not be the same name as any of the intrinsic functions. Also not all of the intrinsic functions provided at one computer installation will necessarily be available at another, so beware of portability problems here.

2.8 Summary

- List-directed I/O statements are simple statements to read data from the default device and write data to it. The statements are of the form

  READ *,*list*   and   PRINT *,*list*

where *list* is a list of symbolic names representing the locations in memory to which the data are to be input or from which the results are to be output.
● Arithmetic expressions consist of operands joined by the arithmetic operators

+

−

*

/

**

● Arithmetic assignments are of the form

VARIABLE = EXPRESSION

● The **STOP** statement stops the execution of the program.
● FORTRAN provides intrinsic functions such as **SQRT, SIN, COS**, etc. for commonly required operations.
● Arithmetic operators have an order of precedence, i.e.

**	is performed first
* /	are performed second
+ −	are performed last

This order may be overridden by the use of parentheses in expressions.

Exercises 2

1. Express the following algebraic equations as FORTRAN arithmetic assignment statements:

   1.1

   $$a = \frac{3xy^2(z+1) + \frac{1}{2}yz}{1 + x + x^3}$$

   1.2

   $$b = \frac{3}{2}x(x-1)[7y - \log_e(\cos x)]^{\frac{1}{2}}$$

   1.3

   $$i = \frac{k}{j}\left[10^2x - \frac{1}{3.0}\frac{(k^2)}{j}\right]$$

   1.4

   $$z = \frac{5x^2[\cos^3(x^2 - y^2) + \tan^{-1}(x \cos x)]^{\frac{1}{2}}}{(e^{x+1}e^{y+1} + 1)}$$

   Assume that all variables beginning with letters *i* to *n* are to be represented by FORTRAN integer variables and that all others are real variables. Do

not use mixed mode arithmetic. In Example 1.3 use intrinsic functions
REAL and **INT** for type conversion where necessary. Write the expression
in two different ways – one converting the whole expression to real before
evaluation and the other converting each sub-expression to real after
evaluation. Calculate the value assigned to the left-hand side of the
FORTRAN statement equivalent to 1.3 above for $j = 3$, $k = 7$ and $x = 0.5$
for the two different cases.

2. What values will be printed by the following program:

```
PROGRAM EG2
I  = 2
J  = 4
X  = 22.5
Y  = -10.0
Z  = 0.25
P  = Z + X * Y
Q  = P + 2.0 * Y ** I
R  = -Y * 8.0 / REAL(J)
X  = Q + R
Y  = X * 2.0 - Z
Z  = Z * R
J  = INT(3.0 * Z / REAL(I))
I  = I + 6
PRINT *,I,J,X,Y,Z
PRINT *,P,Q,R
STOP
END
```

3. Write the program designed in Exercises 1, number 5. Since we have not
yet described how to write selections in FORTRAN, use the formula

    INT(AREA/10.0 + 0.999999)

to compute the number of tins required if the area of the triangle is **AREA**.

4. Write a program to read a temperature in degrees Fahrenheit and convert
it to degrees Centigrade using the formula

$$C = \frac{5}{9}*(F - 32)$$

5. Write a FORTRAN program to calculate the total interest earned by
investing a sum of money at a fixed interest rate for a given number of
years using the expression

$$A = P\left(1 + \frac{r}{100}\right)^n$$

where P is the initial capital, r is the percentage rate of interest, n is the number of years for which the sum is invested, and A is the total capital after n years. The program should have as its data:

(i)   the sum invested (in pounds and pence);

(ii) the rate of interest, r;

(iii) the total number of years, n;

and should output the total interest earned both in pounds and pence and in dollars and cents. Assume the exchange rate is 1.8 dollars to the pound.

3

Selections and other control statements

3.1 Introduction

It has been stated already that, in a FORTRAN program, executable instructions will be obeyed in sequence in the order in which they are written. However, this is not always required. In a selection, for example, a sequence of instructions are to be obeyed only if a particular condition is true and must be branched around (or ignored) otherwise. In a repetition, it is required to branch back to the beginning of a sequence of instructions so that they may be obeyed again and to continue doing this until some condition is reached. So, FORTRAN provides control statements which, when obeyed, will cause some change in the usual execution order of the instructions. A transfer of control may be conditional or unconditional, i.e. control will be transferred if some condition is true, or control will be transferred regardless of any condition.

A selection is an example of a conditional transfer of control statement.

3.2 The block-IF statement

In Chapter 1, we described how selections can form elementary logical components in the design of algorithms. In this section we shall see how such logic is expressed in FORTRAN. As a simple example, suppose that we wish to exchange the contents of two storage locations only if the value of the first is greater than the value of the second. The logic for this may be expressed by 'if number 1 is greater than number 2, then exchange number 1 and number 2'. To write this logic in FORTRAN, we use the block-**IF** statement which is of the form:

IF (e) THEN

where *e* is a logical expression. A logical expression is any expression which when evaluated assumes one of two values – either it is true or it is false. One example of a logical expression is the relational expression which compares the magnitude of two arithmetic expressions. For example, the expression 'number 1 is greater than number 2' is a relational expression which is true if number 1 is greater than number 2 (and, of course, is false if number 1 is less than or equal to number 2). The actual comparison performed depends on the relational operator used ('greater than' in this case, but it may equally well have been 'equal to', 'less than', 'not equal to' and so on). Such relational operators are expressed in FORTRAN by two letter mnemonic codes enclosed between dots, e.g. **.GT.** is 'greater than', **.EQ.** is 'equal to' and so on.

So if **NUM1** is the FORTRAN symbolic name for number 1 and **NUM2** is number 2, the above logic is expressed in FORTRAN by

IF (NUM1 .GT. NUM2) THEN

This statement may be followed by any number of FORTRAN statements which are to be obeyed if the logical expression is true (in this case we wish to exchange the two numbers). This sequence of statements is terminated by **END IF**. So the above logic is expressed by the following FORTRAN:

```
IF (NUM1 .GT. NUM2) THEN
    NTEMP = NUM2
    NUM2 = NUM1
    NUM1 = NTEMP
END IF
PRINT *,NUM1,NUM2
```

The **PRINT** statement is obeyed after the numbers have been exchanged.

Notice that the statements obeyed if the logical expression is true have all been indented with respect to the block-**IF** statement. This, of course, is not essential but it does help the reader of the program to see the structure of the logic more clearly. One can tell at a glance which statements belong together.

If the logical expression is false then all the statements between **IF** and **END IF** are ignored completely and the next statement obeyed is the one immediately following the **END IF**, i.e. the **PRINT** statement in this case. So in the above example, if the logical expression is false the numbers are printed, but if the logical expression is true, the numbers are exchanged and printed.

In some cases a selection involves logic of the form 'if some condition is true then do this, otherwise do that'. To implement this logic, the block-**IF** statement may have an alternative clause which uses the word **ELSE** to mean 'otherwise'; this defines statements to be obeyed if the conditional expression is false. Thus a block-**IF** may be of the form

```
IF (e) THEN
    statements 1
ELSE
    statements 2
END IF
```

If *e* is true then *statements 1* are obeyed; *statements 2* are ignored. If *e* is false then *statements 2* are obeyed; *statements 1* are ignored. In either case, the next statement obeyed is the first executable statement following the **END IF**.

As an example of this, suppose that we wish to compute the pay of an employee given the number of hours worked and the hourly rate of pay for that employee. Suppose that any hours worked in excess of 40 are paid at one and a half times the standard hourly rate. Then the statements in FORTRAN which express this logic are as follows:

```
IF (HRS .GT. 40.0) THEN
    PAY = RATE*40.0 + (1.5*RATE*(HRS - 40.0))
ELSE
    PAY = RATE*HRS
END IF
PRINT *,'The pay due is ',PAY
```

If the logical expression (**HRS .GT. 40.0**) is true then the statements between **IF** and **ELSE** are obeyed; following this, the next statement executed is the one immediately following the **END IF** (i.e. **PRINT**). On the other hand, if the logical expression is false, then the statement between the **ELSE** and the **END IF** is obeyed; following this the statement following the **END IF** is obeyed also. Any number of statements may be included in the **THEN** clause and the **ELSE** clause.

More complicated logical constructions can be written by using one or more **ELSE IF** clauses of the form

ELSE IF (e) THEN

where *e* is a logical expression which, if true, will result in the execution of the statements following the **THEN** until an **ELSE**, **ELSE IF** or **END IF** statement is encountered. There may be any number of **ELSE IF** statements following a block-**IF** statement but, at most, there may only be one **ELSE** statement which must follow all the **ELSE IF** statements.

For example, imagine a bank's transaction processing system in which a transaction code and a sum of money are input to the program. If the transaction code is 1, then the sum is used to credit the customer's current account; if the code is 2 then the sum is used to debit the current account; if the code is 3 then the deposit account is credited and if the code is 4 then the deposit account is debited. This may be expressed in FORTRAN by the following block-**IF**:

```
IF (ITCODE .EQ. 1) THEN
    CACCNT = CACCNT + SUM
ELSE IF (ITCODE .EQ. 2) THEN
    CACCNT = CACCNT - SUM
ELSE IF (ITCODE .EQ. 3) THEN
    DACCNT = DACCNT + SUM
ELSE IF (ITCODE .EQ. 4) THEN
    DACCNT = DACCNT - SUM
END IF
```

(where **ITCODE** is the transaction code, **SUM** is the amount input to the program, **CACCNT** is the current account and **DACCNT** is the deposit account).

This is an example of the use of the block-**IF** statement with several **ELSE IF** clauses and no **ELSE** clause. It may well be advisable to include an **ELSE** clause to handle the erroneous case when the transaction code does not lie in the range 1 to 4. This involves inserting the lines

ELSE
    PRINT *,'Invalid transaction ',ITCODE,' requested for ',SUM

before the **END IF**.

Block-**IF** statements may be nested to any level so that complicated logical constructions may be written, e.g.

	Level
IF (*e1*) **THEN**	1
statements 1	1
IF (*e2*) **THEN**	2
statements 2	2
IF (*e3*) **THEN**	3
statements 3	3
ELSE IF (*e4*) **THEN**	3
statements 4	3
ELSE	3
statements 5	3
END IF	3
ELSE	2
statements 6	2
END IF	2
ELSE	1
statements 7	1
END IF	1

Each block-**IF** statement has an implied level number and all statements and clauses belonging to that block-**IF** have the same level number. This number is given in the right-hand column above. So if *e1* is false the **ELSE** clause at level 1 will be obeyed (*statements 7*). Similarly, if *e2* is false, *statements 6* will be obeyed. If *e2* is true, then *statements 2* will be obeyed followed by the **IF** statement at the next level down and so on. Do not forget to end every block-**IF** with an **END IF**; and notice how indentation enables you to tell at a glance which statements belong together.

It should be obvious from this that it is possible to construct very complicated blocks of nested logic in FORTRAN. Try to avoid doing so since too many levels of nested logic can become extremely difficult to follow. It is very easy to make mistakes this way – one loses track of which **ELSE IF** and **ELSE** clauses belong together. Even if you can follow the logic, it may be very difficult for someone else to do so. Indenting statements at each level helps in this respect.

Any block-**IF**, **ELSE** or **ELSE IF** clause may be empty, i.e. no FORTRAN statements need follow. This is equivalent to saying in English, 'if this is true then do nothing'.

3.3 Logical expressions

As we saw in the previous section, one form of logical expression is the relational expression which compares the values of two arithmetic expressions. It is of the general form

e1 r e2

where *e1* and *e2* are both arithmetic expressions and *r* is one of the following relational operators

.EQ.	Equal to
.LT.	Less than
.GT.	Greater than
.LE.	Less than or equal to
.GE.	Greater than or equal to
.NE.	Not equal to

A relational expression has the logical value true if the values of *e1* and *e2* satisfy the relationship specified by *r*, and the logical value false if they do not.

Simple logical expressions may be combined by the logical operators

.AND.
.OR.
.NOT.
.EQV.
.NEQV.

to form more complicated logical expressions.

We can best understand the meaning of these logical operators by the following examples:

IF (Y1 .GT. Y2 .AND. ICOUNT .LT. 20) THEN

This logical expression will be true if both the conditions '**Y1** is greater than **Y2**' and '**ICOUNT** is less than 20' are true. If one (or both) is false, then the whole logical expression is false and the statements following the **THEN** will not be obeyed.

IF (P. EQ. Q .OR. X .LT. 1.0) THEN

This will be true if either P is equal to Q or X is less than 1.0. Only when they are both false will the whole logical expression be false.

IF (.NOT. X1 .GT. X2) THEN

This has the same effect as the statement

IF (X1 .LE. X2) THEN

i.e. the **.NOT.** operator reverses the true value of whatever follows. Therefore the **THEN** clause will be obeyed if the statement 'X1 is greater than X2' is not true.

The **.NOT.** operator may sometimes be found useful in simplifying long and complicated block-**IF** statements since the following are equivalent:

IF (e) THEN
    statements 1
ELSE
    statements 2
END IF

and

IF (e) THEN
    statements 1
END IF
IF (.NOT. e) THEN
    statements 2
END IF

In cases where *statements 1* contain other block-**IF** statements, perhaps extending over several pages of code, this may be a better way to express the logic.

By using combinations of logical and relational operators, complicated logical expressions can be written such as

IF (A .GT. 3.0 .AND. .NOT. C .EQ. D .OR. B .LT. C) THEN

This illustrates two points. First, two logical operators may not appear in sequence unless the second one is a **.NOT.** operator. Second, ambiguities can be introduced into logical expressions just as they can into arithmetic expressions. The above expression could mean either

IF (A .GT. 3.0 .AND..NOT.(C.EQ.D.OR.B.LT.C)) THEN

or

IF ((A .GT. 3.0 .AND..NOT.C .EQ. D) .OR. B .LT. C) THEN

As in the case of arithmetic expressions, ambiguities can be removed by the use of parentheses. In addition, relational and logical operators are given an implicit order of priority in cases where ambiguities are not resolved by the use of parentheses. This hierarchy, in relation to the arithmetic operators, is as follows:

	Priority
Exponentiation	1
Unary minus	2
Multiplication and division	3
Addition and subtraction	4
The relational operators	5
(all of equal priority)	
.NOT.	6
.AND.	7
.OR.	8
.EQV. .NEQV.	9

So the above example actually has the meaning

IF ((A .GT. 3.0 .AND..NOT. C.EQ.D) .OR. B .LT. C) THEN

since the operator **.AND.** is more binding than the **.OR.** operator according to the above table of priorities.

The operators **.EQV.** and **.NEQV.** represent the logical operations of equivalence and non-equivalence. The expression

IF (A.EQV.B) THEN

will be true if A and B are either both true or both false and

IF (A.NEQV.B) THEN

will be true if A is false and B is true or vice versa. The expression

IF (((A.EQ.B).EQV.(C.NE.D)).AND.((E.GT.F).NEQV.(G.LT.H)))THEN

will be true if the relational expressions **A .EQ. B** and **C .NE. D** are both true or both false, and the relational expression **E .GT. F** does not have the same logical value as **G .LT. H** (i.e. if one is true, the other is false).

Clearly it is possible to construct logical expressions with very complicated logic but beware of doing so. Errors in logic can occur so easily and involved logic can be painfully difficult to understand. Beware particularly of doubly negative logical expressions. Use parentheses to clarify the logic whenever possible. In general, it is far better to use parentheses to clarify the logic even if not absolutely necessary. For example,

IF ((Y1 .GT. Y2) .AND. (ICOUNT .LT. 20)) THEN

and

IF ((P .EQ. Q) .OR. (X .LT. 1.0)) THEN

are clearer representations than the equivalent expressions written without the extra parentheses.

Remember that logical operators combine complete relational expressions so that statements of the form

IF (A .LT. B .OR. C) THEN

are definitely not valid. This must be written

IF (A .LT. B .OR. A .LT. C) THEN

which is not always how such logic is expressed in English.

The programmer must also be aware of the problems which may be encountered when comparing two real quantities for equality. Because of rounding inaccuracies in the computer, two quantities which may appear to be equal may not in fact be exactly equal since real values have only an approximate representation in the computer. It is better to replace statements of the form

IF (X .EQ. Y) THEN

by

IF (ABS(X − Y) .LE. 1.0E − 6) THEN

i.e. check whether the difference between the two numbers is less than a very small quantity rather than checking for exact equality.

Obviously integers may be compared exactly for equality since they do have an exact representation in the computer.

The whole question of types in FORTRAN is deferred until Chapter 5. However, for completeness here, it should be pointed out that any arithmetic expression of type integer, real, double precision or complex may be compared with relational operators. Complex character expressions may be compared with the operators **.EQ.** and **.NE.** only. Two character expressions may be compared but an arithmetic expression must not be compared with a character expression or vice versa.

A relational expression is only one form of logical expression. The expression *e* may be any valid logical expression, the simplest form of which is a single logical variable. This will be discussed further in Chapter 5.

Following the discussion of the last two sections, we have now moved even closer towards understanding the example programs of Chapter 1. At line 40 in Fig. 1.4 the block-**IF** statement

IF ((N .GT. 0) .AND. (N .LE. 1000)) THEN

selects the cases when *N* lies between 1 and 1000 inclusive. If this is true, then statements 50 to 100 will be obeyed (i.e. the squares of *N* numbers will be summed). The **ELSE** clause for this block-**IF** is found at line 110; in this case, *N* does not lie between 1 and 1000, an error message is printed (line 120). In either case, the program is then terminated (line 140). The **END IF** statement for this block-**IF** is at line 130.

In the income tax program of Fig. 1.5, a more complicated structure of nested block-**IF** statements can be seen. The statements

IF ((SALARY .GE. 1.0) .AND. (SALARY .LE. 20000.0)) THEN

at line 70 starts a block-**IF** which has its **ELSE** clause starting at line 220 and ending at line 240. This selects out the case when the salary is between £1 and £20 000 inclusively. If true, statements 80 to 210 are obeyed; if false, statement 230 is obeyed (i.e. the invalid salary is printed). The program is then terminated.

The **THEN** clause for the block-**IF** itself contains a nested block-**IF** which begins at line 80, ends at line 200 and has an **ELSE** clause at line 100. This selects out the case when the salary does not exceed £750; the tax is calculated by statement 90. If the salary does exceed £750 then a further nested block-**IF** at line 130 selects out the case when the salary does not exceed £5750; the **ELSE** clause for this handles the case when the salary does exceed £5750.

In all of these cases, provided the salary lies within the range £1 to £20 000 the statement at line 210 is obeyed.

Study this logic carefully and make sure you can follow the execution paths for all the possible conditions. Check also that this structure matches the structural specification given in Chapter 1.

3.4 The logical IF statement

A simplified form of the block-**IF** statement may be used in the special case when only one instruction is to be obeyed if the logical expression is true. This is the logical **IF** statement and in the earlier days of FORTRAN was the only type of logical **IF** statement that was provided (the block-**IF** was introduced with the 1977 enhancements). It is of the form

IF (e) *statement*

where *statement* is any executable statement which is obeyed if the logical expression *e* is true and is ignored otherwise. For example, overtime pay may be calculated, if there is any, from the single logical **IF** statement

IF (HRS .GT. 40.0) OVERTM = 1.5 ∗ RATE ∗(HRS − 40.0)

3.5 The GOTO statement

The block-**IF** statement provides a powerful and structured facility for controlling the execution path of a program. FORTRAN provides other methods of transferring control and these should either never be used or used only under one or two exceptional circumstances. They are provided in the language for compatibility with FORTRAN 66 which do not have the block-**IF** facility. Their indiscriminate use tends to cause a breakdown in program structure producing programs which are difficult to unravel (often called 'spaghetti programming'). The first of these is the unconditional **GOTO** statement which is of the general form

GOTO *n*

where *n* is the label of any executable statement to which control is to be transferred and thus will become the next statement in sequence to be obeyed. Subsequently, the statements following this in sequence will be obeyed until some further transfer of control or end of program is encountered.

It has already been described how any statement in FORTRAN may be labelled with an unsigned integer constant of up to five decimal digits at least one of which must be non-zero. In general, labels may be positioned anywhere in columns 1 to 5 of the line; blanks and leading zeros are not significant so that 15 is the same label as 0015 and no two statements must be given the same label. Note that programs with labels greater than 32 767 may not be portable.

The **GOTO** statement will cause computer control to be transferred immediately to the statement with the nominated label and this may be earlier or later in the program. Programs (particularly large ones) which continually jump from one label to another are extremely difficult to follow, as well as being inefficient. For example, a program which tries to work out the number of Grade A marks obtained by boys and girls from a set of examination results may be written as follows (assuming that the input records contain a sex code of 1 for a girl and 2 for a boy, together with a mark which will be greater than or equal to 70% for a Grade A, and that the program is to terminate when a zero sex code is found):

```
      PROGRAM MARKS
      NGIRL = 0
      NBOY  = 0
30    READ *,ISEX,MARK
      IF (ISEX .EQ. 0) GOTO 40
      IF (ISEX .EQ. 1) GOTO 10
      IF (ISEX .EQ. 2) GOTO 20
      PRINT *,'***Error – Invalid Sex Code ',ISEX
      STOP
10    IF (MARK .LT. 70) GOTO 30
      NGIRL = NGIRL + 1
      GOTO 30
20    IF (MARK .LT. 70) GOTO 30
      NBOY = NBOY + 1
      GOTO 30
40    PRINT *,'There are ',NGIRL,' girls',
     1          ' and ',NBOY,' boys with Grade A marks'
      STOP
      END
```

This is typical of many programs and I hope that this simple example is sufficient to convince you that there has been a breakdown of structure here and the program is consequently more difficult to follow than the equivalent program written using a block-**IF**, i.e.

```
      PROGRAM MARKS
      NGIRL = 0
      NBOY  = 0
  10  READ *,ISEX,MARK
      IF (ISEX .EQ. 1) THEN
          IF (MARK .GE. 70) NGIRL = NGIRL + 1
      ELSE IF (ISEX .EQ. 2) THEN
          IF (MARK .GE. 70) NBOY = NBOY + 1
      ELSE IF (ISEX .EQ. 0) THEN
          PRINT *,'There are ',NGIRL,' girls',
  1                ' and ',NBOY,' boys with Grade A marks'
          STOP
      ELSE
          PRINT *,'***Error - Invalid Sex Code ',ISEX
          STOP
      END IF
      GOTO 10
      END
```

Now we have reduced the number of **GOTO** statements to one and this is used for repetition purposes, i.e. to go to the beginning, read a new record and perform the whole calculation again. We shall see in the next chapter that there are better ways of implementing repetitions in FORTRAN than this.

The unconditional **GOTO** statement is one of the chief causes of infinite loops in programs. Unless it is correctly combined with appropriate conditional tests to stop the repetition, then the program will loop round and round forever and consume vast amounts of computer time. For example, suppose we wish to read integers from successive input records and find the sum and the product of them all. Then a FORTRAN program to do this might be as follows:

```
      PROGRAM ARITH
      NSUM   = 0
      NPRDCT = 1
  10  PRINT *, 'Enter integer number: '
      READ *,NUM
      NSUM   = NSUM + NUM
      NPRDCT = NPRDCT * NUM
      GOTO 10
      PRINT *,'The sum is ',NSUM,' and the product is ',NPRDCT
      STOP
      END
```

Remember that computers may often appear to be clever but in fact they obey the programmer's instructions like morons regardless of how foolish these instructions might be.

You should satisfy yourself that this program will compute the sum and the product of the numbers input but will never stop looping around the section of program between label 10 and the statement **GOTO 10**. In fact, the **PRINT** statement at the end will never be obeyed.

To remedy this, we must use a block-**IF** statement to test some termination condition which will stop the looping after the numbers have been input.

For example, a suitable termination condition may be when a number which is less than or equal to zero is read. The program now becomes

```
      PROGRAM ARITH
      NSUM   = 0
      NPRDCT = 1
10    PRINT *, 'Enter integer number: '
      READ *,NUM
      IF (NUM .GT. 0) THEN
          NSUM   = NSUM + NUM
          NPRDCT = NPRDCT * NUM
          GOTO 10
      ELSE
          PRINT *,'The sum is ',NSUM,' and the product is ',NPRDCT
          STOP
      END IF
      END
```

It can be seen that the **ELSE** clause will be obeyed when a zero or a negative number is read; the result will be printed and the program terminated. From this the necessity for controlled repetitions which will protect against indefinite looping should be apparent.

So, to summarize, the unconditional **GOTO** statement exists in the language but it is wise to avoid using it. If you do find yourself using it, ask yourself if there is a better way of implementing the logic.

Finally, remember that any executable or non-executable statement may be labelled but control may only be transferred to an executable statement. It is worth pointing out here that some compilers may generate error messages or warnings if non-executable statements (excluding **FORMAT** statements) are labelled. Warnings are sometimes also given if a statement is labelled but no transfer of control to that statement takes place. This may or may not be a genuine program error.

3.6 The arithmetic IF statement

Another early FORTRAN statement which has been made redundant by the introduction of block-**IF** statements is the arithmetic **IF** statement which is of the general form

IF (e) *n1,n2,n3*

where *e* is any arithmetic expression (of type integer, real or double precision) and *n1*, *n2* and *n3* are executable statement labels. If the value of expression *e* is negative then control is passed to statement label *n1*, if it is zero then control is transferred to *n2* and if it is positive control is passed to *n3*.

The arithmetic **IF** statement acts as a three-way switch directing the flow of logic of the program into one of three possible paths (which may be all different but not necessarily so). So in the examination mark program of the previous section it would be possible to implement a switch on the sex code by the following statements:

IF (ISEX − 1)40.10.20

where the code at label 10 processes a girl's marks (i.e when **ISEX** is 1), the code at label 20 processes a boy's marks (i.e. when **ISEX** is 2) and the code at label 40 processes a zero sex code. This statement suffers from all of the disadvantages of the **GOTO** statement as well as being an awkward structure in itself.

3.7 The computed GOTO statement

FORTRAN provides a multi-way switch in the form of the computed **GOTO** statement which can direct the flow of logic into one of several different paths depending on the value of an integer expression. It is of the general form

GOTO (*n1,n2,. . .,nm*), *i*

where *n1*, *n2*, . . ., *nm* are executable statement labels and *i* is an integer expression. If the value of *i* is 1 then control goes to *n1*, if it is 2 then control goes to *n2* and so on, e.g.

GOTO (50,22,8,22,65),IQ

will go to label 50 if $IQ = 1$, 22 if $IQ = 2$, 8 if $IQ = 3$, 22 if $IQ = 4$ and 65 if $IQ = 5$. Note that the labels are not necessarily all different.

The value of *i* must lie in the range *1* to *m*. If it is outside this range then the next statement should be executed although, in practice, compilers may behave differently in this respect. The programmer should test for the value of *i* before the computed **GOTO** is executed, thus ensuring that this possible error is trapped.

The comma following the closing parenthesis is defined as optional in the FORTRAN standard but compilers may vary in their treatment of this.

There is no actual syntactic limit to the number of labels which may be used. Continuation lines may be used to extend the computed **GOTO** over several lines. However, in practice, most compilers will impose some reasonable upper limit.

Note that the examination mark switch of the previous section could be implemented by the statement

GOTO (40,10,20),ISEX + 1

Again, this statement suffers from all of the disadvantages of the **GOTO** statement and is best avoided.

3.8 The assigned GOTO statement

The assigned **GOTO** statement is of the general form

GOTO *iv,(n1,n2,. . .,nm)*

where *iv* is an integer variable and *n1, n2, . . ., nm* are executable statement labels. The integer variable *iv* contains a statement label value which must have been set earlier in the program by an **ASSIGN** statement

ASSIGN *l* **TO** *iv*

where *l* is an executable statement label and *iv* is the integer variable to be used subsequently in the assigned **GOTO** statement. This will cause control to be transferred to that label which must be one of the labels in the list *n1, n2, . . ., nm*, e.g.

ASSIGN 15 TO LABEL
GOTO LABEL, (22,6,15,30,1)

will transfer control to label 15.

The first comma and the list of labels in parentheses need not be present, but if they are, the label must be in the list.

The variable, *iv*, may subsequently be assigned an integer value and used as an integer variable.

An **ASSIGN** statement may be used in one other context only – to assign a **FORMAT** statement label for use in an I/O statement (Chapter 6).

This statement, like all the statements of the previous three sections, is definitely not recommended and is included here only for completeness.

3.9 Summary

- According to the FORTRAN standard, there are sixteen control statements in all, i.e.

  Unconditional GOTO
  Computed GOTO
  Assigned GOTO
  Arithmetic IF
  Logical IF

Block IF
ELSE IF
ELSE
END IF
STOP
END
PAUSE
DO
CONTINUE
CALL
RETURN

Of these sixteen, we have now described the first eleven. The **DO** and **CONTINUE** statements will be described in the next chapter. The **CALL** and **RETURN** statements will be deferred until Chapter 8 when we discuss Functions and Subroutines. Of the control statements described so far, the block-**IF** with its associated **ELSE IF**, **ELSE** and **END IF** statements is by far the most important.

● The block-**IF** statement is of the form

IF (e) THEN
    statements 1
ELSE IF (e) THEN
    statements 2
ELSE IF (e) THEN
    statements 3

        .
        .
        .

ELSE
    statements n
ENDIF

● The logical **IF** statement is of the form

IF (e) *statement*

● The **GOTO** statement is of the general form

GOTO *n*

where *n* is a statement label. It should be used sparingly. The use of the Assigned **GOTO** statement and the Computed **GOTO** statement is definitely not recommended.

Exercises 3

1. If $I=1$, $J=2$, $K=3$, $L=4$ and $M=5$ evaluate the truth values of the following expressions:

(a) J .GT. K .OR. L .EQ. M − I

(b) I + J .NE. K∗L .AND..NOT. M .GT. 3 .OR. K .LT. 2

(c) .NOT. (J − 3 .EQ. (−1)) .OR. .NOT.(M .LT. 50 .AND. K .EQ. I + 1)

2. Using a block-**IF** statement, write a program to evaluate the following functions depending on the value of a variable **NOFUN**:

$$(x_1 - x_2^2)^2 + (1 - x_2)^2$$

if **NOFUN** is 1

$$100(x_2 - x_1^2)^2 + (1 - x_1)^2$$

if **NOFUN** is 2

$$100(x_1 - x_2^3)^2 + (1 - x_2)^2$$

if **NOFUN** is 3

$$(x_1 + 2x_2 - 7)^2 + (2x_1 + x_2 - 5)^2$$

if **NOFUN** is 4

3. Write the search program designed in Exercises 1, number 4.

4. Write a program to evaluate the square root of a number using the formula

$$b = \frac{1}{2}\left(\frac{x}{a} + a\right)$$

where b is a better approximation to the square root of x than a. The first approximation should be taken as $x/2$ and the procedure should be repeated until the difference between a and b is less than 0.000001.

5. Write a program which reads a year (e.g. 1987) and determines whether it is a leap year. Print out an appropriate message indicating whether the year input is or is not a leap year. Use the fact that if a year is a leap year, then its number must be divisible by 400 exactly, or the year number must divide by 4 exactly provided it is not also divisible by 100.

4

Repetitions and arrays

4.1 Introduction

In previous chapters we have described how algorithms may be constructed from basic sequences, selections and repetitions. We have explained in more detail what language statements are provided in FORTRAN to implement sequences and selections. We have touched on the need for repetitions in some of our example programs in the text. In this chapter we shall describe how repetitions can be implemented in FORTRAN and how the power of these can be enhanced by means of arrays. By the end of this chapter, you will understand fully all of the statements used in the complete example programs introduced in Chapter 1.

To illustrate how to implement repetitions in FORTRAN, let us consider a program to read a set of magnetic compass readings and convert these to true readings. A magnetic compass is subject to a deviation from the actual magnetic reading because of the magnetic effects of objects around it; this in turn is subject to a variation from the true reading (caused by the fact that the true North Pole and the magnetic North Pole are not in the same position). Both the deviation and the variation may be East or West. Let us suppose that in this example the deviation is 3 degrees East in which case the value of the deviation must be added to the compass reading, in degrees, to give the magnetic reading in degrees. Let us further suppose that the variation is 6 degrees West in which case it must be subtracted from the magnetic reading to give the true reading, also in degrees. Our program is to read a set of N compass readings and produce a table of these readings together with their equivalent magnetic and true readings.

The algorithm to do this reads as follows:

```
Do N times:
    Read a compass reading
    Add the deviation to give
    the magnetic reading
    Subtract the variation to
    give the true reading
    Print the compass, magnetic
    and true readings
End Do N times
```

It was explained in the last chapter how logic of this type could be implemented using the **GOTO** statement and some appropriate **IF** statement to terminate the repetition. Equally this could be implemented by a statement of the form 'Do N times' followed by the statements which have to be obeyed within the repetition together with some appropriate means of indicating which statement is the last one. The statement 'Do N times' can in turn be expressed as 'Do for each value of a counter from 1 to N (in steps of 1)'. Thus the repetition may be implemented as follows:

Set the initial value of some counter, i.e. I = 1.
Test if the calculation has been done the required number of times.
If so, terminate the repetition.
If not, perform the required calculation for the current value of I.
Increment the counter I on completion of the calculation.
Branch back to the beginning to repeat the calculation.

So here, instructions are repeatedly obeyed under the control of a counter until this counter reaches some termination value. Since it is so often required to perform a count controlled repetition of this sort, FORTRAN provides a single instruction to do just this – the **DO** statement. Instead of the word repetition, FORTRAN tends to use the word 'loop' and all of the statements which fall in the range of the **DO** statement form the **DO** loop.

4.2 The DO statement

The **DO** statement is of the general form

   DO *label, i = m1, m2, m3*

where *label* is the label of an executable statement at a later point in the program and *i* is an integer variable representing the counter to be incremented (for completeness here note that it may also be a real or double precision variable). *m1*, *m2* and *m3* may be any general expression (of type integer, real or double precision) such that *m1* represents the initial value of the counter, *m2* represents the final value and *m3* represents the step by which the counter is to be incremented each time through the loop. (Note for completeness that *i* may not be subscripted). A negative step with *m2* less than *m1* is allowed. If *m3* is not explicitly stated it is taken to be 1. In this case the statement is of the form

   DO *label, i = m1, m2*

This has exactly the same effect as

   DO *label, i = m1, m2,1*

The **DO** statement automatically causes execution of all the statements following it, up to and including the statement labelled *label* for values of *i* from *m1* in steps of *m3*. Thus *i* is set equal to *m1*; it is tested against *m2* and if it does not exceed it, the required computation is performed. Then i is increased to $m1 + m3$, the test is made against $m2$ and the calculation repeated. This is continued until i becomes greater than $m2$, when control is transferred out of the loop to the statement immediately following the statement labelled *label*. The sequence of statements which is obeyed within the loop is known as the range of the **DO** statement. The counter i is usually called the index of the loop or sometimes the control variable.

So it can be seen that the requirements for a repetition are all provided by this one statement. Some examples of the **DO** statement are as follows:

DO 10, I = 1,5

will obey all of the statements up to and including statement 10 for I equal to 1, 2, 3, 4 and 5.

DO 20, J = K,N,3

will obey all of the statements up to and including statement 20 for J equal to K, $K + 3$, $K + 6$ and so on until J exceeds N.

DO 30, I = 1,N,2

will obey all of the statements up to and including statement 30 for I equal to 1, 3, 5, etc. until I exceeds N. Note that I need not necessarily ever assume the value N. If N is 8, then this loop is performed for $I = 1, 3, 5, 7$ but not for $I = 9$ since this exceeds N. It is never done for $I = 8$.

The value of the **DO** control variable, i, may not be changed within the loop. It is good practice to ensure that none of the parameters i, $m1$, $m2$ or $m3$ is changed by any other statement within the range of the **DO** statement. They may be changed outside the range provided that no transfer is subsequently made back into the range.

The program example in the previous chapter which computes the sum and the product of N integers can now be written without the **GOTO** statement as follows:

```
PROGRAM ARITH
NSUM   = 0
NPRDCT = 1
DO 10, I = 1,100
    PRINT *,'Enter integer number: '
    READ *,NUM
    IF (NUM .GT. 0) THEN
        NSUM = NSUM + NUM
        NPRDCT = NPRDCT*NUM
    ELSE
        PRINT *,'The sum is ',NSUM,' and the product is ',
1               NPRDCT
        STOP
    ENDIF
```

```
10  CONTINUE
    PRINT *,'***Error — too many integers'
    STOP
    END
```

It can be seen that the statement labelled 10 is the last statement within the range of the **DO** loop. The **CONTINUE** statement is used here for reasons which will be explained in the next section, but for the moment take it that at this point the system will return control back to the **DO** statement and will automatically increment the counter I by 1 and check to see if this exceeds 100. If it does then the loop is completed and the next statement to be performed will be the one immediately following the statement labelled 10, i.e. the **PRINT** statement which prints an error message since this program will only work if there are less than 101 integers terminated by a negative integer. If I does not exceed 100, then the statements within the loop will be performed again.

It will be instructive for you at this point to implement the program to convert compass readings to true readings as follows:

> Read N, the number of compass readings
> DO 10, $I = 1,N$
>> Read the compass reading
>> Add the deviation to give
>> the magnetic reading
>> Subtract the variation to
>> give the true reading
>> Print the compass, magnetic and true readings
> 10   CONTINUE

Note that it is good programming practice to indent all of the statements which fall within the range of a **DO** loop. The structure of the program is then clear at a glance; this becomes particularly important when we discuss nested loops later.

All the examples introduced so far, use the **DO** statement in its simplest form, i.e. **DO** in steps of 1 from 1 to N. In general, more complicated loops may be written. For example, the expressions used in a **DO** statement may be negative, i.e.

DO 10, I = N+1,M*10,−2

is allowed. This obeys the statements in the range of the loop for $I = N+1$, $N-1, N-3, N-5$ until I is less than **M*10**. Note that the step $m3$ must not be zero nor be an expression which ever assumes a value of zero.

In general, the number of repetitions which will be performed for any **DO** loop is given by the formula

$$\mathbf{MAX}\left(0, \mathbf{INT}\left(\frac{m2 - m1 + m3}{m3}\right)\right)$$

For a loop of 1 to N in steps of 1, this formula yields the value N. The intrinsic function **MAX** selects whichever is the larger of the two arguments.

In the **DO** statement, the comma following the statement label is optional but its use is recommended; this avoids the unfortunate error which may arise when a **DO** statement of the form

DO 10 I = 1,5

is accidentally mistyped as

DO 10 I = 1.5

Since spaces are not significant in FORTRAN names, **DO 10 I** is a valid FORTRAN symbolic name for a real variable. So the above statement is a valid arithmetic assignment statement which assigns 1.5 to **DO10I**. This may go undetected for some time and could have catastrophic effects on the execution of a program. The use of a comma, i.e. **DO 10, I** avoids this ambiguity.

Note that the 1977 definition of FORTRAN made an important change to the behaviour of a **DO** loop, and since some of the world's large FORTRAN programs may still be written in FORTRAN 66, you should be aware of this if you have to work with such a program. Consider the case

DO 10 I = 1,N

when N has the value zero.

In FORTRAN 77, this will set I to 1 and if the value of I exceeds N (which it does immediately if N is 0), then control is transferred to the first executable statement outside the range of the **DO** loop, i.e. the statements are never obeyed.

However in FORTRAN 66, I is set to 1, the loop is executed for this value of I and at the end of this first pass I is incremented and tested against N. It is only then that it is found to exceed it and no further repetitions are performed. So in this case a **DO** loop will always be performed once whatever the value of N.

This difference can result in programs producing quite different results if compiled with an old compiler or a new FORTRAN 77 compiler.

The FORTRAN 77 definition also clearly states that the index variable retains the value it holds when the test fails and may be used in subsequent statements which may assume this. Thus the statements

```
      DO 10, I = 1,50
10       ISUM = ISUM + I**2
      J = I
```

would perform the loop until $I = 50$, increment I to 51 and then discover that this exceeds the termination value; thus control will be transferred to the statement immediately after label 10, with the value of I still set to 51. This statement will therefore assign the value 51 to J.

Also note that if any statement causes a jump out of the loop before all of the repetitions are complete, then the value of I will be the value set for the current repetition. It is permitted to jump out of a loop either to a point earlier or later in the program. Note, however, that it is not permitted to jump into a loop from outside it in such a way as to bypass the **DO** statement itself; this would obviously prevent the system from correctly setting up the initial value of the loop counters. Also never change the value of a loop variable i within the range of the loop because the system itself changes this variable.

A popular application for the **DO** loop is in the summation of series. Suppose that we wish to sum the series

$$1 + \frac{n}{1!} + \frac{n^2}{2!} + \frac{n^3}{3!} + \frac{n^4}{4!} + \ldots$$

Then a FORTRAN program to do this is as follows:

```
      PROGRAM SERIES
      PRINT *,'Enter the value of N: '
      READ *,N
      PRINT *,'Enter the number of terms to be summed: '
      READ *,NTERM
      SUM  = 1.0
      TERM = 1.0
      DO 10, I = 1,NTERM - 1
          TERM = TERM * REAL(N) / REAL(I)
10        SUM = SUM + TERM
      PRINT *,'The sum of ',NTERM,' terms of the series is ',SUM
      STOP
      END
```

However, the full power of the **DO** statement will not become apparent until we introduce the concept of arrays and subscripts. But before we do this, a brief word about the **CONTINUE** statement and conditional loops.

4.3 The CONTINUE statement

The **CONTINUE** statement consists merely of the word **CONTINUE** placed anywhere in columns 7 to 72. It is a dummy statement which can be placed anywhere in a program and does absolutely nothing. It can be labelled and can be used to terminate a **DO** loop, but logically it has no effect on the execution of a program. It is a very useful statement for attaching labels to, so that other statements may be inserted easily before it. It is good programming practice to terminate all **DO** loops with a **CONTINUE** statement, e.g.

```
      DO 10, I = 1,NTERM - 1
          TERM = TERM * REAL(N) / REAL(I)
10        SUM = SUM + TERM
```

would be better written as

```
      DO 10, I = 1,NTERM − 1
          TERM = TERM * REAL(N) / REAL(I)
          SUM = SUM + TERM
   10 CONTINUE
```

In the first case, in order to add an extra statement in the range of the **DO** loop it is necessary to edit the 10 off the statement it currently labels and add a new statement with label 10. In the second case it is simply necessary to insert an extra statement.

Some programmers make it a practice to label only **CONTINUE** statements (and **FORMAT** statements which will be described later).

Note that there are specific rules about which statements can terminate a **DO** loop. The last statement in the range of a **DO** statement must not be a **GOTO** statement, an arithmetic **IF** statement, a **RETURN, STOP, END** or another **DO** statement. It may not be a block-**IF, ELSE IF, ELSE** or **END IF** statement. If it is a logical **IF** statement, it may contain any executable statement except **DO**, block-**IF, ELSE IF, ELSE, END, END IF** or another logical **IF** statement.

Note that among the statements which cannot terminate a **DO** loop is the **END IF** statement. Hence the need for a **CONTINUE** statement in the program ARITH in the previous section; without this, the loop would have terminated on the **END IF** statement.

It is now possible for you to understand completely all of the statements in the example programs of Fig. 1.4 and Fig. 1.5. Try running these on your machine; perhaps you can modify the income tax program to calculate the income tax on your own salary so that it becomes of some real practical use to you.

4.4 Conditional loops

There are two useful constructs which are provided in many other languages but which are not provided explicitly in FORTRAN. These are conditional loops of the form

Repeat until (condition)

and

Repeat while (condition)

These in turn cause the loop to be performed either until some condition becomes true or while a condition is true. Although FORTRAN only provides a count controlled loop and does not have the equivalent of these statements, nevertheless, this logic can be implemented in FORTRAN using a combination of the **DO** loop, the logical **IF** statement and the **GOTO** statement as follows:

```
     DO 10, I = 1,N
          IF (condition) GOTO 20
10   CONTINUE
20   CONTINUE
```

which is the equivalent of the 'repeat until' statement (assuming that 'condition' is a logical expression which starts off false and at some stage within the loop becomes true) and

```
     DO 10, I = 1,N
          IF (.NOT.condition) GOTO 20
10   CONTINUE
20   CONTINUE
```

which is the equivalent of the 'repeat while' statement (assuming that 'condition' is a logical expression which starts off true and at some stage within the loop becomes false. Logical expressions will be described more fully in the next chapter).

These examples are given as valid reasons for using the **GOTO** statement.

These two forms of repetition can also be used as valid logical components of a structural specification. So if a repetition represented in a structure diagram is in fact better represented as a **DO** while or **DO** until in a structural specification then use these in preference.

4.5 Nested loops

An inner **DO** statement can be used within the range of an outer **DO** statement; this is generally referred to as a *nest* of loops. So, for example,

```
     DO 20, I = 1,N
          DO 10, J = 1,M
               .
               .
               .
10        CONTINUE
20   CONTINUE
```

illustrates two nested loops. **DO** statements can be nested to any depth. Control can be transferred from the range of an inner **DO** to the outer range without any restriction but must never be transferred from an outer range to an inner range. If in the following diagram, ⊏ represents the range of a **DO** statement, then the arrows indicate possible transfers of control. In the first figure the arrows represent valid jumps, and in the second figure they represent invalid jumps.

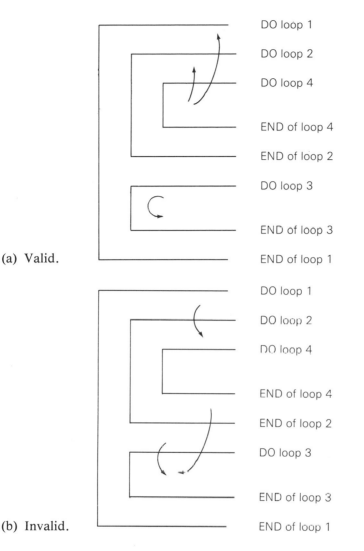

DO loop 1

DO loop 2

DO loop 4

END of loop 4

END of loop 2

DO loop 3

END of loop 3

(a) Valid.   END of loop 1

DO loop 1

DO loop 2

DO loop 4

END of loop 4

END of loop 2

DO loop 3

END of loop 3

(b) Invalid.   END of loop 1

If a **DO** statement is used within a block-**IF**, **ELSE IF** or **ELSE** block then its
range must lie entirely within that block. Conversely, if a block-**IF** statement
is included within a **DO** loop then the corresponding **END IF** statement must
also lie within the **DO** loop. So the following statements

```
      DO 10, I = 1,N
         IF (NUM(I) .LT. 0) THEN
            .
            .
            .
10    CONTINUE
         ENDIF
```

are invalid, as are the statements

```
        IF (NUM(I) .GT. 0)THEN
            DO 10, I = 1,N

                    .
                    .
                    .
        ENDIF
10          CONTINUE
```

and must be written

```
        DO 10, I = 1,N
            IF (NUM(I) .LT. 0) THEN

                .
                .
                .
            END IF
10      CONTINUE
```

and

```
        IF (NUM(I) .GT. 0)THEN
            DO 10, I = 1,N

                .
                .
                .
10          CONTINUE
        ENDIF
```

Nested loops may terminate on the same statement or different statements, e.g.

```
        DO 10, I = 1,L
            DO 10, J = 1,M
                DO 10, K = 1,N

                    .
                    .
                    .
10      CONTINUE
```

or

```
        DO 30, I = 1,L
            DO 20, J = 1,M
                DO 10, K = 1,N

                    .
                    .
                    .
10              CONTINUE
20          CONTINUE
30      CONTINUE
```

From the point of view of good programming practice, the latter representation is much to be preferred.

As we shall see later in this chapter, nested **DO** loops are often used when processing multi-dimensional arrays.

4.6 Arrays and subscripts

So far in our discussion on symbolic names for storage locations we have talked only about assigning one name to one memory location. But suppose that a whole set of consecutive memory locations are all expected to hold the same type of information and are to be referred to with one name. For example, suppose we wish to read in a set of compass readings and hold them all in memory before performing any calculations on them. To explain how we can do this, let us return to our chest of drawers analogy and suppose that all the drawers are painted blue. We can now give instructions to lay the table as follows:

Open BLUE(1)
Take a knife from compartment 0
Close BLUE(1)
Open BLUE(2)
Take a fork from compartment 0
Close BLUE(2)
Open BLUE(3)
Take a spoon from compartment 0
Close BLUE(3)

We can see that we are now referring to individual drawers by means of a name and a number in parentheses where the first drawer is BLUE(1), the second BLUE(2) and so on.

In FORTRAN it is possible to use similar notation to name memory locations. A set of memory locations with the same name is known as an *array*. The name given to these locations is known as the *array name*, and the number given in parentheses after the array name to uniquely identify one location in this set of locations is known as the array *subscript*.

So now we can implement the compass conversion program by reading the compass readings into an array **RCOMP**, storing the magnetic readings in an array **RMAG** and the true readings in an array **RTRUE** as follows:

```
      DO 10, I = 1,N
         READ *,RCOMP(I)
         RMAG(I)  = RCOMP(I) + 3
         RTRUE(I) = RMAG(I)   - 6
         PRINT *,RCOMP(I),RMAG(I),RTRUE(I)
   10 CONTINUE
```

Here the **DO** variable I is set to 1 initially and used as a subscript to the array

RCOMP. Thus the **READ** statement reads a number into **RCOMP(1)**. The corresponding magnetic and true readings are then set up in **RMAG(1)** and **RTRUE(1)**. The next time round the loop, the value of I is 2 and the readings are entered into **RCOMP(2)**, **RMAG(2)** and **RTRUE(2)**. This continues until I exceeds N.

4.7 Dimensioning arrays

Before the compass readings statements of the previous section can be included in a fully working program, we must provide some method of indicating to the compiler how many memory locations are to be reserved for the arrays to be used in the program. This information can be provided in a 'type' statement. We have already described how the names of variables have an implied type given by their first letter (i.e. all names beginning with I to N are integer, all other names are real) and it is not essential to declare the type of a name in a separate statement. However, FORTRAN does provide type declaration statements which can be used to override the implicit naming conventions, e.g. a variable beginning with I can be declared to be real in a type declaration statement for example. These type declarations are discussed in full in the next chapter but we will introduce them briefly here to show how they may be used to dimension arrays.

An integer or real type declaration is of the form

INTEGER *list*

or

REAL *list*

where *list* is a list of variable names or array declarations which are to be given the specified type. Thus

INTEGER COUNT,TEMP,L,I

will declare the four variables to be of type integer (even though the implicit naming conventions of FORTRAN would normally cause **COUNT** and **TEMP** to be real) and

REAL MAG,COMP,INDEX

will declare the three variables to be of type real (even though MAG and INDEX would normally be integer). The list may also include an array declaration which is of the form

name(*d*)

where *name* is a valid FORTRAN symbolic array name and *d* is a dimension declaration which defines how many locations are to be allocated to that array. Thus the statement **INTEGER NUM(5)** defines an integer array of five

locations which can be accessed as **NUM(1)**, **NUM(2)**, **NUM(3)**, **NUM(4)** and
NUM(5). Any particular location is known as an element of that array, e.g.
NUM(3) is the third element of the array **NUM**. All elements of the array must
be of the same type.

Note that array names must be quite distinct from variable names within
the same program. However, both arrays and variables may be declared in
the same type statement, e.g.

REAL RCOMP(1000),COUNT,A(50),I

is a valid statement, but

REAL RCOMP(1000),COUNT,RCOMP,I

is not because **RCOMP** is declared as both an array name and a variable name.

The type declaration statement is a non-executable statement. It must be
placed in the program before any executable statement, i.e. arrays must be
declared before they are used.

Let us suppose that the compass reading program is to process a maximum
of 1000 readings, then a statement to dimension the arrays may be of the form

REAL RCOMP(1000),RMAG(1000),RTRUE(1000)

This informs the compiler that the program wishes to refer to 1000 distinct
sequential locations all identified by the variable **RCOMP**, 1000 identified by
the variable **RMAG** and 1000 identified by the variable **RTRUE**. These
locations can be referred to by **RCOMP(1)**, **RCOMP(2)** and so on to
RCOMP(1000), **RMAG(1)** to **RMAG(1000)** and **RTRUE(1)** to **RTRUE(1000)**. All of
these locations will be reserved for use by the program although the program
may not necessarily use them all. The program must not use more than this.
So the complete program to process compass readings becomes

```
        PROGRAM COMPAS
        REAL RCOMP(1000),RMAG(1000),RTRUE(1000)
        INTEGER I
        PRINT *,'Enter the number of readings: '
        READ *,N
        PRINT *,'Now enter this number of readings one per line: '
        DO 10, I = 1,N
            READ *,RCOMP(I)
            RMAG(I) = RCOMP(I) + 3
            RTRUE(I) = RMAG(I)  - 6
            PRINT *,'Compass = ',RCOMP(I),' Magnetic = ',RMAG(I),
     1                 ' True = ',RTRUE(I)
 10     CONTINUE
        STOP
        END
```

We are now in a position to generalize the simple example program given earlier to read integers and compute their sum and product. All of the numbers can be input and stored in an array as follows:

```
       PROGRAM ARITH
       INTEGER I,NSUM,NPRDCT,NUM(1000)
       NSUM   = 0
       NPRDCT = 1
       PRINT *,'Enter the integers, one per line:'
       DO 10, I = 1, 1000
           READ *, NUM(I)
           IF (NUM(I) .GT. 0) THEN
               NSUM   = NSUM + NUM(I)
               NPRDCT = NPRDCT * NUM(I)
           ELSE
               PRINT *,'The sum is ',NSUM,' and the product is ',
     1                 NPRDCT
           STOP
           ENDIF
    10 CONTINUE
       PRINT *,'***Error — too many integers'
       STOP
       END
```

It is assumed that there will never be more than 1000 integers and that the repetition will be terminated when a negative integer is read.

In this example it is not immediately obvious why we should use arrays but if this code were part of a larger program then it can be appreciated that all of the numbers **NUM(1)** to **NUM(1000)** are held in memory at the same time and can be used for other computations on them. For example, it is possible to add code after label 10, which would find the maximum and minimum of all the numbers. It would be a useful exercise to try this.

Any individual element of an array may be referenced by a subscript expression which must be an integer expression, e.g. **NUM(I + 1)** references the $(i + 1)$th element of the array **NUM**. A subscript expression may itself contain array element references and function references. However, evaluation of a function must not alter the value of any other expression within the same subscript. The value of the subscript expression must lie within the declared dimension or bounds of the array. Failure to do this often results in an execution error with a message 'array bounds exceeded' or something similar. However, it has to be said that not all systems detect such an error, and overflowing the bounds of an array can cause subsequent locations in memory to be overwritten which can in turn cause very bizarre errors in programs. You would be well advised to build in your own tests for array bounds being exceeded. For example, try modifying the **COMPAS** program above to prevent the user from ever entering a value of N which is not in the range 1 to 1000.

In general, FORTRAN array declarations allow the user to specify both the upper and lower bounds of an array subscript.

The statement

INTEGER NUM(5)

defines an integer array **NUM** with five elements **NUM(1)** to **NUM(5)**. The lower bound is always 1. But FORTRAN also permits declarations of the form

d1:d2

where *d1* and *d2* may be integer arithmetic expressions specifying the lower and upper bounds of the array subscript. If the *d1:* is missing then the lower bound is taken to be 1.

Thus the above statement is still a valid FORTRAN statement but could equally well be written

INTEGER NUM(1:5)

Note that *d1* and *d2* must be integer expressions which may be negative, positive or zero. Thus the statement

INTEGER IARR(−5:10),JARR(0:2∗JDIM),ARR(5∗IDIM/IFACT)

declares three arrays. **IARR** contains 16 elements given by

IARR(−5),IARR(−4). . .IARR(0),IARR(1). . .IARR(10)

This is a fixed length array since the dimensions are given by fixed integer constants.

JARR is a variable length array, the second dimension of which depends on the value of the integer variable **JDIM**. If **JDIM** is 5, then this array has 11 elements given by **JARR(0), JARR(1), . . ., JARR(10)**.

ARR is a variable length array with an implied lower bound of 1 since this is not specified. Its size depends on the value of **IDIM** and **IFACT**. If **IDIM** is 4 and **IFACT** is 2 then this array has 10 elements specified as **ARR(1), ARR(2), . . ., ARR(10)**.

In the discussion so far, all of the arrays used have been one-dimensional arrays since elements are identified by the value of one subscript only. Arrays of two or more dimensions may be declared in a similar way. The statement

REAL A(0:5)

declares a one-dimensional real array of six elements A(0), A(1) to A(5) but the statement

INTEGER N(1:5,1:10)

declares a two-dimensional integer array of 50 elements N(1,1) to N(5,10) and

REAL B(10,20,5)

declares a three-dimensional real array of 1000 elements B(1,1,1) to B(10,20,5)

Thus nine consecutive locations could be referenced by means of a one-dimensional array **NUM(1)**, . . ., **NUM(9)** or a two-dimensional array declared as

INTEGER NUM(3,3)

and referenced as **NUM(1,1)**, **NUM(2,1)**, **NUM(3,1)**, **NUM(1,2)**, **NUM(2,2)**, **NUM(3,2)**, **NUM(1,3)**, **NUM(2,3)**, **NUM(3,3)**. The latter can be thought of as an array composed of horizontal rows and vertical columns. The value of the first subscript refers to a particular row and the second to a particular column

$$
\begin{array}{ccc}
\text{NUM(1,1)} & \text{NUM(1,2)} & \text{NUM(1,3)} \\
\downarrow & \downarrow & \downarrow \\
\text{NUM(2,1)} & \text{NUM(2,2)} & \text{NUM(2,3)} \\
\downarrow & \downarrow & \downarrow \\
\text{NUM(3,1)} & \text{NUM(3,2)} & \text{NUM(3,3)}
\end{array}
$$

So **NUM(2,3)** refers to that element in the second row and third column. The arrows indicate the order in which the elements are stored in the computer. They are stored in such a way that the first subscript varies the most rapidly so that the elements **NUM(3,1)** and **NUM(1,2)** are in consecutive locations in memory.

Note that FORTRAN allows a maximum of seven dimensions for an array. For any subscript declaration $d2$ must always be greater than $d1$.

A frequent use of arrays and **DO** loops in mathematical programs is in vector and matrix manipulation. For example, two matrices may be added by nested **DO** loops as follows:

```
      DO 20, J = 1,N
         DO 10, I = 1,M
            C(I,J) = A(I,J) + B(I,J)
10       CONTINUE
20    CONTINUE
```

In this case, J will be set to 1 and the inner loop will be performed for values of I from 1 to M (i.e. $A(1,1)$, $B(1,1)$, $A(2,1)$, $B(2,1)$, . . ., $A(M,1)$, $B(M,1)$ will be summed) before J is incremented to 2 and the inner loop performed again for values of I from 1 to M. This is repeated until J exceeds M.

The columns of a two-dimensional matrix may be summed by

```
      DO 20, J = 1,N
         SUM(J) = 0.0
         DO 10, I = 1,N
            SUM(J) = SUM(J) + ARRAY(I,J)
```

```
10       CONTINUE
20   CONTINUE
```

When using nested **DO** loops always nest them if possible so that the first subscript varies most rapidly. This ensures that the elements of the array will be accessed in the sequence they are held in memory. So the following loop

```
     DO 20, J = 1,500
        DO 10, I = 1,500
           A1(I,J) = B1(I,J) + B2(I,J) + B3(I,J)
           A2(I,J) = A1(I,J) + B2(I,J) + B3(I,J)
10       CONTINUE
20   CONTINUE
```

is more efficient than the statements

```
     DO 20, I = 1,500
        DO 10, J = 1,500
           A1(I,J) = B1(I,J) + B2(I,J) + B3(I,J)
           A2(I,J) = A1(I,J) + B2(I,J) + B3(I,J)
10       CONTINUE
20   CONTINUE
```

If the arrays are larger than can be held in memory, then it may be necessary to read blocks (often called pages) of data in from disc to access the required memory locations. If the memory locations are not accessed consecutively then the number of times this has to be done may increase dramatically thus slowing down the program.

To gain some measure of the difference in efficiency between these on your machine, it is a useful exercise to write two separate programs to do this and measure the run time in each case. Include type statements

```
REAL A1(500,500),A2(500,500)
REAL B1(500,500),B2(500,500),B3(500,500)
```

and initialize the arrays to some suitable values. Find out if your system provides a means of measuring the execution time of a specified part of a FORTRAN program. This is an extremely useful facility when developing large programs; particularly inefficient parts of the program can be isolated and optimized.

Another common use for arrays is to perform 'table lookup'. For example, data values are set up in an array in such a way that the subscript value can be used to obtain a given entry, e.g. the average heights of children from age 1 to 18 years are set up in an array **HEIGHT** of dimension 18 such that **HEIGHT(1)** contains the height for age 1, **HEIGHT(2)** the height for age 2 and so on. Part of a program to read in a child's age and look up the average height for that age would be as follows:

```
REAL HEIGHT(18)
READ *,IAGE
HT = HEIGHT(IAGE)
```

Translation tables which convert information from one form to another use this technique.

4.8 The DIMENSION statement

There is another statement which is provided in FORTRAN which allows you to dimension arrays. This is the **DIMENSION** statement, which is of the general form

DIMENSION *name1(d1),name2(d2), . . .,namen(dn)*

where *name1*, *name2*, . . ., *namen* are valid FORTRAN symbolic names and *d1, d2, . . ., dn* each represent a list of dimension declarations separated by commas.

This statement was the only means by which arrays could be dimensioned in the old ANSI 66 FORTRAN. The introduction of type statements in the ANSI 77 FORTRAN standard effectively made this statement redundant. However, it is included here for completeness since it is still quite often seen.

Thus the following statements are identical:

```
REAL RCOMP(1000),RMAG(1000),RTRUE(1000)
```

and

```
REAL RCOMP,RMAG,RTRUE
DIMENSION RCOMP(1000),RMAG(1000),RTRUE(1000)
```

The latter may simply be written

```
DIMENSION RCOMP(1000),RMAG(1000),RTRUE(1000)
```

since the arrays are real by the implicit naming conventions of FORTRAN.

4.9 A sorting program

As a complete and useful example of array handling, let us consider a program which has to sort an array of integer numbers into ascending numerical order

```
PROGRAM SORT
INTEGER ARRAY(1000),I,N,COUNT,J
INTEGER INTVAL,TEMP
PRINT *,'Enter the number of values to be sorted: '
READ *,N
PRINT *,'Enter this number of values one per line:'
```

```
        DO 10, I = 1,N
           READ *,ARRAY(I)
  10    CONTINUE
        INTVAL = N/2
        DO 20, COUNT = 1,1000
           IF (INTVAL .LE. 0) GOTO 50
           DO 30, I = INTVAL,N – 1
              DO 40, J = I – INTVAL + 1,1, – INTVAL
                 IF (ARRAY(J) .GT. ARRAY(J + INTVAL))THEN
                    TEMP = ARRAY(J)
                    ARRAY(J) = ARRAY(J + INTVAL)
                    ARRAY(J + INTVAL) = TEMP
                 ENDIF
  40          CONTINUE
  30       CONTINUE
        INTVAL = INTVAL/2
  20    CONTINUE
  50    PRINT *,'The array sorted into ascending order is: '
        DO 60, I = 1,N
           PRINT *,ARRAY(I)
  60    CONTINUE
        STOP
        END
```

This program uses the shell sort algorithm, which compares the values of numbers at the beginning and end of the lists and interchanges them if the lower number is numerically greater than the higher number in the list. The interval between elements which are compared is then decreased until consecutive elements are being considered.

4.10 Summary

- Repetitions may be performed in FORTRAN by means of the **DO** statement.
- The **DO** statement is of the general form

    DO *label, i = m1, m2, m3*

    where *label* is the label of an executable statement at a later point in the program; *i* is an integer, real or double precision variable representing the counter to be incremented; *m1*, *m2* and *m3* are integer, real or double precision expressions representing the initial value of the counter, the final value and the step respectively.
- The **CONTINUE** statement may be used to terminate a loop. Loops may be nested.
- FORTRAN does not provide 'Repeat until' or 'Repeat while' statements but this logic can be programmed with a combination of the **DO** statement, a logical **IF** statement and a **GOTO** statement.

- Arrays may be dimensioned in a type statement which is of the general form

    INTEGER *list*

    or

    REAL *list*

    Types other than **INTEGER** or **REAL** may be declared as described later.

    list is a list of variables or array dimension declarations of the form

    name(d1:d2)

    where *name* is a FORTRAN symbolic name, *d1* is an integer arithmetic expression specifying the lower bound of the array, and *d2* is an integer arithmetic expression specifying the upper bound of the array. The lower bound is taken to be 1 if *d1*: is not specified.

- Multi-dimensional arrays may be dimensioned by an array declaration of the form

    name(d1:d2,d3:d4 . . ., dm:dn)

    where *d1*, *d3*, . . ., *dm* represent the lower bound of each subscript and *d2*, *d4*, . . ., *dn* represent the upper bound of each subscript.

- Arrays may also be dimensioned in a **DIMENSION** statement of the form

    DIMENSION *list*

    where *list* is a list of array dimension declarations as described for type statements. In this case the arrays are typed either by the implicit type of *name* or by declaring *name* in a type statement.

Exercises 4

1. What is wrong with the following FORTRAN program which reads in a list of N integers, computes the sums of alternate numbers (**NSMODD**, **NSMEVN**) and forms a new list in which the Ith element $X(I)$ is the arithmetic mean of the $(I-1)$th and $(I+1)$th elements of the original list (NO)? (Assume that $X(1)$ should be set to NO(1)/2 and $X(N)$ to NO(N)/2.)

```
        PROGRAM WRONG
        READ *,N
        DO 10, I = 1,N
            READ *,NO(I)
    10  CONTINUE
        DO 20, I = 1,N,2
            NSMODD = NSMODD + NO(I)
    20  CONTINUE
        NSMEVN = 0     DO 30, I = 2,N,2
```

```
        NSMEVN = NSMEVN + NO(I)
30   CONTINUE
     PRINT *,NSMODD,NSMEVN
     DO 40, I = 1,N − 1
        X(I) = (NO(I − 1) + NO(I + 1))/2
40   CONTINUE
     X(I) = NO(I)
     DO 50, I = 1,N
        PRINT *,X(I)
50   CONTINUE
     STOP
     END
```

2. Write a FORTRAN program to read data into two arrays of numbers N1 and N2. The arrays are 3 columns wide and 5 rows deep. Add these two arrays together to form the sum (array N3). Write this result into an array N4 which is 5 columns wide and 3 rows deep. Print all four arrays.

3. Write a FORTRAN program to read a list of N positive real numbers and to calculate and print the largest, the smallest, the mean and the standard deviation using the formula

$$Standard\ deviation = \sqrt{\left[\frac{\Sigma(number - mean)^2}{N}\right]}$$

4. Write a FORTRAN program which reads in a set of N examination marks for four different subjects into an array of 4 columns and N rows. Scan this array to find out how many of the marks are Grade A ($> 70\%$), how many are Grade B (60 to 70%), how many are Grade C (50 to 60%), how many are Grade D (40 to 50%) and how many are failures ($< 40\%$) for each of the subjects. Print the results and write a structural specification before programming.

5. Write a program which reads in a date as 3 integers (day, month and year) and computes the date of the day 14 days from this date. Set up an array dimensioned with 12 elements which holds the number of days in each month (e.g. element 9 of this array contains the number of days in month 9, i.e. September). Remember that the program must allow for leap years to give the correct number of days in February and will therefore need to use the formula derived in Exercises 3, number 5. Note that this program should only operate on dates in the Gregorian calendar.

5

Types

5.1 Introduction

So far in this book the discussion has been simplified by considering only two basic FORTRAN types – integer and real. The student programmer has been introduced to most of the basic concepts of FORTRAN and should now be able to write simple programs.

In the preceding text, passing references have been made to other FORTRAN types, including character, double precision and logical. In the previous chapter we have shown how type declarations have been used to dimension arrays.

In this chapter we shall describe the whole subject of types in more detail.

5.2 Type statements

It has been described earlier how any FORTRAN name is given an implicit type associated with its first letter. A name beginning with I, J, K, L, M or N is taken to be an integer, and a name beginning with any other letter is taken to be real. However, a programmer may wish to call some real variable by a name which begins with one of the integer letters. For example, it is customary in physics or engineering to denote a current by the letter I and inductance by the letter L, but the FORTRAN variables I and L have an implied integer type whereas current and inductance are real quantities. It would be convenient therefore to have some means of declaring the type of a variable so that the implicit typing is overridden. This would provide a method also of declaring other types in addition to the two implicit types – real and integer.

Types may be declared by means of a type declaration statement which is of the general form

type list

where *type* is a keyword which defines the type and is one of the names

INTEGER
REAL
CHARACTER

DOUBLE PRECISION
LOGICAL
COMPLEX

and *list* is a list of variable names, array names or array declarations separated by commas (the list may include also the names of functions or statement functions, or dummy arguments to statement functions, but these will not be discussed until Chapter 8; parameters may also be typed in this way – see section 5.8).

The names in the list are then declared to be of the defined type, overriding the implicit typing, e.g.

REAL I,L

will declare I and L to be real.

Any name not declared in a type statement will be typed implicitly by its initial letter and no name may appear in a type statement more than once in the same program (or more precisely – in the same program unit).

A type declaration is a non-executable statement and must precede all executable statements.

Arrays may be declared and dimensioned in a type statement. The statements

REAL NO1(50),NO2(100)
DOUBLE PRECISION LONG(100)
COMPLEX IMAG(500)

are equivalent to the statements

REAL NO1,NO2
DOUBLE PRECISION LONG
COMPLEX IMAG
DIMENSION NO1(50),NO2(100),LONG(100),IMAG(500)

and obviously more compact.

A type declaration is simply an instruction to the compiler to reserve in computer memory, for use by the program, a certain number of locations of the appropriate size for that type and allow them to be referenced in the program by the symbolic name.

A character declaration may be of the form

CHARACTER*n *list*

which types all names in *list* as character locations of length n, i.e. capable of storing n characters. If n is 1 then the *n may be omitted.

Before proceeding, a word of warning to those readers who are already familiar with other dialects of FORTRAN. Many compilers allow notation such as **INTEGER*2** (to declare a two byte integer), **INTEGER*4** (a four byte integer), **REAL*4** (a single precision four byte real), **REAL*8** (a double precision eight byte real) and so on. These extensions are definitely non-standard and should be avoided.

5.3 Character type

It has already been described how a character occupies one character storage location which is usually a byte (often consisting of 8 bits). On a 32 bit word-length machine, therefore, 4 characters may be stored in one word.

A character constant is a string of characters enclosed in apostrophes, e.g.

'THIS IS A CHARACTER CONSTANT'

Character constants may contain letters in upper and lower case, e.g.

'This is also a valid CHARACTER constant'

Indeed, any character capable of representation in a computer may form part of a character constant and not simply the characters that form the FORTRAN character set (although you may encounter portability problems if you use characters that are not widely available). The length of the character constant is given by the number of characters in the string. A space is a valid and significant character which contributes to the overall length of the character string. This is an important exception to the general rule that spaces are not significant in FORTRAN. The above character constants are of length 28 and 39 respectively. The apostrophes are used to delimit the character constant and do not form part of the string stored in the computer. An apostrophe within a character constant must be represented as two consecutive apostrophes with no intervening spaces and counts as one character. Thus

'TODAY''S TRANSACTIONS ARE'

is a character constant of length 24 and would be stored on a 32 bit machine (with 4 characters per word) as follows:

T	O	D	A	Word 1
Y		S		Word 2
T	R	A	N	Word 3
S	A	C	T	Word 4
I	O	N	S	Word 5
	A	R	E	Word 6

Note that the length of a character constant must be greater than zero.

Character variables and arrays may be declared in **CHARACTER** type statements and used subsequently in expressions. The declaration statement is of the form

CHARACTER∗n *list*

where *n* is the length of the character variable or array and *list* is a list of names to be declared of type character. *n* may be a positive non-zero integer constant or an integer constant expression (for the record, it may also be an ∗ in parentheses but this will be explained more fully in Chapter 8). An integer constant expression must be enclosed in parentheses. If ∗*n* is not specified then a length of 1 is assumed. The list may contain variable (or parameter) names, array names and array declarations. Functions will be discussed more fully in Chapter 8 but they may also be declared to be of type character.

Any element of *list* may optionally be followed by ∗*n* which specifies the length of that element only and overrides any length set by **CHARACTER∗n**.

Thus the statement

CHARACTER∗6 CHAR,NAME,STRING(5:10),FLAG∗1,SNAME(1:100)∗3

declares the variables **CHAR** and **NAME** to be character variables of length 6 and **STRING** to be a character array consisting of elements **STRING(5)**, **STRING(6)**, . . ., **STRING(10)** all of length 6. But it declares a character variable FLAG to be of length 1 byte and a 100 element array SNAME with each element of length 3 bytes.

CHARACTER statements (and all other type statements) are examples of *specification statements*. There are 14 such statements of which the **DIMENSION** statement and the 6 type statements are examples. All specification statements are non-executable statements and must be placed at the head of the program before any executable statements occur.

Once character variables or arrays have been declared, they may be assigned values in expressions, e.g. assuming the declaration statement above, the statements

```
CHAR      = 'MAGNET'
NAME      = 'MYPROGRAM'
STRING(1) = 'FIRST'
FLAG      = 'A'
SNAME(1)  = 'JIM'
SNAME(2)  = 'JOHN'
```

are all valid assignment statements. In the first statement the character string **MAGNET** which is of length 6 characters is assigned to the character variable **CHAR** which is also of length 6 characters. Thus the characters are entered into 6 character locations as follows:

M	A	G	N	E	T

However, in the second, example, a problem arises. The character string **MYPROGRAM** which is 9 characters long is being assigned to a character location which is 6 characters long. This will not be treated as an error by the compiler. The FORTRAN standard states that if the declared length of the character variable or array does not match the length of the character string assigned to it then the string will either be padded out with spaces on the right or truncated on the right depending on whether it is shorter or longer. In the second example above, the string **MYPROG** will be assigned to **NAME**, i.e. the 3 characters on the right will be truncated. In the third example the string **FIRST** which is of length 5 characters is being assigned to a variable of length 6 therefore the string will be filled out to the right with spaces, i.e. **FIRST**b will be assigned to **STRING**(1) where b is a space or blank. In the remaining examples, A will be correctly assigned to the 1 byte character variable **FLAG**, **JIM** will be assigned to **SNAME**(1) but only the characters **JOH** will be assigned to **SNAME**(2).

Since computers can only store information in memory by setting binary digits to 0 or 1, then obviously pictorial representations of characters cannot be stored. However by allowing 1 byte (or 8 bits) to store a character then any number between 0 and 255 can be used to represent a character, thus allowing 256 possible characters to be so represented. So, when characters are stored in memory they are held internally as numbers, a unique number being assigned to each letter according to the character code used by the computer. As described in Chapter 1, there are two internationally recognized character codes used in computing – the ASCII code and the EBCDIC code. Thus, in the ASCII code, the word **MAGNET** would be stored as follows:

77	65	71	78	69	84

whereas in EBCDIC it would be stored as follows:

212	193	199	213	197	227

ASCII, which is used on many mini-computers, represents characters 0 to 9 by 48 to 57 and the letters A to Z by 65 to 90. It is actually a 7 bit code which defines a total of 128 characters. However EBCDIC, which is used on many mainframe computers, represents characters 0 to 9 by 240 to 249 and letters A to I by 193 to 201, J to R by 209 to 217 and S to Z by 226 to 233. It is an 8 bit code which allows a total of 256 characters. To further complicate matters, there is an 8 bit ASCII code which is a superset of the 7 bit code but provides an extended character set. Also some machines have a 7 bit ASCII code but with an 8th bit set; this has the effect of adding 128 to the 7 bit value, i.e. 0 to 9 is represented by 176 to 185 and A to Z by 193 to 218. All the lower case letters come before the upper case letters in EBCDIC but after the upper case letters in ASCII. The order in which characters are stored in a particular computer is known as the *collating sequence* of that computer. It can be seen that this is not the same for all machines. Notice that it cannot even be assumed that the letters have consecutive numerical values. The ANSI standard does not define a collating sequence except to say that A must be less than Z, 0 must be less than 9, letters and digits must not be intermixed, all of the digits must precede A or all of the digits must follow Z and the space character must be less than A and less than 0. It should be noted therefore that any FORTRAN program which makes any assumptions other than this about the collating sequence is non-standard and therefore may not be portable.

Character operands may be combined to form expressions by the operator // which is known as the collocation operator. For example, the expression

FLAG//CHAR

forms the expression **AMAGNET**. Note that this could be spaced out to the expression **A MAGNET** by the expression

FLAG//' '//CHAR

Similarly, the expression

SNAME(1)//'''S '//CHAR

forms the phrase **JIM'S MAGNET** assuming that **SNAME(1)** contains the name **JIM** as described above. Note the representation of a single quote by a double quote within a character constant. The expression

NAME = 'MY'//'PR'//'OG'

is equivalent to the statement

NAME = 'MYPROG'

and the expression

'IT''S MONDAY TODAY'//' ISN''T IT?'

will yield the result

IT'S MONDAY TODAY ISN'T IT?

The length of the result of a character expression is the sum of the lengths of all of the operands.

Expressions containing more than one operand are evaluated from left to right and, although parentheses may be used, they have no effect on the result. For example,

'ROD,'//'POLE'//' OR PERCH'

yields the string 'ROD, POLE OR PERCH' as do the expressions

('ROD,'//'POLE')//' OR PERCH'

and

'ROD,'//('POLE'//' OR PERCH')

The operator // is assigned a priority less than addition and subtraction but greater than the relational operators in the table given in section 3.3.

Character expressions may be compared using relational operators. The resulting relational expression will be true if the two expressions satisfy the relationship. This depends on the collating sequence of the character set for a particular computer.

An expression $e1$ is considered to be less than $e2$, if $e1$ precedes $e2$ in the collating sequence. As described earlier, only certain assumptions can be made about the collating sequence. Because of this, character relational expressions are a potential source of machine dependence and thus loss of portability.

Note that when character expressions of the same length are compared, they are compared character by character until the condition is determined, e.g.

'FRANCIS' .LT. 'FRANCES'

is false because the sixth letter I in the first word is later in the collating sequence than the sixth letter E in the second word.

'SMITH-EVANS' .LT. 'SMITH-JONES'

is true since the E in EVANS precedes the J in JONES.

If two character strings of unequal length are compared then the comparison takes place as if the shorter string were padded out on the right with blanks or spaces (which precede any of the letters or digits). Thus

'TOKAM' .LT. 'TOKAMAK'

is true as is

'THE' .LT. 'THEORY'

A substring may be extracted from a longer character string by specifying the lowest (l) and the highest (h) character positions of the substring to be extracted. This is specified in the form

($l:h$)

placed after the name of a character variable or array element. So the expression

EQN = 'MAXWELL"S' // 'EQUATIONS'

will set up the character string **MAXWELL'S EQUATIONS** in the variable **EQN** and the expression

PART(1) = EQN(1:9)
PART(2) = EQN(10:18)

will assign the string **'MAXWELL"S'** to **PART(1)** and **'EQUATIONS'** to **PART(2)**.

If l is not specified then 1 is assumed. If h is not specified then the length of the character string is assumed. Note that both l and h may be integer expressions.

Substrings cannot be extracted from constants (or parameters). They must be assigned to a variable and then extracted.

In a substring assignment, a character variable or array element substring may not be used on both sides of the assignment if it refers to the same character locations, e.g.

STRING(1) = STRING(1)(3:5)

is invalid in FORTRAN. Similarly,

STRING(1)(1:4) = STRING(1)(2:5)

is invalid, but

STRING(1)(1:4) = STRING(1)(7:10)

is valid since the same character locations are not referenced on both sides.

FORTRAN provides two useful intrinsic functions to convert a character to its equivalent integer and vice versa. They are

CHAR   which converts an integer argument to the corresponding character depending on the collating sequence of the machine.

ICHAR   which converts a character argument of length 1 to the corresponding integer depending on the collating sequence of the machine.

Using the **ICHAR** function, a FORTRAN program which prints out the collating sequence for all the letters and digits for your machine may be written as follows:

```
      PROGRAM COLLAT
      INTEGER I
      CHARACTER*36 ALPHA
      ALPHA = 'ABCDEFGHIJKLMNOPQRSTUVWXYZ0123456789'
      DO 10, I=1,36
10       PRINT *,ICHAR(ALPHA(I:I)),' ',ALPHA(I:I)
      STOP
      END
```

Try running this on your machine to see what the collating sequence is.

Comparison for equality is useful when character strings are assigned to character variables. For example, a program which reads records until it finds a record beginning with **START**, and then counts the number of records until a record beginning with **END** is found, might read as follows:

```
PROGRAM COUNT
INTEGER NREC,I
CHARACTER*80 RECORD
NREC = 0
DO 10, I = 1,10000
    READ *,RECORD
    IF (RECORD(1:5) .EQ. 'START')THEN
        NREC = 0
    ELSE IF (RECORD(1:3) .EQ. 'END')THEN
        PRINT *,'Number of records = ',NREC
        STOP
    ELSE
        NREC = NREC + 1
    END IF
10  CONTINUE
    STOP
    END
```

The character type is of particular use in text processing programs which manipulate characters. In the age of the word processor, it is particularly interesting to note that FORTRAN 77 can be used to program many of the functions of a word processor. For example, in a particular section of text it is noticed that the word 'THE' has been mistyped 'HTE' every time. Suppose that we wish to write a FORTRAN program to change every occurrence of HTE to THE. Then a structure diagram for such a program might be as shown on the opposite page, which in our formal specification language is

```
Do until end of text
    Read a line
    Do until end of line
        Read a word
        If word is HTE then
            change to THE
        Endif
    End do end of line
        Print line
End do end of text
Stop
```

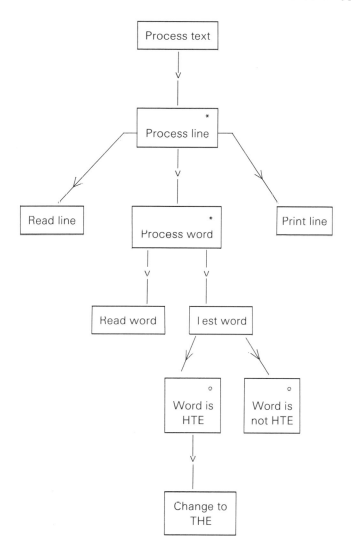

A FORTRAN program to do this reads as follows:

```
PROGRAM WORD
INTEGER N LINE, I, J
CHARACTER*82 LINE
PRINT *,'Enter the number of lines of text: '
READ *,NLINE
DO 10, I = 1,NLINE
    LINE = ' '
    READ (*,'(A80)') LINE(2:81)
    IF (LINE(2:4) .EQ. 'END') STOP
```

(section 6.6.2 for format A80)

```
        DO 20, J = 1,78
            IF (LINE(J:J + 4) .EQ. ' HTE ') LINE(J:J + 4) = ' THE '
20      CONTINUE
        PRINT *,LINE(2:81)
10  CONTINUE
    STOP
    END
```

This assumes that no line of text contains more than 80 characters and that the program is to terminate either when the required number of lines is processed or when the word **END** is found in the first three columns of the line. Try this out on a paragraph of text of your own choice. Note the way that a long character variable can be cleared to spaces by assigning one space to it. This uses the fact that if a short character constant is assigned to a longer character variable then the rest of that character variable will be flushed out with spaces.

Intrinsic character functions are provided to perform frequently required operations; apart from **CHAR** and **ICHAR** described earlier, these include

LEN   which returns an integer which is the length of the character string argument.

INDEX   which searches the character string given by argument 1 for the substring given by argument 2 and returns an integer which is the starting position of the first occurrence of the substring.

In addition to these functions, there are logical functions for character string comparisons described in section 5.6.

5.4 Double precision type

Real entities in FORTRAN programs are allocated one numeric storage location in computer memory. This is usually one computer word. This sets an upper limit on the accuracy to which any number can be held (7 decimal digits on a 32 bit word machine, for example). Thus it can be seen that an expression such as 2.00000002 − 1.00000001 would not necessarily yield the result 1.00000001. So in a long numerical computation involving small differences between numbers, appreciable errors can be introduced and the same program could well give different results on different machines.

Therefore, if you wish a program to be both accurate and portable it may be advisable to declare all real entities to be double precision. This will ensure that two numeric storage locations are allocated to them (but note that they are treated logically in the program as one unit). Thus on a 32 bit machine, 64 bits will be allocated to a double precision entity; of these perhaps 16 bits will be allocated to the exponent and 48 bits to the mantissa (including the sign). Such a machine could hold real numbers to an accuracy of 14 decimal digits, i.e. twice the single precision accuracy.

A program may be converted from real to double precision by performing the following operations:

Convert all real constants in the program to double precision constants.

Declare all real variables, arrays, etc. to be double precision in a type declaration.

Perform all real I/O with double precision format specifications (Chapter 6).

Use double precision functions.

Double precision constants must be written in floating point form with the letter D, instead of the letter E, used to denote the exponent, e.g. 1.62D4 represents the number 16200.0 held to double precision or 0.6582975831D0 represents 0.6582975831 held to double precision, but note that it is not sufficient to write the number in this form without the D exponent (in this case it would be taken as a real constant and truncated).

The rules which apply to the formation of double precision constants are exactly the same as for single precision constants with an E exponent (section 1.8).

Variables and arrays may be declared to be double precision in a type declaration, e.g.

DOUBLE PRECISION LARGE,SMALL,DARRAY(500)

will declare two double precision variables (**LARGE** and **SMALL**) and a double precision array (**DARRAY**) of 500 elements. Arithmetic assignment statements and expressions may be written in the usual way using double precision entities, e.g.

DARRAY(1) = LARGE + SMALL*5.7234D2

The same operators are used and the same rules of precedence apply.

A discussion of mixed mode arithmetic including the mixing of double precision types with other types is given in section 5.10.

Functions can be declared to be double precision by preceding the word **FUNCTION** with the type specification **DOUBLE PRECISION** (Chapter 8).

Note that FORTRAN 77 has introduced generic names for intrinsic functions so that the same name may be used regardless of the type; the type of the argument determines the function type. A full list of intrinsic functions is given in Appendix A. So for example, the function **SIN** will find the sine of a real argument and return a real result; but if the argument is double precision, it will return a double precision result.

Parameters (section 5.8) and dummy arguments (Chapter 8) may also be declared to be double precision.

Note that there is a performance penalty with double precision. Programs written in double precision can take as much as 50% longer to run compared with their single precision equivalents. They also require more memory of course.

5.5 Complex type

A complex number is represented in the computer as a pair of real numbers, the first being the real part and the second being the imaginary part. A complex constant consists of two real numbers (which can be any valid real constant) separated by commas and enclosed in parentheses. Thus the constant (5.6,3.2) represents the complex number $5.6 + 3.2i$.

A complex variable must be declared to be complex by the type statement **COMPLEX**, which must appear before any executable statement. The initial letter of the variable name then has no particular significance. Two words will be allocated to the complex variable and their contents will be two real quantities.

Arithmetic can be performed with complex variables using the operators $+ - * /$. Consider the complex variables A and B where $A = a + bi$ and $B = c + di$. Then the arithmetic operators have the following effect:

$$A + B = (a + bi) + (c + di) = (a + c) + (b + d)i$$
$$A - B = (a + bi) - (c + di) = (a - c) + (b - d)i$$
$$A * B = (a + bi)*(c + di) = (ac - bd) + (ad + bc)i$$
$$A / B = (a + bi)/(c + di) = \frac{ac + bd}{c^2 + d^2} + \frac{(bc - ad)i}{c^2 + d^2}$$

In FORTRAN 77, complex quantities may be mixed with real or integer quantities in expressions; the rules for mixed-mode arithmetic are described in section 5.10.

The operator $**$ can be used to raise a complex quantity to an integer power. FORTRAN 77 also allows a complex number to be raised to a complex power (or to a real power by converting to a complex power with an imaginary part of zero).

Functions can be declared complex by preceding the word **FUNCTION** with the type specification **COMPLEX**. Also generic intrinsic functions such as **SQRT, SIN, COS**, etc. can be used with complex arguments. Special intrinsic functions which only operate on complex arguments include **AIMAG(X)** which finds the imaginary part of X and **CMPLX** which converts the argument to complex.

An extensive description of functions may be found in Chapter 8 and in Appendix A.

Note that some FORTRAN compilers do allow a double precision complex type but this is not standard.

Complex quantities may be compared in relational expressions but since they are in effect pairs of real numbers the same pitfalls apply when comparing them for exact equality as described in Chapter 3.

5.6 Logical type

In section 3.3 logical expressions were introduced, and it was described how a logical expression could be constructed from relational expressions and the logical operators

.AND. .OR.   .NOT.
.EQV. .NEQV.

Logical constants, variables and arrays may also be used as operands in logical expressions. A logical constant can have one of two values – true or false. The logical constant **.TRUE.** represents the value true, and **.FALSE.** represents the value false. Logical variables and arrays may be declared by means of a **LOGICAL** type declaration, e.g.

LOGICAL VAL,EOF,START,FLAGS(10)

declares the variables **VAL**, **EOF** and **START** to be of type logical and a logical array **FLAGS** of ten elements given by **FLAGS(1)** to **FLAGS(10)**.

Logical values may be assigned to a logical variable or array element by means of a logical assignment statement of the general form

LOGICAL VARIABLE = LOGICAL EXPRESSION

where the logical expression can be a logical constant, variable or array element, a relational expression or any combination of these using the logical operators. The left-hand side may also be a logical array element.

A common use of logical variables is as flags to test a particular condition in a program. For example, it may be that a program has to carry out a specific action the first time control passes through a particular section of it but never subsequently. A way of testing for this would be to set a logical flag to the value **.TRUE.** at the beginning of the program, i.e.

LOGICAL FLAG
FLAG = .TRUE.

At some later point a test of the form

IF (FLAG) THEN

would enable codes to be obeyed only when the flag is set to true (i.e. the first time through) but subsequently the statement

FLAG = .FALSE.

would set the logical value of **FLAG** to false and the **IF**-block would then never be obeyed subsequently. Note that the above statement could equally well be written

FLAG = .NOT.FLAG

but this would reverse the truth value of **FLAG** each time through that section of the program.

As a complete example of the use of flags, take **PROGRAM COUNT** which counts the number of records between **START** and **END**, but modify it so that it counts records between **BLOCK** and **ENDBLOCK** but not otherwise. There may be several **BLOCK/ENDBLOCK** blocks between **START** and **END**. Then this can be written as follows:

```
PROGRAM COUNT
INTEGER NREC,I
LOGICAL SFLAG,BFLAG
CHARACTER*80 RECORD
SFLAG = .FALSE.
BFLAG = .FALSE.
DO 10, I = 1,1000
    READ *,RECORD
    IF (RECORD(1:5) .EQ. 'START') THEN
        NREC = 0
        SFLAG = .TRUE.
    ELSE IF (RECORD(1:3) .EQ. 'END') THEN
        PRINT *,'Number of records = ',NREC
        STOP
    ELSE IF (RECORD(1:5) .EQ. 'BLOCK') THEN
        BFLAG = .TRUE.
    ELSE IF (RECORD(1:8) .EQ. 'ENDBLOCK') THEN
        BFLAG = .FALSE.
    ELSE IF (SFLAG .AND. BFLAG) THEN
        NREC = NREC + 1
    ENDIF
10  CONTINUE
    STOP
    END
```

Relational expressions can be assigned to logical variables so that statements of the form

```
LOGICAL L1,L2
L1 = IA.EQ.5 .OR. B.GT.C
L2 = X .LT. 0.0
IF (L1 .AND. L2) THEN
```

may be written. This uses logical variables to preserve the result of evaluating a logical expression so that it need only be evaluated once. Logical variables can also be used to produce more readable codes. For example, returning to the examination mark example of section 3.5, it is possible to store the sex of the candidate as a logical variable, e.g.

```
LOGICAL GIRL,BOY,EOF
GIRL = ISEX.EQ.1
```

```
BOY = ISEX.EQ.2
IF (GIRL) THEN
    .
    .
    .
ELSE IF (BOY) THEN
    .
    .
    .
ELSE IF (EOF) THEN
    .
    .
    .
ELSE
    .
    .
    .
ENDIF
```

One numeric storage location is allocated to a logical type. Logical intrinsic functions are provided in FORTRAN 77 to compare two character expressions. These are **LGT, LLT, LGE** and **LLE** which return the value **.TRUE.** if the first operand is greater than, less than, greater than or equal to, or less than or equal to the second operand. These depend on the collating sequence of the machine (section 5.3).

5.7 The IMPLICIT statement

FORTRAN provides the **IMPLICIT** statement which allows the programmer to override the default data-typing specified by the initial letter of a name. The statement is of the form

IMPLICIT *type(list),type(list),* . . .

where *type* is one of the data type names given in section 5.2 and *list* specifies the letters which if used as an initial letter of a name will cause that name to be of the specified type. These letters may be listed explicitly and separated by commas, e.g.

IMPLICIT REAL(I,J,K,L,M,N)

will ensure that all variables will be of type real even if they begin with any of the letters *I* to *N*. A sequence of consecutive letters may be indicated by −, e.g.

IMPLICIT REAL(I − N)

has the same effect as the previous statement and

IMPLICIT REAL(A − Z)

will ensure that all names in the program are real.

Many types may be specified in one **IMPLICIT** statement and any letters not specified will automatically assume the default FORTRAN type, e.g.

> **IMPLICIT DOUBLE PRECISION (A – H),REAL(I – N),COMPLEX(O,P,Q),**
> 1   **INTEGER(R,S,T)**

will cause names beginning with

A, B, C, D, E, F, G or H	to be double precision
I, J, K, L, M or N	to be real
O, P or Q	to be complex
R, S or T	to be integer
U, V, W, X, Y or Z	to be real

If an **IMPLICIT** statement is used it must precede all other specification and executable statements in the program. It will not affect the type of any intrinsic system functions. Explicit type declarations will override implicit typing. Note that the danger of using an implicit statement function is forgetting that you have done so and that the type therefore is not necessarily provided by the initial letter.

5.8 The PARAMETER statement

The **PARAMETER** statement allows a constant to be assigned a symbolic name which may be used subsequently in place of the constant itself. It is of the form

> **PARAMETER** (*name* = *constant,name* = *constant, . . .*)

where *name* is a symbolic name which may have been previously typed in a type statement (or has the default FORTRAN type) and *constant* is any constant expression appropriate to the associated name. It may contain constants, parameter names which have been declared previously, or may be a constant expression. It may not contain function references.

A parameter is a named constant so that it may be used anywhere in the program where a constant may be used except in formats or **FORMAT** statements (Chapter 6). It may not be used to form a complex constant.

The use of the **PARAMETER** statement is to be encouraged since it provides a good documentation aid and can also improve program portability. Constants which may be machine dependent can be declared at the head of a program in a **PARAMETER** statement and the name used throughout the program. If it is required to move the program to a new machine then the value of the constant may be changed once at the head of the program instead of everywhere throughout the program. A common use would be in programs that refer to the internal character values of a particular computer, e.g.

> **IMPLICIT INTEGER(A – Z)**
> **PARAMETER (A = 65,B = 66,C = 67,D = 68,E = 69)**

and so on would define the ASCII character set. Then a simple test to find out whether a character is a letter can be written as follows:

IF (CHAR .GE. A .AND. CHAR .LE. Z)THEN

The statements

IMPLICIT INTEGER(W,C)
PARAMETER (WLNGTH = 32,CHARWD = 4)

would define the word length and the number of characters per word for a particular machine and

PARAMETER (PI = 3.14159265)

would define the constant **PI**. Since expressions can be used in **PARAMETER** statements then the statement **PARAMETER (PIBY4 = PI/4.0)** is valid, for example. Note that expressions can only contain ⏐ ＊ / and ＊＊ (provided the exponent is an integer).

Parameters may be used to dimension arrays, specify character string lengths (and so on) in subsequent statements, e.g.

PARAMETER (N = 500,M = 100,LEN = 4)
REAL ARRAY(N,M)
CHARACTER＊(LEN) CHAR1,CHAR2

Note the convenience of dimensioning arrays and so on with parameters. If it is required to change the dimension of all arrays in the program, this may be done simply by changing the parameter statement.

5.9 The DATA statement

The contents of memory locations may be set to initial values during program execution by assignment or input statements. Alternatively, the **DATA** statement may be used to set initial values of memory locations before program execution commences. This is of the general form

DATA *list1* /*d1*/,*list2*/*d2*/. . . .

where *list1*, *list2*, etc. are lists of variables or array element names and *d1*, *d2*, etc. are the lists of values to which these named locations are to be initialized, e.g.

DATA A,B(1,1),C/67.87,54.72,5.0/

will set A to 67.87, 54.72 to B(1,1) and 5.0 to C.

The **DATA** statement is not an executable statement and initialization of locations takes place as the program is being loaded into memory.

The above statement could be written thus

DATA A/67.87/,B(1,1)/54.72/,C/5.0/

this is a matter of personal preference.

Character constants may be assigned to character locations in **DATA** statements, e.g.

CHARACTER*1 DOT,X,BLANK
DATA DOT,X,BLANK/'.','X',' '/

assigns the character '.' to **DOT**, 'X' to **X** and ' ' (space) to **BLANK**. Note that if the character string is shorter than the location to which it is assigned, then it will be left adjusted and the remainder filled out with spaces. If the character string is longer then it will be truncated on the right.

Note that character strings should be assigned to character locations only and you should avoid mixing types in **DATA** statements. Assign a constant of a given type to a location of the same type. FORTRAN 66, which did not have character variables, allowed character strings to be assigned to integer locations but this is not to be recommended.

All locations used in a FORTRAN program must be initialized in some way before they are used. It is bad programming practice to assume that locations in memory will be cleared to zero before execution commences. This may be done at some computer installations and programs written to take advantage of this. Such programs may no longer work, however, when a new computer is installed or when the program is moved to another installation.

Some non-standard extensions to FORTRAN 66 and FORTRAN 77 allow data to be initialized in a type declaration statement when the rules and syntax of the **DATA** statement apply but often with some restrictions imposed. If you wish your program to be portable, however, it is safer to initialize variables in **DATA** statements only.

If several names in a **DATA** statement are to be initialized to the same value then a repetition factor may be used. This consists of an integer constant followed by an asterisk and precedes the data value, e.g.

DATA I,J,K,L,M,N/6*1/

will initialize variables, I, J, K, L, M and N to 1.

FORTRAN 77 allows array names and substring names to be initialized in **DATA** statements. Parameters which have been declared previously may also be used. For example,

DIMENSION A(20),Z(5)
DATA A,Z,J/20*0.0,5*1.0,3/

initializes the 20 elements of array A to 0, the 5 elements of array Z to 1.0 and J to 3.

CHARACTER*15 TITLE
PARAMETER (N = 50)
REAL ARRAY(N)
DATA TITLE/'SECTION'/
DATA ARRAY/N*0.0/,TITLE(8:11)/' ONE'/

will initialize the 50 elements of **ARRAY** to zero and will set the string 'SECTION ONE' in the character variable **TITLE**.

Implied **DO** loops may be used in FORTRAN 77 **DATA** declarations to initialize parts of an array but this will be described in Chapter 6.

Types may be mixed in **DATA** statements. Where types differ, the rules described for assignment statements in the next section apply.

Rules for initializing data in **COMMON** will be described in Chapter 9.

DATA statements must appear after all specification statements. It is usual to place them before the first executable statement.

5.10 Mixed mode arithmetic

So far in this book, the programmer has been advised to avoid mixing data types in expressions, assignment statements, etc. However, FORTRAN does allow mixed mode arithmetic and rules for this are defined in the ANSI 77 standard. A description of these rules is given here. Consider the following examples:

i. A/B both operands real.
ii. I/J both operands integer.
iii. A/J first operand real, second integer.
iv. I/B first operand integer, second real.

For $A = 5.5, B = 2.0, I = 3$ and $J = 2$ these expressions have the following values

i.   2.75
ii. 1
iii. 2.75
iv. 1.5

In case (i) no problems arise. The operands are both real and therefore the resulting value of the expression is a real number. In case (ii) both the operands are integer, and therefore the result of the operation is an integer. So although the actual result of dividing 3 by 2 is 1.5, when this division is performed in integer mode, the value returned is the integral part only, i.e. 1 (note that it is not rounded up to 2). In cases (iii) and (iv) the expressions are mixed. Since real and integer numbers are held in different forms in the computer, arithmetic operations cannot be performed directly between them. Thus if an expression is mixed the integer number is first converted to a real number and then real arithmetic is performed. Hence I and J will be converted to the real numbers 3.0 and 2.0 respectively, and expressions (iii) and (iv) will be carried out as if both operands were real and will yield real results.

This principle holds in more complicated expressions. An expression of the form

    R + S*I/J + N/3

will be computed by first multiplying S and I together, giving a real result (I having first been converted to a real number). J will then be converted to a real number and divided into the result of S*I to give a real result. This will be added to the real number R giving a real result. Finally, $N/3$ will be evaluated as an integer expression giving an integer result. This will then be converted to a real number and added to the previous result. The whole expression will produce a real answer. For $R = 10.6$, $S = 3.5$, $I = 5$, $J = 2$ and $N = 7$ the result will be

$$R + S*I/J + N/3 = 10.6 + 3.5*5.0/2.0 + 7/3$$
$$= 10.6 + 8.75 + 2.0$$
$$= 21.35$$

Note the effect of the truncation in the integer division $N/3$.

This expression would give the result 21.68333 if it were evaluated throughout in real arithmetic. Since some compilers may in fact evaluate it this way, a good rule is never to write an expression which would give different results if evaluated in a different order. Use intrinsic functions for type conversion to make clear your intention.

Mixed assignment statements may be written in the form

    INTEGER VARIABLE = REAL EXPRESSION

or

    REAL VARIABLE = INTEGER EXPRESSION

If the result of a real expression is assigned to an integer variable, then truncation will occur before assignment takes place and any fractional part will be lost. On the other hand, if an integer result is assigned to a real variable it is first converted to a real result (with the fractional part equal to zero) before the assignment. Consider a statement of the form

    X = A/B

If A is 9.0 and B is 5.0, then X will be given the value 1.8. However, if the statement had been of the form

    M = A/B

M would have been assigned the value 1 (i.e. any fractional part is ignored). So it can be seen that statements of these forms could introduce considerable error into a calculation if they were written without due care and, moreover, since they are grammatically quite correct, they would not be detected by the FORTRAN compiler.

To summarize:

Subexpressions containing real and integer types are evaluated in real arithmetic (by converting the integer to real) and yield a real result.

Subexpressions containing double precision mixed with real or integer types are evaluated in double precision (by converting the real or integer to double precision) and yield a double precision result.

Subexpressions containing complex types mixed with real or integer are evaluated in complex (by converting the real or integer to complex with a zero imaginary part) and yield a complex result.

Complex types may not be mixed with double precision.

Character and logical types may not be mixed with any other type.

These rules apply regardless of the context in which the expression is used.

The exception to this general rule applies to the exponentiation operator which may be used to raise a real, double precision or complex entity to an integer power.

5.11 Binary, octal and hexadecimal types

Before leaving the subject of types it should be pointed out that FORTRAN does not provide facilities for binary, octal or hexadecimal constants, input/output, etc. although many compilers do provide this as an extension. For example, the letter Z before a constant, e.g. Z00A0D135 may be used to represent a hexadecimal constant, or a colon, e.g. :10753, to represent an octal constant on some machines. These are definitely non-standard extensions and it is better to use the corresponding decimal constants rather than use these facilities if you wish the program to be portable.

5.12 Summary

● FORTRAN names may be typed by any of the following statements:

    INTEGER *list*
    REAL *list*
    CHARACTER*n *list*
    DOUBLE PRECISION *list*
    LOGICAL *list*
    COMPLEX *list*

where *list* is a list of variable names, array names or array declarations separated by commas.

● Default typing of names can be overridden by

    IMPLICIT *type(list),type(list), . . .*

where *type* is one of the above data type names and *list* is a list of letters.

- Constants may be assigned to names by

  PARAMETER (*name = constant,name = constant, . . .*)

  where *name* is any valid FORTRAN name which may be used in place of a constant and *constant* is any valid FORTRAN constant to be referred to by the corresponding name.

- Data may be set to initial values by

  DATA *list1/d1/,list2/d2/, . . .*

  where *list1*, *list2*, . . ., etc. are variables, array names, array elements or character substrings which are to be initialized and *d1*, *d2*, . . ., etc. are the constant expressions representing the initial values.

Exercises 5

1. Which of the following are, (a) valid, and (b) invalid FORTRAN constants. Give reasons for (b).

   ```
   'ALL'S WELL THAT ENDS WELL'
   'TODAY''S DATE IS 15:10:81'
   'THE VALUE OF X =
   2.35675D2
   .TRUE.
   (3.65,2E5)
   (5.3 2.1)
   .F.
   ```

   What are the lengths of the valid character constants?

2. In the following sequence of statements, what strings are assigned to C1, C2, C3 and C4?

   ```
   CHARACTER C1*4,C2*7,C3*10,C4*24
   CHARACTER*40 SAYING
   SAYING = 'England expects every man to do his duty'
   C1      = SAYING(37:)
   C2      = SAYING(30:32)//SAYING(27:27)//SAYING(33:35)
   C3      = SAYING(:4)//SAYING(34:35)//SAYING(33:33)//'men'
   C4      = C3//SAYING(29:32)//'their '//C1
   ```

3. Write character assignment statements which rearrange the string 'before tomorrow note the questions that arise' into the string 'to be or not to be that is the question'.

4. Write a FORTRAN program to translate a paragraph of text which is secretly encoded according to the rules of Caesar's cipher, i.e. each letter of the alphabet is replaced by the letter that comes three places before it. The program should be able to decode or encode input text depending on

whether the word **DECODE** or **ENCODE** is the first line of the data. The input text should be terminated by a line beginning with **** in columns 1 to 4.

5. Write a program which will sort an array of names into ascending alphabetical order using the shell sort algorithm given in section 4.9.

6

Formatted I/O

6.1 Introduction

A FORTRAN program must in general provide at least three items of information in order to input or output data, i.e.

a. the logical number of the I/O unit to be used (which is related to an actual physical device by system Job Control commands outside the FORTRAN program);
b. the names of locations to which the data are to be input or from which results are to be output;
c. the types of the data to be input or output.

Item (a) specifies where to find the data to be read (or where to send the results to be written); item (b) specifies where to store the data after it has been read (or where the data to be written is stored); and item (c) specifies how the data values are to be interpreted, e.g. as integers, or as real numbers, or as character strings, etc.

In the examples and exercises so far we have considered only the simple case when the I/O unit used is the default unit (usually the on-line terminal) and the type of each data element is the same as the type of the corresponding variable in the I/O list, i.e. list-directed I/O. So, for example, the statement

READ *,SALARY

does not specify the I/O unit (item (a)) but assumes that the data values are to be read from the default device; it specifies item (b) as the location **SALARY** and uses the asterisk to specify item (c), i.e. the data type is real, the same type as **SALARY**. Similarly the statement

PRINT *,SALARY

will print the value of **SALARY** on the default output device but with the layout determined by the system and not by the programmer, e.g. £20,000 may be printed as 20000.00 or +20000.000 or 20000. etc. So list-directed I/O does not permit the programmer any control over the layout or *format* of the data (as no doubt you have already discovered in the programs you have written). So how does FORTRAN allow the programmer to specify the format of the data on input or output, and how can data be transferred to or from I/O units other than the default unit?

The answer lies in the general forms of the **READ** and **WRITE** statements which are

READ(*control list*)*list*

and

WRITE(*control list*)*list*

where *control list* is a list of control information specifiers separated by commas. A control information specifier is of the general form

keyword = *value*

and is used to provide additional information about the I/O transfer.

So, for example, the I/O unit may be defined by a specifier of the form

UNIT = *u*

where *u* is an integer expression (greater than or equal to zero) defining the unit number. Thus the statement

READ(UNIT = 1,*)SALARY

is identical to the statement

READ *,SALARY

if unit 1 is the default device.

Similarly, the data format may be defined by a specifier of the form

FMT = *f*

where *f* is a format identifier. Format identifiers will be fully described later in this chapter, but for the moment take it that a real number of total width 8 characters with 2 digits after the decimal point can be described by the format identifier F8.2. This can be included as a character expression in the **READ** or **WRITE** statement. So if it is required to read **SALARY** from unit 1 not with the default format provided for list-directed I/O but with a format of F8.2, then this may be achieved with a statement of the form

READ(UNIT = 1,FMT = '(F8.2)')SALARY

Note that the format identifier must be included in parentheses within a character expression.

Control list information may be specified in any order provided that the keywords are always used. Thus

READ(FMT = '(F8.2)',UNIT = 1)SALARY

is equally valid. However, the keywords **UNIT** and **FMT** may be omitted in which case the unit number must be specified in the first position and the format in the second position, i.e.

READ(1,'(F8.2)')SALARY

is valid but

READ('(F8.2)',1)SALARY

is not and neither is

READ('(F8.2)',UNIT = 1)SALARY

In any I/O statement, when the unit is not specified, the default device is assumed and the simplified forms of the I/O statements may be used, i.e.

READ *f,list*

and:

PRINT *f,list*

Note that the **PRINT** statement is used for output to the default device, i.e. there is no **WRITE** $f,list$ statement.

When f is an asterisk specifying list-directed I/O, then these statements become the simple statements with which we have already become so familiar

READ *∗,list*

and

PRINT *∗,list*

Thus if unit 1 is both the default input unit and the default output unit then the following statements are equivalent:

READ (1,∗)X,Y,Z   READ ∗,X,Y,Z   and   READ(∗,∗)X,Y,Z

as are

WRITE(1,∗)A,B,C   PRINT ∗,A,B,C   and   WRITE(∗,∗)A,B,C

Note that the ANSI standard does not specify any rules for which input or output unit numbers should be used for specific devices. It is widespread practice to use input unit 5 for reading card images from a file, unit 6 for writing card images to a file, unit 7 for printing lines on the lineprinter and unit 1 for the on-line terminal (the default device). However this is by no means standard and can be a cause of machine dependence (and thus loss of portability) in a program.

A format specification itself may contain literal strings, e.g.

WRITE(6,'("TIME = ",I4,"VOLTS = ",I5)')ITIME,IVOLTS

This illustrates the point that any quotes included within the character constant format specification must be represented by two quotes. If the character literal itself includes quotes this results in the following rather awkward, error-prone syntax

WRITE(6,'("TODAY""S TRANSACTIONS")')

Note that special characters (called carriage control characters) which give instructions directly to a lineprinter may be included in character literals, e.g.

WRITE(7,'("0",F0.3/"1 NEW PAGE")')X

will cause the '0' and the '1' to be interpreted as carriage control characters assuming that the lineprinter is connected to unit 7. Lineprinter control characters will be discussed more fully later in this chapter when format specifications are studied in greater detail.

   If a format identifier is specified in the **READ** or **WRITE** statement then the statement is a *formatted* I/O statement; if f is not specified then the statement is an *unformatted* I/O statement. In the former, some editing is carried out on the data before the I/O transfer takes place according to the formats specified in f. In the latter, unformatted data is input or output completely unchanged in some machine dependent way; unformatted data may be a mixture of any of the FORTRAN data types and will be read or written in binary. It follows from this that unformatted data must be read by a statement similar to the statement with which it was originally written. The following are unformatted I/O statements

READ(8)X,Y

which reads data previously written by a statement of the form

WRITE (8)X,Y

and

WRITE(6)ARRAY,MEM

which writes data from two complete arrays (**ARRAY** and **MEM**); this may subsequently be read back by the statement

READ (6)ARRAY,MEM

or may be read into different arrays of the same dimension by a statement of the form

READ (6)NEWARR,NEWMEM

6.2 The FORMAT statement

When formatted I/O is used rather than list-directed I/O then a format identifier must be provided for each item of data in the I/O list. These may be either included in the **READ** or **WRITE** statement as a character expression (as shown in the examples of the previous section) or included in a **FORMAT** statement which is of the general form

    label   **FORMAT**(*format specifier list*)

where *format specifier list* is a list of format specifications separated by commas and *label* is a FORTRAN statement label (in columns 1 to 5) which is used as the format identifier in the associated **READ** or **WRITE** statement. Thus the statement

    READ(5,'(F8.2)')SALARY

may equally well be written

    READ(5,10)SALARY
  10 **FORMAT(F8.2)**

or

    READ(UNIT = 5,FMT = 10)SALARY
  10 **FORMAT(F8.2)**

Note that the format specification f can be an integer constant representing the label of a **FORMAT** statement or an integer variable containing a **FORMAT** statement label set up by an **ASSIGN** statement (although this is not particularly recommended).

The introduction of formats as character expressions in I/O statements has tended to make the FORMAT statement redundant although it is still widely used.

Since the format specification can either be a character expression in the **READ** or **WRITE** statement or be specified in a **FORMAT** statement, there are many ways in which the same I/O statement can be written. The following statements are all examples of the way the same data containing a mixture of text and numbers can be written

    WRITE (1,10)IRD,ISEC,RMAG,TEMP
  10 **FORMAT(' AFTER',I4,' READINGS IN',I4,**
    1   **' SECONDS THE MAGNETIC FIELD WAS',**
    2   **F8.3,' AND THE TEMPERATURE WAS ',F8.3)**

or

    PRINT '(" AFTER",I4," READINGS IN",I4,
    1   **" SECONDS THE MAGNETIC FIELD WAS",F8.3,**
    2   **" AND THE TEMPERATURE WAS",F8.3)',**
    3   **IRD,ISEC,RMAG,TEMP**

or

```
FMT1 = '(" AFTER",I4," READINGS IN",I4," SECONDS"'
FMT2 = '" THE MAGNETIC FIELD WAS",F8.3,'
FMT3 = '" AND THE TEMPERATURE WAS ",F8.3)'
FMT4 = FMT1//FMT2//FMT3
PRINT FMT4,IRD,ISEC,RMAG,TEMP
```

This assumes that **FMT1**, **FMT2**, **FMT3** and **FMT4** are declared as character variables of the appropriate length and that **IRD**, **ISEC**, **RMAG** and **TEMP** contain values for the number of readings, the number of seconds, the magnetic field and the temperature respectively.

6.3 The I/O list

In its simplest form the FORTRAN I/O list consists of a series of variables, array names, array element names or character strings (or substrings) separated by commas. In unformatted I/O the data transfer takes place without modification, to or from the named locations in the order in which they appear in the list.

However, in formatted I/O, the items in the list are paired with the format specifications in the associated format identifier, e.g.

READ(5,'(I5,F8.3,F9.4)')I,X,Y

will read I according to format I5 (which specifies an integer of 5 digits), X according to format F8.3 (which specifies a real number of total length 8 digits with 3 digits after the decimal point) and Y according to format F9.4 (which specifies a real number of total length 9 digits with 4 digits after the decimal point). The format specifications and the I/O list keep in step, and items are input one after another from the same data record until the end of the input list is reached. This example is straightforward since the number of items in the I/O list is exactly the same as the number of format specifications and the types correspond (i.e. the integer is input with the I format and the reals are input with the F format). A new data record is selected when a **READ** (or **WRITE**) statement is encountered and all the numbers are read from the one record. Note that here, the format specifications are specified as a character string within the **READ** statement; they could equally well have been specified in a labelled **FORMAT** statement of the form

```
    READ(5,10)I,X,Y
10  FORMAT(I5,F8.3,F9.4)
```

In some cases, the **READ** or **WRITE** statement and the associated format specifications do not match exactly. Programmers sometimes find it convenient in a FORTRAN program to use one **FORMAT** statement with several **READ** or **WRITE** statements. For example,

```
        READ (5,10)I,AREA,J,WIDTH
   10   FORMAT(I5,F8.4,I3,F7.4)
        . . .
        . . .

        . . .
        READ (5,10)NO,VEL,ICOUNT
        READ (5,10)I,LENGTH,COUNT,WIDTH,VOLUME,RESULT
```

In the first **READ** statement the I/O list and the format specifications match exactly. I is input with a format of I5, **AREA** with F8.4, J with I3 and **WIDTH** with F7.4. In the second **READ** statement there are more format specifications than elements in the list. In this case, the first three specifications are matched with the corresponding elements in the I/O list, and the last part of the **FORMAT** statement is ignored. Therefore a data record containing:

bbb22b96.1569b58

(where *b* represents a blank or space) will be correctly input with the integer 22 read into **NO**, the real 96.1569 into **VEL** and the integer 58 into **ICOUNT**.

In the third **READ** statement there are two complications. The first is that there are more elements in the list than there are format specifications in the **FORMAT** statement. In a situation like this the **FORMAT** statement is repeatedly scanned from the beginning until the input list is exhausted, each rescan causing a new data record to be selected. The first scan of the **FORMAT** statement will cause input to **I, LENGTH, COUNT** and **WIDTH**. A new record is selected and data will be input to **VOLUME** and **RESULT** according to the I5 and F8.4 specifications which appear at the begining of the second scan of **FORMAT** statement 10. The input list is then exhausted so any remaining format specifications in the **FORMAT** statement will not be used.

The second complication in this case is that the type of the FORTRAN variables in the list does not always coincide with the corresponding format specification. Thus data is being read into the integer variable **LENGTH** with a format specification F8.4, into **COUNT** (real) with an I3 specification (integer) and into **VOLUME** (real) with an I5 specification (integer). This is illegal; the format specification and the form of the data on the input record must correspond in type with the corresponding I/O list entry.

These more complicated situations have been described here for completeness but programmers (and particularly beginners) are advised to avoid them. Keep your I/O and **FORMAT** statements simple. In particular, be careful to ensure that you are selecting a new record only when you intend to do so. This will occur:

a. whenever a new **READ** or **WRITE** statement is encountered;
b. whenever a format specification list is exhausted but the I/O list is not;
c. whenever a slash separator is met in the **FORMAT** statement.

So the statements

```
    READ (5,10)I,J,K
10  FORMAT(I5,I8,I7)
```

will read three integers from one record. But the statements

```
    READ(5,10)
    READ(5,20)
    READ(5,30)
10  FORMAT(I5)
20  FORMAT(I8)
30  FORMAT(I7)
```

will read three integers from three consecutive records and the statements

```
    READ(5,10)I,J,K,L,M,N
10  FORMAT(I5,I8,I7)
```

will read 6 integers from 2 consecutive records (with 3 integers per record).

Note that a record is a generalized term for a unit of input/output. On input it could be a card or a card image in a file and on output a line of printing. There is a maximum limit to the size of a record for any particular device (e.g. 80 characters on input and 132 characters on output) depending on the physical characteristics of that device.

A slash in a **FORMAT** statement may also be used to select a new record, e.g.

```
    READ(5,10)I,J,K
10  FORMAT(I5/I8/I7)
```

would have the same effect as the second of the two examples above, i.e. three integers will be read from three consecutive records. Notice that the slash is a separator used in place of a comma and not as well as a comma.

Finally, note that an input list may not contain expressions (since this is meaningless) but an output list may, e.g.

```
READ(5,10)A + B
```

is illegal but

```
WRITE(6,10)A + B
```

is perfectly valid.

Either an input or an output list may be empty, e.g.

```
READ(5,10)
```

would simply skip over an input record and

```
WRITE(6,10)
```

would write a blank record or may write some output not associated with an I/O list item, for example, a character string

```
    WRITE(6,10)
10  FORMAT('This is the end')
```

Long character constants may be spread across more than one record. The end of the record will not be interpreted as a space in this case but any blank columns will be. Thus

```
    WRITE(6,*)' This is an example
1               of what to avoid'
```

will be written with 48 spaces between the word 'example' and the word 'of'. This results from the 37 spaces following the word 'example' up to column 72 of the first record and the 11 spaces from column 7 to the word 'of' on the second record.

If list-directed I/O is used on output, then the values in the output list are converted to a default format according to their type. If it is used on input then the values on the record must have the same form as a constant of the corresponding type in the input list. Values on the input record must be separated by spaces or commas. There may be any number of spaces between values; there is no concept of a field width as in formatted I/O. Two adjacent commas with nothing but spaces between will cause the corresponding item in the input list to remain unchanged.

If a slash is used to separate values on a data input record, then the execution of the input statement will be terminated when the first slash is encountered.

The important point to note about list-directed I/O is that the value read or written for any given type is in exactly the same format as for a constant of that type. It follows that character constants on an input record must be enclosed between apostrophes but the apostrophes are not present on output. Each output record begins with a blank for carriage control. This also results in some differences in representation between formatted and list-directed I/O.

For example,

```
REAL A,B,X
INTEGER NUM
COMPLEX ROOTS
DOUBLE PRECISION ACCUR
LOGICAL FLAG
CHARACTER*8 MESS
READ *,A,B,X,NUM,ROOTS
PRINT *,A,B,X,NUM,ROOTS
READ *,FLAG,MESS,ACCUR
PRINT *,FLAG,MESS,ACCUR
```

would read two records with the following content:

```
23.569   8.7631   2.36E02   3096   (2.3,5.6)
.TRUE.   ' THE END'   2.6137892D02
```

and produce the following output records:

```
23.5690   8.76310   236.000   3096   (2.30000,5.60000)
T THE END   261.3789200000
```

(or something very similar depending on the machine used). Note the difference between the external representation of a complex number input or output with list-directed I/O (when it is two real numbers enclosed in parentheses and separated by a comma) and with formatted I/O when it is input or output as two separate real numbers with an F format specification for example.

Also in list-directed I/O, blanks in numeric fields are never interpreted as zeros; by default, embedded blanks are not permitted in numeric constants.

6.4 Repetition factors

Any format specification may be preceded by an unsigned integer constant which defines the number of times that field is to be repeated. For example,

READ(5,'(F8.4,F8.4,F8.4)')A,B,C

demands that the field F8.4 be used three times in succession for input to A, B and C. This may be written with a repetition factor as follows:

READ(5,'(3F8.4)')A,B,C

Groups of format specifications in parentheses may be repeated. For example,

READ(5,'(I5,F9.3,I5,F9.3)')I,A,J,B

may be written

READ(5,'(2(I5,F9.3))')I,A,J,B

Group specifications can be nested, i.e. a group can appear within another group.

The group format specification also affects the order in which the format codes are used. Earlier in this chapter (section 6.3) the situation in which there are more variables in the I/O list than format specifications in the format list was discussed. It was stated then that the format list is repeatedly scanned from the beginning until the I/O list is exhausted. This is perfectly valid unless the format list contains group format specifications in parentheses. In this case the format list is rescanned from the last nested group (taking into account any repetition of that group). This is illustrated by means of the following examples:

READ(5,'(I5,2(I3,F10.6))')I,J,A,K,B,L,C,M

is equivalent to inputting data to I with format I5, J with I3, A with F10.6, K with I3 and B with F10.6. The format specification is then exhausted, a new record is selected and the last nested group specification (i.e. 2(I3,F10.6)) is rescanned. L is input with format I3, C with F10.6 and M with I3. The I/O list is now exhausted, and so the rest of the format list is ignored. In the following situation:

READ(5,'(I5,(I2,F9.3),I6)')I,J,A,K,L,B,M,N

I is input with format I5, J with I2, A with F9.3 and K with I6. The format list is now exhausted, a new record is selected and the format list is rescanned from the group (I2,F9.3). So L is input with format I2, B with F9.3 and M with I6. The format list is again exhausted, a new record is taken and the statement is rescanned from the group (I2,F9.3). N is input with format I2 and the input list is now exhausted.

The general rule which applies is that the format list is always rescanned from the beginning of the format specification terminated by the last preceding right parenthesis, or to the first left parenthesis if there is no right parenthesis (always reusing any repetitions attached to the group within the parentheses).

Slashes may appear within group specifications to select new records.

Note that a repetition factor may not be zero, and some compilers will not accept a number greater than 255.

Formats should not be nested more than three deep for the sake of portability.

Repeated values in data may be represented on the input record in the form

r∗*c*

where *r* is an unsigned, non-zero, integer constant representing the repetition factor and *c* is the data value to be input *r* times, e.g.

READ(5,∗)I,J,K,A,(C(I),I = 1,10)

will read the data record

3∗20,,10∗3.1412

such that I, J and K are set to 20, the value of A is unchanged since it corresponds to no data and the ten elements C(1) to C(10) of the array C are all set to 3.1412.

If two or more successive values on output are the same, then the option is given to output these with the repeat specifier *r*∗*c*. This will depend on the compiler used.

6.5 The implied DO statement

Data can be input to individual array elements by specifying subscripted variables in the I/O list, e.g.

READ(5,'(F10.5,F8.4,F9.4)')A(I,J),B(I),C(J)

This statement requires that the appropriate values of I and J have been set at some point earlier in the program. It is quite legal for these values to be input by the same **READ** statement provided that this is done at a point in the I/O list before any reference to them, e.g. the statement

READ(5,'(2I5,F10.5,F8.4,F9.4)')I,J,A(I,J),B(I),C(J)

corresponding to an input record

*bbb*35*bbbb*5*bbb*1.18360*bb*2.3924*bb*20.9721

would read 35 into I, 5 into J, 1.18360 into A(35,5), 2.3924 into B(35) and 20.9721 into C(5). Note the use of a repetition factor here before the I5 specification.

Data may be input to an entire array by specifying the unsubscripted array name only in the I/O list, e.g.

REAL ARR(25)
READ(5,'(F10.5)')ARR

would read 25 numbers into consecutive elements of the array **ARR** according to format specification F10.5. The numbers would be read, one per record, from 25 consecutive records since a new record is selected each time the input list is exhausted. Note that the array must have been dimensioned at some earlier point in the program.

Values could be read into specified elements of an array (or indeed a whole array) by a **DO** loop of the form

```
    DO 10, I = 1,10
        READ(5,'(F8.3)')A(I)
10  CONTINUE
```

However, FORTRAN provides an implied **DO** statement to enable data to be input to selected elements of an array more conveniently. The implied **DO** statement is analogous to the **DO** loop. The statements

READ(5,'(F8.3)')(A(I),I = 1,10)

have the same effect as the above **DO** loop but is more efficient.
    Similarly,

READ(5,'(6F8.3)')(A(I),I = 15,25,2)

will read six real numbers from one record into elements A(15), A(17), A(19),

A(21), A(23) and A(25) of the array A, according to format specification F8.3.

Implied **DO** loops can be nested. For example, statements of the form

```
    DO 20 I = 1,10
        DO 10 J = 1,5
            READ(5,'(F10.4)')A(J,I)
10      CONTINUE
20  CONTINUE
```

can be written in the form

READ(5,'(F10.4)')((A(J,I),J = 1,5),I = 1,10)

These would both input data into the two-dimensional array A in the order A(1,1), A(2,1), A(3,1), A(4,1), A(5,1), A(1,2), A(2,2) and so on to A(5,10). Note the use of commas and parentheses in nested implied **DO** statements.

In general, an implied **DO** statement is of the form

$(list, i = m1, m2, m3)$

where *list* is an I/O list and i, $m1$, $m2$ and $m3$ are as defined in section 4.2. If nested, this may be generalized to

$((list, i = m1, m2, m3), j = m4, m5, m6)$

and so on. None of the entities $m1$, $m2$, $m3$, etc. may have their values changed within the loop. In practice this means that statements of the form

READ(5,10)(N,A(I),I = N,100)

are not allowed.

For completeness it should be noted that FORTRAN also allows **DATA** statements to include implied **DO** statements.

The examples of the **READ** statement in this section apply equally well to the **WRITE** statement. Note that a statement of the form

READ(5,10)(I,A(I),B(I),I = 1,N)

is invalid on input but is valid on output, i.e.

WRITE(6,10)(I,A(I),B(I),I = 1,N)

6.6 Format specifications

We have already introduced the idea of format specifications earlier in this chapter and seen how numeric specifications such as I5 or F8.3 can be used. In this section we shall discuss each format specification for each of the FORTRAN data types in greater detail.

Most format specifications consist of two parts – a letter which describes the type of data to be input or output and a number which specifies the field width of the data (i.e. the number of column positions occupied).

6.6.1 Numeric fields

Integers may be input and output by means of the I format code

Iw   or   **Iw.m**

where w and m are both unsigned integer constants greater than zero. w is the field width or the number of columns occupied by the number on input or output; this must include the sign position and any blanks. The plus sign may or may not be present for positive integers but space for it must be allocated in the field width. Decimal points are not allowed in integer fields. On input, m has no significance and Iw.m is identical to Iw; however on output, integers will be output with at least m digits in the field w (m of course must be less than or equal to w). Leading zeros will be printed if necessary.

On input, leading, trailing and embedded blanks are taken as zero so care must be taken to right justify the integer in the field. For example, four data records contain the following integers typed in column 1 onwards

    −1265
    +53
    bb762
    bb8b3

where b is a blank or a space.

The format specification I5 would input the integers −1265, +5300, +762 and +803. This may not be what is required. To read −1265, +53, +762, +83 the input records must be

    −1265
    bb + 53
    bb762
    bbb83

If the number occupies more than w positions on input, then only those digits within the field will be read and the remainder will be taken as part of the next field, e.g.

    b15784bb32

will be read as 1578 and 40032 with a format specification of 2I5.

On output, if the field width w is greater than the magnitude of the number then the left of the field will be padded out with blanks if the m specification is not used. If the magnitude of the number is greater than w then compilers will vary in the action they take. Some will print out a line of asterisks in the field.

Real numbers can be transmitted with or without an exponent part. The F format is used for numbers without an exponent and is of the form

Fw.d

where *w* represents the total field width and *d* is the number of places after the decimal point. The total field width includes the sign, decimal point and spaces. Leading, trailing and embedded blanks are taken as zero. Suppose successive data records contain

+253.9562*bb*
*bbb*63.2*bbbb*
*bbb*63200*bbb*
*b*1.95682573
*b*25.29*bbbbb*

then a format specification of F9.4 will input +253.9562, +63.200, +63.2000, +1.956825 and +25.29000.

This illustrates several points. If a decimal point is not punched in the field then the format specification will determine the position of the decimal point. If a decimal point is present in the field, then its position will override that specified in the format specification should the two differ. If the number is larger than the specified field width, then the extra digits will be taken as part of the next field.

On output, *d* positions will be printed to the right of the decimal point. If the fractional part is larger than this, then it will be rounded up, e.g.

−532.675928

printed with format F10.5 will be output as −532.67593. The field width *w* must allow for the decimal point and sign. Note that one digit is always printed to the left of the decimal point even if it is zero. If the number is smaller than the field width, it will be printed with leading spaces; if it is larger then asterisks may be printed in the field, but compilers will vary in this respect.

Real numbers with an exponent are transmitted by means of the E format specification. This is of the form

Ew.d   or   Ew.dEe

where *w* is the total field width, including the sign, decimal point, exponent and any blanks; *d* specifies the number of digits after the decimal point and *e* is the number of digits in the exponent. On input, four positions are reserved for the exponent, so the rest of the number should contain no more than *w* − 4 characters. A number with less than four positions in the exponent can be input with this specification. However, since trailing blanks (as well as leading and embedded blanks) are taken as zero, it is important that the number should be right justified in the field. The decimal point need not be present, but if it is, its position overrides that given in the format specification. With a format specification of E11.4 the numbers 0.5632E + 03, +0.2986E04b and −0.652E − 2bb will be input as +0.5632E + 03 (correct), +0.2986E040 (incorrect since trailing blanks are read as zero) and −0.652E − 200 (incorrect since the position of the decimal point in the data overrides that specified in the format code and trailing blanks are taken as zero).

Note also that on input the two formats above are identical.

On output, d significant digits are printed to the right of the decimal point. If there are more than this in the number, then the fractional part will be rounded up. An allowance should be made in w for one sign to the left of the decimal point and an exponent taking four positions. Thus a minimum of seven print positions is required for the E format, i.e. +0.E + dd.

If the additional Ee specification is used on output, then the exponent will be output with at least e digits.

Real numbers also may be input or output by means of the general format specification

Gw.d   or   **Gw.dEe**

On input, these are identical to Fw.d. On output, the rules seem complicated but, in general, mean that Gw.d is identical to Fw.d for numbers which are not too large or too small for the field, but acts like Ew.d (with an appropriate adjustment of the exponent) if the numbers are large or small.

For example, the table

Number	*F10.3*	*E10.3*	*G10.3*
−12556.0	−12556.000	−0.126E 05	−0.126E 05
67.25	67.250	0.673E 02	67.3
0.000150723	0.000	0.151E − 03	0.151E − 03
1126753	1126753.0	0.113E 07	0.113E 07
−102.3876	−102.388	−0.102E 03	−102.
1732981.0	**********	0.173E 07	0.173E 07

shows the format of several numbers output with E10.3 and G10.3. If the exponent of the number when normalized lies between 0 and d then the Fw.d format is used on output (as for 67.25 which when normalized is 0.6725E2) otherwise the E format is used. However, the number is left adjusted in the field by four places (as if E 00 were present but not output). So 67.250 is output as:

$bbbb$67.250

with F10.3 format but as

bb67.3$bbbb$

with G10.3 format.

It can be seen from this table, that one disadvantage of the G format is that it will not necessarily produce neat tabulated results with the decimal points of all the numbers aligned as the E format will. Note however the advantage of the last example where the number is too large for the field in the F format and so a line of asterisks is printed but the E and G formats both produce a truncated form of the number.

The format specification for double precision data is of the form

Dw.d

where w is the field width and d the number of digits after the decimal point. The specification is analogous to the E format and the same rules apply except that the letter D (rather than E) specifies the exponent. The number input is of the form

$+0.n\ n\ .\ .\ .\ n\ D + d1d2$

where $d1$ and $d2$ are the two digits of the exponent.

A complex number consists of a pair of separate real numbers representing the real and imaginary parts. Such numbers may be input or output by two successive F, E or D format specifications which may be different for the two parts.

Finally, note that all numeric format specifications may be preceded by a repetition factor as described in section 6.4.

The printing of a plus in numeric fields may be controlled by means of the S, SS and SP formats.

SP	will cause a plus to be produced wherever one may optionally appear.
SS	no plus will be produced in fields where one may optionally occur.
S	the local system default for optional plus is used.

Whenever SP, SS or S is used it remains in operation for all fields until it is explicitly altered.

Similarly BN and BZ may be used to control the handling of blanks in numeric fields on input.

BZ	will cause all but leading blanks to be converted to zeros.
BN	will ignore all blanks. The number will be right adjusted in the field. A field of all blanks will be treated as zero.

(These format specifiers override any **BLANK** = option used when a file is opened – Chapter 7. The effect is temporary. When the **READ** statement is complete the **BLANK** = value will be restored.) BN and BZ have no effect on output.

As an exercise in the use of numeric format specifiers do Exercise 6.1.

6.6.2 *Character fields*

Character strings may be output in FORTRAN by simply enclosing the string in quotes, for example,

```
    WRITE(6,10)
10  FORMAT('THE ROOTS ARE')
```

or

```
WRITE(6,'("THE ROOTS ARE")')
```

will cause one record containing the specified character string to be written to output unit 6. Character strings may be used in format statements on output only and there must be no element in the I/O list corresponding to them. Such strings may be used to label and annotate printed results. Note that the character strings are constants and may not be altered by the program.

Character strings may be mixed with other format specifications to produce records of annotated results, e.g. the record

```
TIME = 1430   250VOLTS   10AMPS   2500WATTS
```

may be written by the statements

```
    WRITE(6,10)ITIM,IVOLTS,IAMPS,IWATTS
10  FORMAT(' TIME = ',I4,I5,'VOLTS',I4,'AMPS',I6,'WATTS')
```

Tabulated results may be output similarly, e.g.

```
    WRITE(6,10)
    WRITE(6,'(" ",4I6)')ITIM,IVOLTS,IAMPS,IWATTS
10  FORMAT(' TIME VOLTS AMPS WATTS')
```

would produce

```
TIME   VOLTS   AMPS   WATTS
1430    250     10    2500
```

if output to a lineprinter. (Note that a blank carriage control character is placed in the **FORMAT** statement for the beginning of each record.)

In an example such as this, it is obviously important to space out the headings and results so that they are neatly tabulated in columns. Sufficient spaces may be included in the field specifications to allow for this, but to ease the task FORTRAN provides the specification

w**X**

specifically for transmitting w spaces on output or skipping w columns on input. It is a positional format specification since it indicates that the next character is to be transmitted, to or from the record, w positions forward from the current position.

The previous example may be written thus

```
    WRITE(6,10)
    WRITE(6,'(" ",4I6)')ITIM,IVOLTS,IAMPS,IWATTS
10  FORMAT(' TIME',2X,'VOLTS',2X,'AMPS',1X,'WATTS')
```

Note that the first character position in the first format of the record is used to transmit the carriage control character. The X format must be preceded by a number even if it is 1, i.e. X alone must not be used to mean 1X. Note also that X is not needed to skip the remainder of an input or output record. The input or output record will automatically be terminated when the I/O list and/or format specifications are exhausted.

Characters may be input to any named memory location by means of the A format specification

Aw

where w is the number of characters to be input, e.g.

```
    CHARACTER*80 CARD
    READ(5,'(A80)')CARD
```

These characters then become accessible to the program.

Characters may be output from named locations by this format also, e.g.

```
    WRITE(6,'(A80)')CARD
```

In theory, there is no limit to the number of characters w which may be input or output with the A format but in practice most compilers impose a limit. Some will not accept a number greater than 255.

If the width of the field is not specified (i.e. A alone is used) then the length of the corresponding character item in the I/O list will be taken as the number of characters to be read or written.

If w is specified and the length of the corresponding item in the list is l then the effect is as follows:

On input: If $w \geq l$ then the rightmost l characters are taken from the input field.
If $w < l$ then w characters are input and left justified. The rest of the character location is padded out with blanks.
On output: If $w > l$ the characters are output right justified in the field and preceded by blanks.
If $w \leq l$ the leftmost w characters are output.

For example,

```
    CHARACTER*8 RUNNO
    READ(5,'(A5)')RUNNO
```

will input the record

RUN*b*1

as RUN*b*1*bbb* in the character variable **RUNNO** which is of declared length 8 characters.

If the record

NEW*b*RUN*b*1

were read in this format then NEW*b*R*bbb* would be input to **RUNNO**.

In FORTRAN 66, the Hollerith format specification (H) was used to output character strings. This has effectively been made redundant by the introduction of character strings enclosed in quotes in FORTRAN 77. The H format has in fact been deleted from the FORTRAN 77 standard and so should never be used. However, many compilers do provide it as an enhancement to ensure compatibility with earlier versions of FORTRAN. It is included here for completeness in case you meet it in old programs. It differs from the A specification in that it is not used to transmit characters to or from locations in memory. It is used only to output literal character strings which are not accessible to the program in any other way.

For example,

```
    WRITE(6,10)
10  FORMAT(14H THE ROOTS ARE)
```

would write the string **THE ROOTS ARE** to unit 6. It is identical to the statement

```
    WRITE(6,10)
10  FORMAT(' THE ROOTS ARE')
```

This may be done also by the statements

```
    CHARACTER*14 MSG
    READ(5,10)MSG
10  FORMAT(A14)
    WRITE(6,10)MSG
```

but in this case the message **THE ROOTS ARE** must be provided on a data record on unit 5.

If the character string itself contains an apostrophe, then it must be represented by two successive apostrophes, e.g.

```
10  FORMAT(' THE EQUATION''S ROOTS ARE')
```

is equivalent to

```
10  FORMAT(25H THE EQUATION'S ROOTS ARE)
```

Character strings may be assigned to character variables and then output using the A format, e.g.

```
      CHARACTER*25 MSG
      REAL ROOTS(5)
      INTEGER I
      MSG = ' THE EQUATION''S ROOTS ARE'
      WRITE(6,10)MSG,(ROOTS(I),I=1,5)
   10 FORMAT('1 TABLE OF RESULTS',//A25,5F10.4)
```

will result in a new page being selected on a lineprinter (remember that the first character of a **FORMAT** specification may be used for carriage control and 1 represents paper throw). The heading

TABLE OF RESULTS

will be output followed by two new lines. The line

THE EQUATION'S ROOTS ARE *n1 n2 n3 n4 n5*

will then be output (where *n1* to *n5* are the contents of **ROOTS(1)** to **ROOTS(5)**).

To test out the use of character formats, annotate the table of Fahrenheit and Centigrade in Exercise 6.1.

6.6.3 Carriage control characters

When a record is output to certain devices (for example, the lineprinter), the first character of the record is not printed but is used to determine vertical line spacing. The remaining characters, if any, are printed on the line beginning at the left margin.

Special characters, known as carriage control characters, may be used in the first position and have the following effect:

b	select a new line before printing
0	select two new lines before printing
1	select a new page before printing
+	no paper movement
	(print the current line on top of the previous one)

Either Hollerith format specifications or quotes may be used to transmit these characters, e.g.

FORMAT(1H1,F12.6,I3,F10.5)

or

FORMAT('1',F12.6,I3,F10.5)

will both cause three numbers to be printed at the top of the next page.

FORMAT('0ENDЬOFЬRUNЬ',I3)

will select two new lines and then print the character string and an integer on the line.

Another line may be printed on top of this, e.g.

FORMAT(' +',70X,'SPECTRUM',I4)

These carriage control characters will be obeyed only on certain devices such as lineprinters which provide carriage control. If the same record is sent to any other output device then the effect is undefined, but the carriage control character may appear literally in the output record, e.g. **0END OF RUN**.

Note that systems may vary in the way they treat these control characters, particularly the + which may sometimes be interpreted as meaning 'append to the current line'.

Remember that slashes may be used anywhere in **FORMAT** statements to select a new record. Several slashes can be placed in succession to begin several new records. The effect of slashes at the beginning or end of a **FORMAT** statement is additional to the automatic beginning of a new record with each **READ** or **WRITE** statement. This frequently confuses beginners. For example,

    WRITE(6,10)(A(I),I = 1,10)
10   FORMAT(F9.4)

will cause each element of A to be printed on a new line whereas

    WRITE(6,10)(A(I),I = 1,10)
10   FORMAT(F9.4/)

will cause each element of the array to be printed on a new line, followed by a blank line.

On input, *n* consecutive slashes at the beginning or end of a **FORMAT** statement cause *n* consecutive records to be skipped. Slashes are separators and should not themselves be separated by commas.

It should be pointed out that compilers may vary in the way they treat slashes at the end of **FORMAT** statements and so for portable programs it is wise to avoid them. Remember also that carriage control characters will be expected after every slash for those devices which require carriage control.

6.6.4 Logical fields

Logical data types may be input or output by means of the format specification

   Lw

where *w* represents the total width of the field. The corresponding I/O list item must be of type **LOGICAL**.

On input, a valid field consists of optional blanks followed by a T or F which will cause either **.TRUE.** or **.FALSE.** to be assigned to the corresponding input list element. Any characters following this in the field will be ignored. The logical constants **.TRUE.** and **.FALSE.** are valid forms on input also.

On output, the field consists of $w - 1$ blanks followed by a T or F depending on whether the corresponding I/O list element is true or false.

6.6.5 Positional editing

In section 6.6.2, the X format specification for transmitting spaces was described. This can be used to skip columns on input or output and is a form of positional editing.

FORTRAN 77 provides additional T format specifications for positional editing. The format

Tc

specifies that column c is the position at which the next character is to be written or read (where c is an unsigned integer constant which cannot be zero).

TLc

will position the character pointer so that the next character will be read or written c column positions left (or backward) from the current position.

TRc

will position the character pointer so that the next character will be read or written c column positions right (or forward) from the current position.

6.6.6 Colon editing

It has been described earlier how format specifications are repeatedly scanned until the I/O list is exhausted – each rescan causing a new record to be selected.

The rescan will start at the beginning of the format if there are no embedded format groups, e.g.

READ(5,'(I5)')I,J,K

but will start at the first left parenthesis back from the end of the format specification if there are embedded groups, e.g.

READ(5,'(2F9.3,4(2X,F10.3))')X,Y,(A(I),I = 1,N)

will repeatedly scan the format 4(2X,F10.3) until N elements of A(I) have been input.

This may sometimes cause problems on output when an output list is exhausted, e.g.

WRITE(6,'(2("NUMBER = ",I3))')(NUM(I),I = 1,N)

will output

NUMBER = 105   NUMBER = 256
NUMBER = 172   NUMBER =

if *N* is 3. Obviously the programmer needs to suppress the output of **NUMBER =** if the output list is exhausted.

FORTRAN 77 provides the colon edit descriptor to do this. If a colon is encountered in a format list and the output list is exhausted, all subsequent output will be suppressed. It has no effect until the list is exhausted. So the above example can be rewritten

WRITE(6,'(2(:"NUMBER = ",I3))')(NUM(I),I = 1,N)

Another interesting example of this is in the printing of character variables where the actual significant length (excluding any trailing blanks) is unknown but it is required to print it without any superfluous blanks, e.g.

```
CHARACTER*80
READ *,RECORD
WRITE(*,'(80(:A))')RECORD
```

6.7 Scale factors

A scale factor *n*P can be used to move the position of a decimal point of a real number when it is transferred to or from a memory location. The power of 10 by which the number is to be scaled is given by *n* which may be a signed or unsigned integer constant.

On input it can be used with the F, E, G or D format. For example,

*n*P**F***w.d*

where *w* and *d* are as defined in section 6.6. If *n* is positive, the decimal point is moved *n* positions to the left. If it is negative the decimal point is moved *n* positions to the right. The external number 336.295 would be held internally as 3.36295 if input with a format specification −2PF8.3. The effect on output with F format is similar but the decimal point is moved in the opposite direction, e.g. 3.36295 will be output as 336.295 with a format 2PF8.3. So note that the scale factor changes the actual value of the number on input or output with F format.

If a number with an exponent is input with E, G or D format, the scale factor has no effect on the value of the number, e.g. 53.172E + 02 input with E11.3 or 2PE11.3 will be held internally as 0.53172E + 04.

If a scale factor is used on output with E or D format the overall value of the number will not be changed but the decimal point will be printed in a different position and the exponent adjusted accordingly. For example, the number 53.172 output with E11.4 and 1PE11.4 will be printed as 0.5317E + 02 and 5.3172E + 01 respectively, i.e. in general the mantissa is multiplied by 10**n when a positive scale factor nP is used. Note that extra significance is obtained on output when the scale factor format is used.

The effect on output with the G format depends on whether F mode or E mode output is used. With F mode output the scale factor will have no effect so that the overall value of the number is maintained. For E mode output with the G format, the scale factor operates as for E or D format.

A repetition factor can still be used if a scale factor is used, i.e. 2P3F10.4 is equivalent to 2PF10.4, 2PF10.4, 2PF10.4.

Once a scale factor has been set, it remains set and applies to all subsequent specifications in the same **FORMAT** statement until removed by a 0P scale factor. For example, 2PF10.4, 0PF10.4 would input the data −2098.5632 and +1382.9685 in the form −20.985632, +1382.9685.

6.8 Run-time format statements

It was stated earlier that in formatted I/O statements of the form

READ(u,f)list   or   **WRITE(u,f)**list

f may be the name of a character string containing a format specification.

These formats can be set up as character strings within the program. Alternatively a data record may contain a format specification such as

(I5,2(F10.4,3X),E16.6)

and this may be input to an array by means of the A format, e.g.

CHARACTER*22 FMT
READ(5,'(22A1)')FMT

This format may be used subsequently, e.g.

READ(5,FMT)I,A,B,X

This provides a means of changing format statements as the program requirements are changed. For example, variable length records of text may be input and subsequently printed. If each record is preceded by another record containing up to three characters which specify the length of the following record (which never exceeds 80), then run-time format statements may be used as follows:

CHARACTER FMT*7,TEXT*80
FMT = '(A1)'
READ(5,'(A3)')FMT(2:4)

```
READ(5,FMT)TEXT
WRITE(6,FMT)TEXT
```

6.9 STOP and PAUSE

An extension to the **STOP** statement enables it to perform limited output, i.e.

STOP *n*

where *n* is optional and may be a character constant or a number of not more than five digits. At the time of termination *n* is accessible and may be output, e.g.

STOP 'END OF PROGRAM'

or

STOP 5

may typically result in

****STOP END OF PROGRAM

or

****STOP 5

being output at the terminal. The exact effect will depend on the compiler used.

FORTRAN 77 provides the additional statement

PAUSE *n*

where *n* is optional and is as defined for **STOP**.

The **PAUSE** statement causes a temporary halt in the execution of the program. At this time *n* is accessible and may be output at the terminal. Execution may be resumed by some means outside the program. The way this is done will depend on the particular computer installation used. For example, on one system the statements

PAUSE 'END OF FIRST ITERATION'

or

PAUSE 10

will cause

****PAUSE END OF FIRST ITERATION

or

****PAUSE 10

to be printed at the on-line terminal. If the user replies with **START**, program execution will be resumed.

This statement can provide a method of monitoring the execution path of a program. However, since different systems may implement **PAUSE** in different ways, its use may result in loss of program portability.

6.10 Summary

● I/O statements are of the general form

  READ(*control list*)*list*
  WRITE(*control list*)*list*

  where *control list* is a list of control information specifiers and *list* is the I/O list.
● The I/O unit may be defined by a specifier of the form

  UNIT = u

  where *u* is an integer expression specifying the unit number. If the default unit is used, then this field need not be present.
● The data format may be defined by a specifier of the form

  FMT = *f*

  where *f* is the format identifier.
● I/O may be unformatted in which case the **FMT** specifier is not used.
● A **FORMAT** statement is of the form

  label **FORMAT**(*format specifier list*)

  where *format specifier list* is a list of format specifications separated by commas.
● *f* may be a character expression or the label of a **FORMAT** statement.
● The format may be specified in the I/O statement or in a separate **FORMAT** statement.
● If *f* is an asterisk, then list-directed I/O is specified and the statements

  READ *,list*   and   **PRINT** *,list*

  may be used.
● The implied **DO** statement can be used to transfer data to or from arrays. This is of the general form

  (*list, i = m1, m2, m3*)

● Formats are specified by the format specifiers I, F, E, G, D, X, A, L, T, TL, TR.
● Special carriage control characters may be used to control printer movement.

Exercises 6

1. Write a program to produce a table of Fahrenheit and equivalent Centigrade temperatures for every degree Fahrenheit from 1 to 100. Print this out in five columns across the page.

2. A survey of people's drinking and smoking habits results in a set of data records of the following format:

        Name   Character*20
        Age   I2
        Sex   Character*1
        Address   Character*25
        Marital Status   Character*7
        Units/week   I4
        Cigarettes/day   I3

where each of the above fields is separated by a single space.

Units/week gives the number of units of alcohol consumed each week. Assume that for females, light drinkers consume less than 8 units per week, moderate drinkers consume 8 to 14 units per week and heavy drinkers consume more than 14 units per week. The corresponding figures for males are less than 11, 11 to 20 and greater than 20 units respectively.

Cigarettes/day gives the number of cigarettes smoked per day. Assume that for females, light smokers consume less than 8 cigarettes per day, moderate smokers consume 8 to 14 cigarettes per day and heavy smokers consume more than 14 cigarettes per day. The corresponding figures for males are less than 11, 11 to 20 and greater than 20 cigarettes respectively.

Write a program to read and analyse the data. Print the number of females who are light, moderate or heavy drinkers and the number who are light, moderate or heavy smokers. Produce similar figures for males. (Assume that the data is terminated by 999 in the first 3 columns.)

Also print the name, age, sex, address and marital status of those people who are both heavy drinkers and heavy smokers together with the number of units/week and cigarettes/day they consume.

3. Write a FORTRAN program to plot a graph of the cosine function from 0 to 2π in 0.05π increments using the lineprinter. Assume that the lineprinter prints 120 characters in a line and that the variables AST and BL contain the character constants * and b which can be printed in A1 format. Try to improve the appearance of the graph by printing axes and by marking the 0, $\pi/2$, π, $3\pi/2$ and 2π axes and the 0, ±0.5 and ±1 ordinates. Assume unit 7 is connected to the lineprinter.

4. Write a program to read a floating point number as characters (allowing for an integer part, followed by a dot, followed by a fractional part, followed by an exponent part). Convert this input to the corresponding numeric value and print it out using E format. Allow for any valid format of FORTRAN floating point constants on input and detect invalid input. Treat embedded blanks as zeros.

5. Write a FORTRAN program to calculate the orbital speed (in miles per hour) of an artificial satellite which is to orbit the earth. Use the equation

$$v^2 r = \gamma E$$

where v is the orbital speed, r is the radius of the orbit from the centre of the earth, E is the mass of the earth and γ is the gravitational constant (take the product γE to be $1.44*10**12$ miles^3/hr^2 and the radius of the earth to be 3960 miles).

Compute the orbital speed for orbits from 1000 to 250 000 miles in units of 1000 miles, and also the number of days it would take a satellite to orbit the earth at each of these heights (where the length of orbit is $2\pi r$ for a satellite of height r).

Tabulate the results. If the distance of the moon from the earth is 250 000 miles, use the table to determine how many days it takes for the moon to orbit the earth.

7

Files

7.1 Introduction

During the fifties and sixties, the most commonly used medium for inputting both programs and data to the computer was the punched card. Results were produced on the lineprinter or punched on cards for resubmission to the computer as data. The ANSI 66 definition of I/O reflected this.

Since that time, cards have become almost obsolete and magnetic media such as discs and tapes are used more and more. Programmers now input programs and data from on-line devices (such as terminals or visual display units) to disc files. Results may be output to disc files or tape as well as printing devices such as the lineprinter.

FORTRAN 77 has catered for this by providing a very much more powerful and generalized I/O system for handling files.

The general term for a unit of input or output is a logical record. An input record may be a card or card image on disc; an output record may be a line of print or a line on a magnetic medium such as a disc or tape. A sequence of records is known as a file; this may be lines of print or a deck of cards but more usually a file refers to a sequence of records stored on disc or tape.

There is an important difference between magnetic tapes and discs. Records on tapes are written and read one after the other from the beginning of the tape to the end as the tape winds past the read/write heads; for this reason tapes are known as serial devices. Discs on the other hand rotate under read/write heads which can move across the surface and position on any track; this allows records to be written in any order at any position and for this reason discs are known as direct access devices (or sometimes random access devices). Thus in FORTRAN, records in a file may be read or written in one of two modes – either sequentially or randomly. The first mode is called sequential access, i.e. n records are written to a file one after another from record 1, 2, 3, . . ., n and must be read sequentially in this order. The second mode is called direct access, i.e. a file contains n records but these may be written and read in any order by reference to a record number which is a positive integer in the range 1 to n and is specified when the record is read or written.

All files must be considered as having a file pointer. When a file is first accessed or opened this pointer points to record 1, the first physical record in the file whether the file is sequential or direct access. With each sequential access, the pointer moves sequentially through the file until a specially formatted record called the endfile record is encountered. With each direct access, the file pointer is moved to the specified record number.

Records are of three types – they may be formatted, unformatted or specially formatted endfile records. Formatted records are written by formatted output statements, unformatted records are written by unformatted output statements (as discussed in the last chapter) and endfile records are written by the ENDFILE statement which will be described later.

In a sequential file, records must all be of the same type, i.e. either all formatted or all unformatted. They need not all be of the same length.

In a direct access file, records must also all be of the same type. They must be accessed by direct access I/O statements which differ from sequential access statements. They must all be of the same length.

Files may be given a name and must be connected to a given input or output unit identified within a FORTRAN program by a logical unit number. It is the programmer's responsibility to create the file, name it and connect it to the required unit. Some devices (such as the default input and output device) may be taken as preconnected and do not have to be explicitly connected by the programmer.

7.2 Control information specifiers REC, ERR, END and IOSTAT

Many of the additional features required to access files either sequentially or randomly, are provided by means of additional control information specifiers in the control lists of the **READ** and **WRITE** statements. For example, direct access I/O is provided by means of an additional entry **REC** = r in the **READ** or **WRITE** statement to specify the record number r which is to be read or written. This may be a positive integer expression.

The statement

READ(5,'(I5,3F6.2,2I3)',REC = 15)N1,R1,R2,R3,N2,N3

will read record 15 from the direct access file on unit 5 using the specified formats. Similarly, the statement

WRITE(6,'(I5,3F6.2,2I3)',REC = 15)N1,R1,R2,R3,N2,N3

will write record 15 to the file on channel 6.

If a record is read or written, the transfer may or may not be carried out successfully. The programmer may detect an unsuccessful transfer and take some action to recover from the error or print out a warning message that such an error has occurred. To do this the clauses

IOSTAT = *ios*   and   **ERR** = *s*

may be included in the **READ** or **WRITE** statement, where *ios* is an integer variable or array element which will be set to zero if no error occurs or end of file not found. If an error is detected then a positive value will be assigned to *ios*. Different numbers may be assigned for different types of error but the actual error numbers used depends on the compiler; there are no rules about this in the ANSI standard. If end of file is detected, then a negative value is returned in *ios*.

The error number returned may be tested after the **READ** or **WRITE**, e.g.

```
READ(5,'(I5,3F6.2,2I3)',REC = 15,IOSTAT = I)N1,R1,R2,R3,N2,N3
IF (I.EQ.0) THEN
. . .
ELSE IF (I.GT.0) THEN
. . .
ELSE IF (I.LT.0) THEN
. . .
END IF
```

The **THEN** clause of the block-**IF** will include the instructions to be obeyed if the read is successful; the first **ELSE IF** clause will include the instructions to be obeyed if there is an error on the read; the second **ELSE IF** clause will include the instructions to be obeyed if end of file is detected.

The additional control information specifier **ERR** = *s* may be included also. *s* is the label of an executable statement to which control is to be transferred if an error occurs. The **IOSTAT** variable will be set if such an error occurs. If the **ERR** = clause is used then the statements that test for error conditions need not follow the **READ/WRITE** statement immediately, e.g.

```
READ(5,'(I5,3F6.2,2I3)',REC = 15,IOSTAT = I,ERR = 30)N1,R1,R2,R3,N2,N3
. . .
. . .
. . .
30  statements to test the value of I, the IOSTAT variable
```

Similarly, the **END** = *s* control information specifier may be included so that control is transferred to statement label *s* if end of file is detected. If the **IOSTAT** clause is present also then a negative value will be assigned to *ios*. A typical example may be to read a set of values in a **DO** loop as follows:

```
    DO 10,I = 1,1000
        READ(5,'(F8.3)',END = 999)RVALUE(I)
10  CONTINUE
        .
        .
        .
999 Control comes here when end of file is reached
```

This removes the need for a special end of data terminator record.

The items on the control list in the **READ** and **WRITE** statements may appear in any order provided the keywords 'END = ', 'ERR = ', 'REC = ', 'IOSTAT = ' or 'FMT = ' are included. If 'UNIT = ' is omitted then the unit number must be the first item in the list. If 'FMT = ' is omitted then the format label must be the second item in the list and the first item must be the unit number without the identifier 'UNIT = '. These are the only two items for which the identifying keyword may be omitted.

7.3 OPEN and CLOSE

Before a file can be accessed by any I/O statement on a particular logical unit, it has to be created and connected to that logical unit. Most computer systems provide methods of doing this outside the FORTRAN program in Job Control statements. For example, unit 5 and unit 6 may be connected to disc files before the FORTRAN program is entered. Thus a **READ** or **WRITE** statement will cause a data transfer to take place on that unit without any further action on the part of the program. Files connected outside the program are known as preconnected files. The default input and output units are always preconnected.

However, in more complicated programs which require many input and output units, the programmer may need to control the file connections from within the program.

FORTRAN provides **OPEN** and **CLOSE** statements to enable the programmer to do this. **OPEN** will create a new file and connect it to the specified unit or will connect an existing file to a unit. A data communication channel is then opened between the program and the file. At any time in the execution of the program, this data channel may be closed and the same file may be connected to another channel. One file may not be connected to more than one channel at any time but many different files may be connected to many different channels up to a maximum limit defined by the system.

Units not closed at the end of program execution should be closed automatically by the system (but it is bad programming to assume this; the program itself should close all files). If the program opens a preconnected file then no error will occur but in general all files must be closed before they are re-opened, either on a different unit or on the same unit (perhaps with different properties).

The **OPEN** statement is of the form

OPEN(*openlist*)

where *openlist* may contain any of the following items:

```
UNIT   = u
FILE   = name
STATUS = stat
```

```
ACCESS = acc
FORM   = fm
RECL   = rl
BLANK  = blnk
ERR    = s
IOSTAT = ios
```

separated by commas. The items may be placed in any order. The phrase
'**UNIT** = ' may be omitted but if so the unit number must the first item on the
list. The unit number must be specified always but all other items on the list
are optional and may not appear more than once in any statement.

u is an integer expression defining the unit number.

name   is a character expression. Its value is the name of the file to be con-
         nected to the unit. Trailing blanks are removed. If the file does not
         exist it may be created (depending on the defaults of the computer
         installation). If a name is not given then a default system name will
         be used. This will be different at different computer installations.

stat   is a character expression which is assigned either the value '**OLD**' (in
         which case the file must already exist) or the value '**NEW**' (in which
         case the file must not exist and will be created) or the value
         '**SCRATCH**' (in which case an unnamed file will be connected to the
         unit but will be deleted either when the unit is closed or at the end of
         program execution) or the value '**UNKNOWN**' (in which case the
         status of the file will depend on the defaults at the computer installa-
         tion used). If the **STATUS** = phrase is omitted then '**UNKNOWN**' will
         be the assumed value.

acc   is a character expression with the value '**SEQUENTIAL**' if a sequential
         file is to be connected to the unit or the value '**DIRECT**' if a direct
         access file is to be connected to the unit. Trailing blanks are ignored.
         If this item is omitted then '**SEQUENTIAL**' will be assumed.

fm   is a character expression with the value '**FORMATTED**' if the file
         is to be accessed with formatted I/O statements or the value
         '**UNFORMATTED**' if the file is to be accessed with unformatted
         I/O statements. Trailing blanks are ignored. If this item is omitted
         then '**FORMATTED**' is assumed for sequential files and
         '**UNFORMATTED**' is assumed for direct access files.

rl   is a positive integer expression defining the record length for direct
         access files. This length is the number of characters per record for a
         formatted file. For unformatted files, the length is in units defined
         by the computer installation. This item must be included for direct
         access files, but otherwise must be omitted.

blnk   is a character expression with the value '**NULL**' if all blanks in
         numeric fields are to be ignored (except that a field of all blanks is
         zero) or '**ZERO**' if blanks in numeric fields are to be treated as zeros.

This item may be specified only for formatted files. For compatibility with FORTRAN 66 'ZERO' must be specified. If the item is omitted then 'NULL' is assumed.

s   is the label of an executable statement to which control is to be transferred if an error occurs.

ios   is an integer variable or array element which will be positive if an error occurs and zero otherwise (note that the end of file condition does not apply here).

The following examples illustrate the use of the OPEN statement

OPEN(10,FILE = 'BESSEL')

will connect a file called **BESSEL** to unit 10. By default, it will be a sequential file of formatted records. Its status will be **UNKNOWN** which may mean that it will be created if it does not exist but this depends on the defaults set for a particular computer installation. Blanks in numeric fields will be ignored. It must be read and written with formatted I/O statements.

OPEN(10,FILE = 'INTEGRALS',STATUS = 'NEW')

will create a new file called **INTEGRALS** on unit 10. The file must not already exist. It will have the default properties described for the previous example. The statement

OPEN(10,FILE = 'MYFILE',STATUS = 'OLD',ACCESS = 'DIRECT',RECL = 80)

will open an existing direct access file called **MYFILE** on unit 10. It will consist of unformatted records of length 80 units. Blanks in numeric fields will be ignored. The statement

OPEN(UNIT = 5,STATUS = 'SCRATCH',ACCESS = 'DIRECT',RECL = 80,
1   **FORM = 'FORMATTED',BLANK = 'ZERO',IOSTAT = IERR,ERR = 100)**

will open a direct access scratch file (unnamed) on unit 5 with formatted records of length 80 characters. Blanks in numeric fields will be treated as zeros. Any error in opening this file will cause control to be passed to statement 100 and **IERR** will be assigned a positive error number. Scratch files are used by programs for temporary workspace, e.g. to hold intermediate results. They will be deleted when the file is closed either by a **CLOSE** statement on that unit or at the end of program execution.

A file may be disconnected from a unit by the **CLOSE** statement which is of the form

CLOSE(*closelist*)

where *closelist* may contain any of the following:

UNIT   = *u*
IOSTAT = *ios*

ERR   = *s*
STATUS = *stat*

where

u, *ios* and *s* have been defined already,

stat   is a character expression with the value '**KEEP**' if the file is to be
            kept after it is closed or '**DELETE**' if the file is to be deleted after it is
            closed. Trailing blanks are ignored. The default specifier is **KEEP** if
            this item is omitted. Files opened with status **SCRATCH** may not be
            closed with status **KEEP**. Scratch files will always be deleted.

Note that the same file may be opened again in the same program, either on
the same or a different unit, provided it is first closed and then re-opened.

The unit number must always be specified. The phrase '**UNIT =** ' may be
omitted, in which case *u* must be the first item on the list. All other items are
optional and may appear in any order. Note that files are not closed by name.

The following examples illustrate the use of the **CLOSE** statement

CLOSE(10)

will close and keep the file on unit 10.

CLOSE(UNIT = 20,STATUS = 'DELETE',ERR = 100,IOSTAT = IERR)

will close and delete the file on unit 20. If an error occurs, control will be
transferred to label 100 and **IERR** will contain a positive error number.

```
      OPEN(UNIT = 6,FILE = 'RESULTS',STATUS = 'NEW',ACCESS = 'DIRECT',
    1        FORM = 'FORMATTED',RECL = 80,BLANK = 'ZERO')
      CLOSE(6,ERR = 999,IOSTAT = IERR,STATUS = 'KEEP')
      OPEN(5,FILE = 'RESULTS',STATUS = 'OLD',ACCESS = 'DIRECT',
    1        FORM = 'FORMATTED',RECL = 80,BLANK = 'ZERO')
```

creates and opens a direct access file called **RESULTS** on unit 6; this file is
subsequently closed and kept; it is then re-opened on unit 5. In this way,
results can be written out from a program and subsequently read back as
data.

7.4 INQUIRE

At any time during the execution of a program, the properties of a particular
file may be determined from within the program by means of the **INQUIRE**
statement. The inquiry may refer to the file by its name or by its unit number
and may be carried out either before, after or while the file is connected to a
unit.

The **INQUIRE** statement is of the general form

INQUIRE (*inquiry list*)

where *inquiry list* is a list of items separated by commas.

The inquiry can be by unit or by name but not both. If the file is not connected to a unit when the inquiry takes place then the inquiry must, of course, be by name.

If the inquiry is by the name of the file then this list must contain one file specifier of the form

FILE = *name*

where *name* is a character expression whose value is the name of the file. Trailing blanks are ignored.

If the inquiry is by unit, then the list must contain one unit specifier of the form

UNIT = *u*

In either case, the list may contain other items which will now be described in turn.

In addition to a **FILE** or **UNIT** specifier, the inquiry may contain any of the following items:

IOSTAT	= *ios*
ERR	= *s*
EXIST	= *e*
OPENED	= *o*
NUMBER	= *n*
NAMED	= *nmd*
NAME	= *fn*
ACCESS	= *acc*
SEQUENTIAL	= *seq*
DIRECT	= *dir*
FORM	= *fm*
FORMATTED	= *fmt*
UNFORMATTED	= *unf*
RECL	= *rl*
NEXTREC	= *nr*
BLANK	= *blnk*

where

ios   is an integer variable or array element which will be positive if an error occurs and zero otherwise.

s   is the label of an executable statement to which control is to be transferred if an error occurs.

e   is a logical variable or array element which is set to **.TRUE.** if the file exists (for inquiry by name) or the unit exists (for inquiry by unit) and **.FALSE.** otherwise.

o   is a logical variable (or array element) which is set to **.TRUE.** if the file is open (for inquiry by name) or the unit is open (for inquiry by unit) or set to **.FALSE.** otherwise.

n   is an integer variable (or array element) which is set to the number of the unit connected to the file. If no unit is connected then this variable is undefined.

nmd   is a logical variable (or array element) which is set to **.TRUE.** if the file has a name and to **.FALSE.** otherwise.

fn   is a character variable (or array element) which is set to the file name. If there is no name or the file is not connected then the variable becomes undefined.

acc   is a character variable (or array element) which is set to **'SEQUENTIAL'** if the file is connected for sequential access or **'DIRECT'** if it is connected for direct access. The variable is undefined if there is no connection.

seq   is a character variable (or array element) which is assigned the value **'YES'** if the file can be connected for sequential access, **'NO'** if it cannot. If the system is unable to determine this then the value **'UNKNOWN'** is set.

dir   is a character variable (or array element) which is assigned the value **'YES'** if the file can be connected for direct access, **'NO'** if it cannot and **'UNKNOWN'** if this cannot be determined.

fm   is a character variable (or array element) which is set to **'FORMATTED'** if the file is connected for a formatted data transfer and **'UNFORMATTED'** for an unformatted transfer. The variable is undefined if the file is not open.

fmt   is a character variable (or array element) which is assigned the value **'YES'** if the file consists of formatted records, **'NO'** if unformatted and **'UNKNOWN'** if this cannot be determined.

unf   the equivalent of *fmt* for unformatted records.

rl   is an integer variable (or array element) which is set to the record length of the connected file. It is undefined if the file consists of variable length records or is not connected for direct access.

nr   is an integer variable (or array element) which is set to $n + 1$ where n is the record number of the last record read from or written to a file connected for direct access. The variable is undefined if the file is not connected for direct access.

blnk   is a character variable (or array element) which is set to **'ZERO'** if blanks in numeric fields are converted to zeros or **'NULL'** if blanks are ignored. The variable is undefined if the file is not open for formatted data transfer.

Note the difference between **EXIST** and **OPENED**. A file exists if it has already been created in your filing system by whatever method (e.g. by a FORTRAN program or by an operating system command or editor); it need not be connected to a unit of the program issuing the **INQUIRE** statement. However, a file is only **OPENED** if it exists and is connected to an I/O unit.

So an **INQUIRE** statement could be written to determine whether a file exists and is connected to the required unit. If not, it can be created and connected to that unit, e.g.

```
    INQUIRE(FILE = 'MYFILE',EXIST = FEXIST,OPENED = FOPEN,
1          NUMBER = FUNIT)
    IF (FOPEN) THEN
        PRINT *,'MYFILE is opened on unit ',FUNIT
    ELSE IF (FEXIST) THEN
        OPEN(UNIT = 5,FILE = 'MYFILE',STATUS = 'OLD')
    ELSE
        OPEN(UNIT = 5,FILE = 'MYFILE',STATUS = 'NEW')
    ENDIF
```

The program example in Fig. 7.1 illustrates many of the features of FORTRAN file handling. Suppose it is required to update or add records to a direct access file called **RANDOM**. The program must first check that the file exists and create it if it does not. An existing file must be checked to ensure that direct access is allowed. The first record of the file holds the total number of records in the file, in I6 format. The program reads as data the record number to be updated or the character string **NEXT** if a record is to be added. The program to do this illustrates the use of **OPEN, CLOSE** and **INQUIRE**. It also uses internal files which will be described in the next section.

7.5 Internal files

So far in this discussion we have talked only of external files, i.e. files on some peripheral device external to the program. FORTRAN provides the concept of an internal file which is a way of using an area of the program's memory as if it were a file which can be read or written. To do this, the name of an area in memory must be specified in a **READ** or **WRITE** statement in place of the file unit number, e.g.

```
    READ(IBUF,'(5(9X,I5))')(A(I),I = 1,5)
```

or

```
    WRITE(IBUF,'(5(9X,I5)')(A(I),I = 1,5)
```

The **READ** or **WRITE** is obeyed as usual (and all the normal rules apply) except that the data to be transferred is read from (or written to) the specified area in memory instead of the peripheral device. This area is termed an 'internal file' and must be a character variable, character array element, character array or substring. If it is a character variable, character array element or substring, it may contain only one record which is the length of the corresponding character variable (or array element or substring) but if it is a character array it may contain a sequence of records. Only sequential, formatted I/O

```
************************************************************************
*                         PROGRAM UPDATE                              *
*                                                                     *
************************************************************************
      PROGRAM UPDATE
      CHARACTER*80 A
      CHARACTER*4 REPLY
      INTEGER CHAN,ERR,I,NREC,LREC
      LOGICAL FEXST
      CHARACTER*6 FACC
*
* Inquire if file exists
*
      INQUIRE(FILE='RANDOM',EXIST=FEXST)
*
* If it exists then open for direct access on unit 8
*
      IF (FEXST) THEN
         OPEN(UNIT=8,FILE='RANDOM',STATUS='OLD',ACCESS='DIRECT',
     1       RECL=80,ERR=10,IOSTAT=ERR,FORM='FORMATTED')
         CHAN=8
         PRINT '(''Existing file opened'')'
         INQUIRE(UNIT=CHAN,ACCESS=FACC)
*
* Check that direct access is allowed
*
         IF (FACC .EQ. 'DIRECT')THEN
*
* If it is then read first record containing the number of records
* in the file
*
            READ(CHAN,'(I6)',REC=1)LREC
            PRINT '(''NO. OF RECORDS IN FILE '',I5)',LREC
         ELSE
*
* Otherwise print error message and close file
*
            PRINT '(''File is not direct access file'')'
            CLOSE(CHAN)
            STOP
         END IF
      ELSE
*
* If it does not exist then create a new direct access file
*
         OPEN(UNIT=8,FILE='RANDOM',STATUS='NEW',ACCESS='DIRECT',
     1       RECL=80,ERR=10,IOSTAT=ERR,FORM='FORMATTED')
         CHAN=8
*        PRINT '(''New file created'')'
*        LREC=1
         WRITE(CHAN,'(I6,74X)',REC=1)LREC
      ENDIF
      LREC = LREC+1
*
* Prompt user to type the number of the record to be updated or
* the character string 'NEXT'
*
      PRINT '(''TYPE RECORD NUMBER'')'
*
* Note that the reply is read into a character variable
*
      READ '(A4)',REPLY
      IF (REPLY .EQ. 'NEXT') THEN
         NREC = LREC
      ELSE
```

(figure continues)

FIG. 7.1 A FORTRAN program to update records in a direct access file

144   Files

```
*
* If the reply is not 'NEXT' then it should be a record number
* This is read from the character variable reply as an internal
* file with blanks ignored.
*
        READ(REPLY,'(BN,I4)',ERR=20)NREC
      ENDIF
*
* Check that the record number is valid
*
      IF (NREC.GT.LREC.OR.NREC.LT.2) THEN
         PRINT '(''Invalid record number'')'
         CLOSE(CHAN)
         STOP
      END IF
*
* Now read the required record and write to the required position
*
      PRINT '(''Type record'')'
      READ '(A80)',A
      WRITE(CHAN,'(A80)',REC=NREC)A
*
* Update record 1 if the number of records in the file has increased
*
      IF (NREC.GE.LREC)THEN
         WRITE(CHAN,'(I6,74X)',REC=1)LREC
      END IF
      PRINT '(''File updated'')'
      CLOSE(CHAN)
      STOP
   10 CONTINUE
      PRINT '(''I/O Error on file - status word is'',I6)',ERR
      CLOSE(CHAN)
      STOP
   20 CONTINUE
      PRINT '(''Invalid record number'')'
      CLOSE(CHAN)
      STOP
      END
```

FIG. 7.1 *contd*

statements can be used with internal files. They must not be read or written with list-directed I/O.

When the **READ** or **WRITE** statement is executed, format conversion will take place according to the format specifications provided. Thus the internal file facility provides a useful means of converting from one format to another. For example, an integer or real number (held in variables **INTNUM** and **RNUM** respectively) may be converted to its character string equivalent by the statements

CHARACTER*10 CHARST
WRITE(CHARST,'(I9)')INTNUM
WRITE(CHARST,'(F7.2)')RNUM

Another use of internal files may be to read the same record from the internal file in several different formats whilst only using one peripheral transfer. The file pointer returns to the beginning of the record after each **READ** or **WRITE** so for example a data record may be read into **IBUF** with format A80 and subsequently read as five integers as follows:

```
CHARACTER*80 IBUF
INTEGER A(5)
READ(5,'(A80)')IBUF
  . . .
  . . .
  . . .
READ(IBUF,'(5(9X,I5))')(A(I),I = 1,5)
```

If the input record contains five integers starting in columns 10, 24, 38, 52 and 66 then these five integers will be read into A(1) to A(5) with format I5.

For those familiar with **ENCODE** and **DECODE** in FORTRAN 66 extended compilers, then the internal file facility in ANSI 77 provides an alternative method of performing the same function.

Another typical use would be where several input records have to be read with different formats depending on a particular character set in column 1. By inputting each record with format A80 into a character variable, testing column 1 and then reading from the character variable as an internal file with different format specifications, the programmer may achieve the required result.

7.6 The ENDFILE statement

As stated earlier, files contain a specially formatted record called the endfile record which is physically the last record of the file and marks its end. Such records are written by a special **ENDFILE** statement which is of the form

ENDFILE u

or

ENDFILE(*list*)

where *u* is the unit number to which the endfile record is to be written and *list* is a list of control information specifiers separated by commas. The control information specifiers which may be used in this statement are **UNIT** = *u*, **ERR** = *s* and **IOSTAT** = *ios* as defined in previous sections. Any attempt to read or write past the end of this record will be detected as an error which may be trapped by the **ERR** or **IOSTAT** specifiers. Once positioned at end of file, it is necessary to rewind or backspace the file in order to read from it or write to it again. Statements to do this will now be described.

7.7 BACKSPACE and REWIND

It has already been explained that a file consists of *n* records numbered 1, 2,

. . ., *n*. A file pointer moves through the file as records are read or written. This pointer is positioned at record 1 when the file is first opened. For sequential access, the pointer will move to record 2, 3, 4, etc. as records are successively read or written. At any time the **BACKSPACE** statement will position the file pointer before the preceding record. It is of the form

BACKSPACE *u*

or

BACKSPACE(*list***)**

In this statement (as in the **ENDFILE** statement described earlier) *u* is a unit number and *list* is a list of control information specifiers separated by commas. This list must contain a unit specifier of the form

UNIT = *u*

(where the phrase '**UNIT** =' is optional) and the optional specifiers

IOSTAT = *ios*
ERR   = *s*

may be included. *ios* is an integer variable or array element which will be positive if an error occurs and zero otherwise; *s* is the label of an executable statement to which control is to be transferred if an error occurs.

If **BACKSPACE** is issued and there is no preceding record in the file, then the position of the file pointer remains unchanged.

The file pointer may be positioned at its initial point (record 1) at any time by the **REWIND** statement

REWIND *u*

or

REWIND(*list***)**

where *u* and *list* are as defined for **ENDFILE** and **BACKSPACE**. If the file is already at its initial point, then this statement is allowed but has no effect. Note that if the file is on magnetic tape, this statement will physically rewind the tape.

If the file does not exist, then execution of the **ENDFILE** statement will create the file. Execution of the **BACKSPACE** statement is not allowed if the file does not exist. Execution of the **REWIND** statement is allowed but has no effect.

Note that all these statements are used on sequential files only. The files may not be written with list-directed I/O if **BACKSPACE** is to be used.

The following program illustrates the use of **BACKSPACE** and **REWIND** to add some new records to the end of an existing file and then print the file from the beginning:

Open existing file
Do until EOF of existing file
    Read and ignore records
End Do until EOF
Backspace one record
Open file of new records
Do until EOF of new records
    Read a record
    Write to the end of the old file
End Do until EOF of new records
Close file of new records
Rewind updated file
Do until EOF of updated file
    Print record
End Do until EOF of updated file
Stop

```
      PROGRAM APPEND
      INTEGER FILSZ1,FILSZ2
      PARAMETER (FILSZ1 = 10000,FILSZ2 = 100)
      CHARACTER*80 RECORD
      INTEGER I,OLDERR,NEWERR,CLSER1,CLSER2,UPDERR
*
* Open the file to be updated
*
      OPEN(5,FILE = 'OLDFIL',STATUS = 'OLD',ACCESS = 'SEQUENTIAL',
     1      ERR = 990,IOSTAT = OLDERR)
*
* Read and ignore records until end of file
*
      DO 10, I = 1,FILSZ1
          READ(5,'(A80)',END = 20, ERR = 991)
  10  CONTINUE
*
* Position unit 5 before the end of file record
*
  20  BACKSPACE 5
*
* Open the file containing the records to be appended
*
      OPEN(6,FILE = 'NEWFIL',STATUS = 'OLD',ERR = 992,
     1      IOSTAT = NEWERR)
*
* Read records from this file and append them to the file on unit 5
* until end of file on unit 6 is found.
*
      DO 30, I = 1,FILSZ2
```

```
            READ(6,'(A80)',ERR = 993,END = 40)RECORD
            WRITE(5,'(A80)',ERR = 994)RECORD
   30   CONTINUE
   40   CLOSE(6,ERR = 996,IOSTAT = CLSER2)
*
* Rewind and print the updated file
*
        REWIND 5
        DO 50, I = 1,FILSZ1
            READ(5,'(A80)',ERR = 996,END = 999,
   1             IOSTAT = UPDERR)RECORD
            PRINT *,RECORD
   50   CONTINUE
  990      .
  991      .
  992      .
  993   Statements to handle errors
  994      .
  995      .
  996      .
  999   CLOSE(5)
        STOP
        END
```

7.8 Summary

- A unit of input or output is a record.
- A sequence of records is a file.
- Files may be sequential or direct access.
- Records may be formatted, unformatted or endfile records.
- Files may also be internal files, i.e.

    READ or WRITE(*internal file,f*)*list*

  where *internal file* is a variable, array element, array or substring of type **CHARACTER**.

- Additional control information specifiers **REC**, **ERR**, **END** and **IOSTAT** are provided for file handling, i.e.

    REC   = r
    ERR   = s
    END   = s
    IOSTAT = ios

  where r is a positive integer expression, s is the label of an executable statement and *ios* is an integer variable or array element which is zero if no error occurs and positive otherwise.

- Files may be opened and connected to the required unit by the **OPEN** statement, i.e.

>   **OPEN(UNIT** = *u*,**FILE** = *name*,**STATUS** = *stat*,**ACCESS** = *acc*,
> 1   **FORM** = *fm*,**RECL** = *rl*,**BLANK** = *blnk*,**ERR** = *s*,**IOSTAT** = *ios*)

Files are closed and disconnected from the logical unit by the **CLOSE** statement, i.e.

>   **CLOSE(UNIT** = *u*,**IOSTAT** = *ios*,**ERR** = *s*,**STATUS** = *stat*)

Information about a file can be obtained by the **INQUIRE** statement, i.e.

>   **INQUIRE(UNIT** = *u*,**IOSTAT** = *ios*,**ERR** = *s*,**EXIST** = *e*,**OPENED** = *o*,
> 1   **NUMBER** = *n*,**NAMED** = *nmd*,**NAME** = *fn*,**ACCESS** = *acc*,
> 2   **SEQUENTIAL** = *seq*,**DIRECT** = *dir*,**FORM** = *fm*,
> 3   **FORMATTED** = *fmt*,**UNFORMATTED** = *unf*,
> 4   **RECL** = *rl*,**NEXTREC** = *nr*,**BLANK** = *blnk*)

If the inquiry is by name rather than by unit, then the term **UNIT** = *u* is replaced by the term **FILE** − *name*.

- Files may be backspaced and rewound by the **BACKSPACE** and **REWIND** statement, i.e.

>   **BACKSPACE** *u*   or   **BACKSPACE(***list***)**
>   **REWIND** *u*   **REWIND(***list***)**

Endfile records may be written by the **ENDFILE** statement, i.e.

>   **ENDFILE** *u*   or   **ENDFILE(***list***)**

where *u* is the unit number and *list* is a list of control information specifiers (only **UNIT**, **ERR** and **IOSTAT** apply here).

Exercises 7

1. Which of the following FORTRAN I/O statements are invalid and why?
   (a) **WRITE(ERR** = 900,6,'(I5)')I
   (b) **READ(∗,∗,IOSTAT** = IOST)X,Y,A,B,I,J
   (c) **INQUIRE(FILE** = 'FILENAME',**UNIT** = 6,**EXIST** = EXST,**OPENED** = OPND)
   (d) **OPEN(6,FILE** = 'FILENAME',**ACCESS** = 'SEQUENTIAL',**RECL** = 80)
   (e) **CLOSE(UNIT** = 8,**STATUS** = 'DELETE')

2. Rewrite Exercise 6.1 so that it writes its results to a file on unit 6.

3. Write the sorting program of Exercise 5.5 so that it reads the names to be sorted from a file on unit 5 and writes the sorted list to a file on unit 6.

4. Write a typical weekly payroll program to update a master file of employee records with the current week's input and to print a payslip for

each employee. Assume that the weekly payroll data is read from a file on unit 5, that the master employee file is read on unit 6 and the payroll slips are printed to the file on unit 7. Errors should be printed on the default output unit. Assume that the employees are paid at a fixed rate for 40 hours' work and at 1.5 times that rate for hours in excess of this. The weekly data contains the employee number and the number of hours worked that week. The master file contains the employee number, the employee name, the annual tax-free allowance and the tax rate for each employee as well as the gross pay to date, the net pay to date and the number of hours worked to date. The pay slips contain the employee number, the employee name, the number of hours worked, the gross pay and the net pay for that week. For simplicity, assume one standard tax rate of 30%.

5. A bank account file contains

   Account number   Customer number   Balance

   A customer file contains

   Customer number   Name   Address   Permitted overdraft

   Scan these files to determine all the people with a negative balance (overdrawn) and check whether this exceeds the permitted overdraft for that customer. Print the names and addresses of all customers who have exceeded their permitted overdraft.

8

Functions and subroutines

8.1 Introduction

In this book so far, the program examples and exercises have consisted of one block of FORTRAN statements commencing with a **PROGRAM** statement followed by declaration statements and executable statements and terminated by **END**.

This is an acceptable structure for small programs. But large programs written in this way can become difficult to manage; it would be more convenient if FORTRAN provided a method of dividing the program into smaller, more manageable units which could be developed and tested independently. Furthermore, it may be that different FORTRAN programs need to carry out many of the same functions. It would save time and effort if a block of FORTRAN statements could be included easily in many different programs.

FORTRAN provides facilities that enable the programmer to do these things.

A FORTRAN program must consist of one main program but may include a number of subprograms which can be called by the main program (or by other subprograms) to carry out some well-defined task. All the programs so far in this book have consisted of one main program with no subprograms.

A main program or a subprogram are both examples of program units. Subprograms can be functions or subroutines. There are, in fact, four types of subprogram:

i.   Intrinsic functions.
ii. Statement functions.
iii. External functions (or function subprograms).
iv. Subroutines.

Each of these will be described in turn in the following sections.

Before proceeding, note that it is good programming practice to limit any program unit to one or two pages of text, partly so that it will be easier to write, understand and manage, and partly because most compilers impose an upper limit on the size of a program unit that can be compiled; large units may cause loss of program portability. It is also good software engineering practice to limit the complexity of any subprogram to aid human comprehension. Do not forget the importance of structured design for each subprogram. It is at the design stage that the complexity of each program unit can be assessed and division into several smaller, less complicated units can be effected where necessary.

8.2 The main program and the PROGRAM statement

All FORTRAN programs must contain one and only one main program. This is terminated by **END**. It may contain one or more **STOP** statements to terminate execution (or this may occur in a subprogram). If no **STOP** statement is present then **END** is taken as an executable statement implying **STOP**.

The main program may be headed by an optional statement of the form

PROGRAM *name*

where *name* is any valid FORTRAN symbolic name used to identify the program. Thus the program name is limited to six characters as all FORTRAN names are. The **PROGRAM** statement is optional but, if present, must be the first statement of the main program. The program name must not duplicate the name of any data item in the main program nor the name of any subprogram (or **COMMON** block – Chapter 9). If the **PROGRAM** statement is not used, most systems will allocate a default system name to the main program.

Between the start of a main program and **END**, the FORTRAN statements must follow the order described in the next section. Calls on other subprograms may be included.

A main program and subprograms in FORTRAN are independent units of compilation. That is the source text of a FORTRAN program unit may be submitted alone to the FORTRAN compiler which will produce an object module for that unit. Any number of separate compilations may be carried out on different program units and object modules will be produced for each unit. When a program is ready to run then the object modules for the main program, and as many subprograms as the program requires, are collected or linked together to form an executable program which may be run. Object modules provided by other programmers or by system libraries of subprograms may be linked in at this point. Exactly how this is done depends on the computer used and the Job Control statements provided. However, it should be obvious that the provision of the subprogram facility potentially saves programming effort since programmers can share program units.

The facility of independent compilation has permitted the establishment of large libraries of subroutines (such as the NAG library or the Harwell subroutine library) which provide standard solutions for a wide selection of problems.

8.3 Statement ordering

The FORTRAN 77 standard defines rules for the ordering of statements between the header and the end of any program unit. In addition to the rules in the standard, it is wise to follow a recommended ordering for the sake of clarity and portability as follows:

PROGRAM (or subprogram) header
IMPLICIT statements
Type statements and PARAMETER statements
EXTERNAL and INTRINSIC statements
DIMENSION statements
COMMON statements
EQUIVALENCE statements
DATA statements
Statement function statements
Executable and FORMAT statements
END

Note that **IMPLICIT** statements must precede all other statements except the header. Many of the above statements have not been described so far in this book but will be introduced later in this chapter or Chapter 9. The ANSI standard allows **DIMENSION, COMMON, EQUIVALENCE** and **EXTERNAL** or **INTRINSIC** to be intermingled; **DATA** statements may be placed anywhere after type and **PARAMETER** statements but before **END** (i.e. intermingled with declaration or executable statements). However, **DATA** statements initialize memory locations before execution of the program begins and so their position in the program does not imply the point at which initialization will occur. **DATA** initialization statements are not executable statements but they will be obeyed in order; it is common practice to group them all at the head of a program unit in the position shown above.

FORMAT statements, if used, may be interspersed anywhere between the header and **END**. Some programmers prefer to group them together immediately before the **END** and others place them after the I/O statement to which they belong; this is a matter of personal taste.

ENTRY statements may be placed anywhere between the header and **END** (see later).

The **PARAMETER** statement may be interspersed with **IMPLICIT** and Type statements but must precede all **DATA** statements, statement functions and executable statements.

Comment lines may be included anywhere. They may precede the header but must not follow the **END** statement.

8.4 Intrinsic functions and the INTRINSIC statement

The concept of intrinsic functions has already been introduced in section 2.7.

Any FORTRAN expression may include a call on an intrinsic function by including the name of the function at the appropriate point in the expression. This function will be obeyed at the point it occurs and will return a result which is used as the operand value at that point in the evaluation of the expression.

The FORTRAN language defines a range of intrinsic (or built-in) functions which must be provided with all implementations of the language. These include commonly used trigonometric functions, square root and so on. A complete list of available functions is given in Appendix A.

Intrinsic functions may have arguments which provide values on which the functions must operate when called. For example, **SQRT(X)** finds the square root of the value of the argument X, e.g.

   Y = SQRT(X) − Z

This means 'transfer control to the **SQRT** function passing the value of X to it; return from the function with the square root of X; subtract Z from this value and assign the result to Y'.

A function may have one or more arguments enclosed in parentheses, separated by commas and following the function name.

In FORTRAN 66, a particular function could have several different names depending on the type of the arguments, e.g. **SQRT** finds the square root of a real argument, **DSQRT** finds the square root of a double precision argument and **CSQRT** finds the square root of a complex argument. These names were called the specific names of the function.

FORTRAN 77 also provides these specific function names (for the sake of upward compatibility) but in addition provides generic function names which may be used with arguments of any type. For example, **INT** and **REAL** (to convert any real argument to integer or any integer argument to real respectively); **DBLE** and **CMPLX** (to convert any numeric argument to double precision or complex); **AINT, ANINT** or **NINT** (to convert a real or double precision argument to a truncated integer, the nearest whole number or the nearest integer respectively); **ABS, MOD** and **SIGN** (to find the absolute value of a numeric argument, or the remainder when the two arguments are divided, or to transfer the sign of the second argument to the first argument respectively); **DIM** (to find the positive difference between the first and second arguments or return zero if negative) and **MAX** and **MIN** (to find the maximum or minimum of n arguments of any numeric type). These are useful generic functions provided in addition to square root, logarithmic, trigonometric and character functions introduced already.

The FORTRAN programmer is advised to use generic names for intrinsic functions in preference to specific names. It is these names only which are given in Appendix A.

Any intrinsic function used in a program unit may be declared in an **INTRINSIC** statement declaration which is of the form

INTRINSIC *list*

where *list* is a list of intrinsic function names separated by commas, e.g.

INTRINSIC SQRT,LOG,TAN,ABS

It is essential to declare in an **INTRINSIC** statement any intrinsic function name which is to be passed as an argument to another subprogram (see later) but not all intrinsic functions may be passed as arguments. The rules may be summarized as follows:

i.   Specific and generic function names may be declared in an **INTRINSIC** statement. Any name may appear once only in an **INTRINSIC** statement in any program unit (and may not also appear in an **EXTERNAL** statement – see later).
ii. Any function name passed as an argument to another subprogram *must* appear in an **INTRINSIC** statement.
iii. Generic function names may not be passed as arguments to subprograms.
iv. Specific names of functions for type conversion (**IFIX, FLOAT,** etc.), lexical comparison (**LLE, LLT,** etc.) and for selecting maxima or minima (**MAX0, MIN0,** etc.) may not be passed as arguments.

It is good programming practice to declare the names of all intrinsic functions called in a program unit in an **INTRINSIC** statement. This provides a good documentation aid and will result in an immediate error message if the program is compiled on a system which does not provide all the required functions, since not all computer installations necessarily provide all of the intrinsic functions available at another installation.

8.5 The statement function

Any FORTRAN program may require to perform the same function several times. This function may not be available as an intrinsic function and must be written by the programmer and be included in a program unit as a user supplied function. If such a function may be performed by a single statement then a statement function can be used to define it.

A statement function declaration is of the form

name(*argument list*) = *expression*

where *name* is the function name and obeys the usual FORTRAN naming conventions. The *argument list* is a list of arguments separated by commas and included in parentheses.

This statement function declaration defines the function to be performed. It must follow all **IMPLICIT** and type statements but precede all executable statements.

Any executable statement within the same program unit (be this the main program or a subprogram) may reference this function by including the name and arguments in an expression.

The arguments in the statement function definition are *dummy arguments* which will be replaced by actual arguments when the function is called. For example, suppose it is required to calculate the function

$$ax^2 + by^2 + cxy + d$$

at several points in a program. A statement function statement could be defined for this function, i.e.

QUAD(X,Y) = A*X**2 + B*Y**2 + C*X*Y + D

At this stage, no actual computation is performed. This is simply a definition. If it is required to calculate this function at two points X1,Y1 and X2,Y2 then statements of the form

F1 = QUAD(X1,Y1)
F2 = QUAD(X2,Y2)

may be written. The function is evaluated at points (X1,Y1), (X2,Y2) and the actual arguments X1,Y1 and X2,Y2 will be used in place of the dummy arguments X,Y in the definition. A main program to do this can be constructed as follows:

```
PROGRAM STATFN
REAL X,Y,A,B,C,D,F1,F2,X1,Y1,X2,Y2
QUAD(X,Y) = A*X**2 + B*Y**2 + C*X*Y + D
READ *,X1,Y1,X2,Y2,A,B,C,D
F1 = QUAD(X1,Y1)
F2 = QUAD(X2,Y2)
PRINT *,F1,F2
STOP
END
```

The statement function can equally well be defined in any subprogram.

The expression on the right-hand side of a statement function definition may be any valid FORTRAN expression containing constants, variables, array elements, character expressions, parameters and intrinsic functions. It may contain references to previously defined statement functions (and to external functions) but may not reference itself.

Dummy argument names obey the usual FORTRAN naming conventions. It is advisable to ensure that all the arguments are actually used in the expression.

A dummy argument name applies only to the statement function definition in which it is used. If the same name is used in another statement function definition or elsewhere in the program unit, the names have no connection. Note that a dummy argument may be a variable or array name of any type but may not be a constant, array element or expression. Dummy arguments may or may not appear in a type statement preceding the statement function.

The actual arguments must correspond in order, number and type to the equivalent dummy arguments. Actual arguments may be expressions (i.e. constants, variables, array names, array elements or combinations of these).

Statement functions may be called only in the program unit in which they are defined. They may not be passed as arguments to other subprograms.

If the expression on the right-hand side of a statement function definition contains names that do not appear in the argument list, e.g. A, B, C and D in the above example, then values must have been assigned to these before the function is called. That is A, B, C and D must be declared and assigned values in the calling program or subprogram.

If the expression contains references to external functions these must not change the values of their arguments (or of **COMMON** locations – see later).

A complete program which uses statement functions might be structured as follows:

```
PROGRAM STFUNC
INTRINSIC SQRT,MAX
REAL A,B,C,D
REAL X1,Y1,Z1,X2,Y2,Z2
REAL F1,F2,F3,F4
QUAD(X,Y) = A*X**2 + B*Y**2 + C*X*Y + D
EXPR(X,Y,Z) = SQRT(X) + MAX(Y,Z)
READ *,A,B,C,D
READ *,X1,Y1,Z1
READ *,X2,Y2,Z2
F1 = QUAD(X1,Y1)
F2 = QUAD(X2,Y2)
F3 = EXPR(X1,Y1,Z1)
F4 = EXPR(X2,Y2,Z2)
PRINT *,F1,F2
PRINT *,F3,F4
STOP
END
```

8.6 The FUNCTION subprogram and RETURN

The statement function is labour-saving in that it enables the programmer to define once an expression which appears many times in a program. However, it is a very limited facility since it can consist of only one statement.

FORTRAN provides an extension to this facility by allowing the programmer to define a function subprogram consisting of a sequence of statements.

Such a subprogram consists of a **FUNCTION** header followed by any FORTRAN declaration and executable statements (in the order described in section 8.3) followed by **END**.

The function header is of the form

FUNCTION *name(argument list)*

where *name* is the function name and *argument list* is a list of dummy arguments separated by commas as described in the previous section; any element of this list may be a dummy variable, array or subprogram name.

The name of the function defines the function type since it obeys the usual FORTRAN naming conventions.

The implied typing of the name may be overridden by preceding the word **FORTRAN** by a type declaration (**INTEGER, REAL, DOUBLE PRECISION, LOGICAL** or **CHARACTER**) or by means of **IMPLICIT**.

For example,

INTEGER FUNCTION FN(X,Y,Z)

will define an integer function FN whereas

FUNCTION FN(X,Y,Z)

defines a real function, FN. The statements

FUNCTION FN(X,Y,Z)   or   **FUNCTION FN(X,Y,Z)**
IMPLICIT INTEGER(F)   **INTEGER FN**

would define an integer function also.

Suppose a FORTRAN program is required to calculate the following two functions

$$100(x_2 - x_1^2)^2 + (1 - x_1)^2$$

and

$$(x_1 - x_2^2)^2 + (1 - x_2)^2$$

Then a program to do this could be structured as follows:

```
PROGRAM FUNCTS
REAL F1,F2,X1,X2,FX1,FX2
READ(5,'(2F10.4)')X1,X2
F1 = FX1(X1,X2)
F2 = FX2(X1,X2)
WRITE(6,'(2F10.4)')FX1,FX2
STOP
END
```

```
FUNCTION FX1(X,Y)
REAL FN1,FN2,X,Y
FN1 = Y - X*X
FN2 = 1.0 - X
FX1 = 100.0*FN1*FN1 + FN2*FN2
RETURN
END

FUNCTION FX2(X,Y)
REAL FN1,FN2,X,Y
FN1 = X - Y*Y
FN2 = 1.0 - Y
FX2 = FN1*FN1 + FN2*FN2
RETURN
END
```

Note that the value of the function is returned to the calling program (in this case the main program but in general this could be any program unit) by assigning this value to the name of the function during the execution of the **FUNCTION** subprogram. Its value on exit is the value of the function that is returned to the calling program unit. It follows that the function name should be declared to be of this same type in all the program units that call it.

Thus a **FUNCTION** subprogram is of the general form

type FUNCTION *name(argument list)*

.
.
.

name = *expression*

.
.
.

      RETURN
      END

where *type* and *argument list* are optional. A complete FORTRAN program may consist of a main program and many **FUNCTION** subprograms, each contained between a header and **END** (note that unlike a statement function, a **FUNCTION** subprogram is not declared within another program unit; it is called from it).

The sequence of statements following a **FUNCTION** statement is referred to as a subprogram since it is treated as an entirely separate program in compilation, i.e. it may be held in a totally separate disc file and may be submitted alone to the FORTRAN compiler without the main program or any other subprogram that calls it or is called by it. Alternatively, several program units could be held in one disc file and submitted to the compiler together.

The former method has two advantages. A large FORTRAN program is difficult to correct and test. By breaking it down into subprograms it may be written and tested in manageable sections; only when all separate parts are working satisfactorily will the entire program be run. This is also more economical in computer time since only the subprograms which have errors need be corrected. Remember also that a subprogram is a self-contained unit and may be removed from one program and included in another program without any alteration.

Try typing up the above three program units on your computer and compile them independently; then link them all together and run the resulting program.

The FORTRAN variables used within a subprogram are local to that subprogram unless they are declared to be global in a **COMMON** statement (this will be discussed more fully in the next chapter). So a local variable X used in one subprogram is quite different from a local variable X in a different subprogram. Local variables may be assigned values only in the program unit in which they are declared unless they are passed as actual arguments to other subprograms.

When the execution of a subprogram is complete, control must be returned to the point in the calling program where the subprogram was called. The **RETURN** statement is used to indicate the point in the execution path at which control is returned. There may be more than one **RETURN** statement in a subprogram each indicating the end of a possible execution path in the program. If no **RETURN** statement is present, **END** is often taken to imply **RETURN**.

A function is activated by using its name as an operand in an expression. At that point in the evaluation of the expression, the function subprogram is entered and executed. The function value is returned as the value of the operand at that point in the expression. Control is always returned to the point in the expression immediately following the function reference. This is true no matter which **RETURN** statement is obeyed in the body of the subprogram.

Character functions may also be defined; the character function must have an associated length (which is taken to be 1 if not defined), e.g.

```
CHARACTER*40 FUNCTION CONCAT(CHAR1,CHAR2,CHAR3,CHAR4)
CHARACTER*10 CHAR1,CHAR2,CHAR3,CHAR4
CONCAT = CHAR1//CHAR2//CHAR3//CHAR4
RETURN
END
```

is a character function to concatenate four character variables of length 10 into one character string of length 40. Remember that the function name should be declared to be of this same length in all the program units that call it, i.e. in this case a statement is required of the form:

```
CHARACTER*40 CONCAT
```

Functions without arguments are allowed, in which case the function name must be followed by empty parentheses both when defined and when called, e.g.

X + FX() ∗ Y

calls a function of the form

FUNCTION FX()
    .
    .
    .
FX =
    .
    .
    .
RETURN
END

8.7 The SUBROUTINE subprogram and the CALL statement

FUNCTION subprograms are referenced only as operands in expressions. The function name returns one result to the calling program and has an associated type.

A **SUBROUTINE** subprogram is a more generalized facility and may return many results to the calling program (via its argument list) or perhaps none at all. A subroutine subprogram has the general structure

SUBROUTINE *name(argument list)*
    .
    .
    .
RETURN
    .
    .
    .
END

where *name* is any valid FORTRAN name by which the subprogram is identified. A subroutine does not have an associated type. The name therefore does not carry an implied type with it and the word **SUBROUTINE** may not be preceded by a type statement. No value is ever assigned to the name. The name must not appear anywhere in the body of a subroutine; it must be of maximum length six characters.

The *argument list* is a list of dummy arguments separated by commas. There need not necessarily be any arguments for a subroutine (in which case the parentheses may or may not be present, e.g. **SUBROUTINE EXIT** and

SUBROUTINE EXIT() are equally valid as alternative ways of defining the same subroutine header).

A dummy argument may be a variable, array or subprogram name; it may also be an asterisk as will be discussed later in this section.

The **SUBROUTINE** statement must be the first statement in the subprogram and may be followed by a sequence of any valid FORTRAN statements (except a **FUNCTION, SUBROUTINE, PROGRAM** or **BLOCK DATA** statement). The **END** statement must be the last statement in the subprogram and it must contain at least one **RETURN** or **STOP** statement. If there is no **RETURN** statement then **END** will imply **RETURN**.

Values from the subprogram may be returned to the calling program by means of one or more arguments in the argument list. So arguments may be used to pass values to the subprogram and return values from it. The same argument may be used for both purposes. Any argument used to return a result must be assigned a value in the subprogram.

Two typical subroutines are

```
SUBROUTINE ROOTS(A,B,C,X1,X2)
REAL A,B,C,X1,X2,B24AC
B24AC = B*B - 4.0*A*C
IF (B24AC .LT. 0.0) CALL ERROR
B24AC = SQRT(B24AC)
IF (B .GE. 0) B24AC = -B24AC
X1 = (-B + B24AC)/(2.0*A)
X2 = C/(A*X1)
RETURN
END


SUBROUTINE ERROR
WRITE(6,'("1 Roots are complex"/" Program terminated")')
STOP
END
```

Note that in these examples the dummy arguments A, B, C are used to supply information to the subroutine, whereas the dummy arguments X1, X2 are used to return the results to the calling program. **ERROR** is an example of a subprogram which does not require any dummy arguments since it returns no results; it does not contain any **RETURN** statement since the **STOP** statement terminates execution.

A **SUBROUTINE** subprogram is activated by means of a **CALL** statement of the form

> **CALL** *name (argument list)*

where *name* is the name of a subroutine and *argument list* is a list of actual arguments separated by commas. There may be no arguments in which case the empty parentheses ( ) may be used but they are optional, e.g.

SUBROUTINE ERROR may be entered by **CALL ERROR** or by **CALL ERROR** ().

The subroutine will be entered at the first executable statement (this is known as the entry point) and the statements in the body of the subprogram will be obeyed in the usual FORTRAN sequence until a **STOP** or **RETURN** statement is encountered. When **RETURN** is encountered, control will be returned to the statement in the calling program immediately following the **CALL** statement. FORTRAN 77 provides a method of specifying alternative entry points and alternative return points and this will be described in section 8.10.

A subroutine may be called from a main program or from another subprogram. If it is required to calculate a function (FX) and its derivative (G) at some point X, then a subroutine could be written of the form

SUBROUTINE CALCFG(X,FX,G)
.
.
.
(coding to calculate the function and its derivative)
.
.
.
RETURN
END

This subroutine could be entered at two different points in the main program by writing

.
.
.
CALL CALCFG(X1,FX1,G1)
.
.
CALL CALCFG(X2,FX2,G2)
.
.
.

This would calculate the function and its derivative at the points X1 and X2, returning the results in FX1, G1 and FX2, G2.

Similarly, **SUBROUTINE ROOTS** above could be called by a statement of the form

CALL ROOTS(1.0,3.0,2.0,ROOT1,ROOT2)

Note that FORTRAN is not a recursive language, i.e. a function or subroutine subprogram may not reference or call itself in any way. This not only includes the case when a subprogram calls itself, but also the case when a subprogram calls another subprogram which itself calls the first subprogram.

The actual arguments of a subroutine call must agree in order, number and type with the corresponding dummy arguments. An actual argument may be an expression, an array name, an intrinsic function name or the name of another subprogram. A dummy argument which is an array may be passed an array element as an actual argument. This then becomes the first element of the dummy array. FORTRAN also permits an alternative return specifier as an actual argument (section 8.10).

Avoid writing subprograms with long lists of arguments. Apart from the fact that such subprograms may be difficult to understand and use, many compilers have an upper limit to the number of arguments they can handle. In general, limit argument lists to less than about ten entries and use **COMMON** to communicate with other subprograms (Chapter 9). It is also safer to avoid the name **MAIN** for a function or subroutine. Some systems reserve this for the name of a main program which does not have a **PROGRAM** statement provided by the programmer.

The symbolic names of subroutines and functions are global names and must not be the same as any other global name or the same as any local name in the program unit. The symbolic name of a dummy argument is local to the program unit and must not appear in an **EQUIVALENCE, PARAMETER, SAVE, INTRINSIC, DATA** or **COMMON** statement except as a **COMMON** block name (Chapter 9).

Note that in FORTRAN actual arguments which are the names of variables, array elements or substrings are passed to a subprogram by address, e.g.

SUBROUTINE SUB1(X)

and

CALL SUB1(X1)

will cause the address of the memory location corresponding to X1 to be passed to the subroutine dummy argument X; note there is no actual memory location corresponding to X. Thus the statement $X = X + 1$ within the body of the subroutine will increment the contents of location X1 by 1.

The FORTRAN programmer should be warned that this also applies to constants. Never pass a constant as an actual argument to a subroutine which changes the value of that argument, e.g.

SUBROUTINE SUB1   **SUBROUTINE SUB2(J)**

.

.

.   .

$I = 6$.

.   .

.

.

```
CALL SUB2(6)        J = J + 1
     .                   .
     .                   .
     .                   .
K = 6               RETURN
     .              END
     .
     .
```

The call on **SUB2** passes the address of the memory location containing the constant 6 to the subroutine. Unfortunately, this subroutine increments the argument by 1. This in effect changes the constant location 6 to the value 7! Thus whenever the constant 6 is used again it will have the value 7. Back in the calling program, the statement $K = 6$ will set K to 7 and not 6. The programmer will appreciate that the effect of this on the program could be quite catastrophic.

The fact that the address of an actual argument is passed across to the dummy argument of a subprogram can cause problems when arrays are passed as parameters. This is discussed more fully in section 8.9.

8.8 The EXTERNAL statement

If the subprogram requires the name of another subprogram as one of its arguments, then this name must be declared in an **EXTERNAL** statement in the calling program unit. This declaration is of the form

EXTERNAL *list*

where *list* is a list of names of subprograms which are to be passed as arguments to other subprograms, e.g.

```
EXTERNAL SUB1,SUB2
     .
     .
     .
CALL SUBR(X1,SUB1,Y1)
     .
     .
     .
CALL SUBR(X2,SUB2,Y2)
     .
     .
     .
```

could call a subroutine

```
SUBROUTINE SUBR(X,SUB,Y)
     .
     .
     .
```

```
CALL SUB(X,Y)
        .
        .
        .
RETURN
END
```

The first call of **SUBR** would cause **SUB1** to be called, and the second would cause **SUB2** to be called.

Note that a statement function name must not appear in an **EXTERNAL** statement. Statement functions can be referenced only in the program unit in which they are defined. If an intrinsic function is to be passed as an actual argument then it must be declared in an **INTRINSIC** statement (section 8.4) but some functions must never be passed as arguments. If the name of an intrinsic function appears in an **EXTERNAL** statement then it becomes the name of a user supplied function which overrides the intrinsic system function whenever it is used, e.g. you may write your own square root function by

```
EXTERNAL SQRT       FUNCTION SQRT(X)
     .                       .
     .                       .
     .                       .
Y = SQRT(X)         SQRT = ...
     .                       .
     .                       .
     .                       .
                    RETURN
                    END
```

The statement Y = **SQRT(X)** will cause the user supplied **SQRT** function to be called.

Some systems require that all external functions called by a program unit are both typed and declared as external in the calling program, e.g.

```
LOGICAL FLAG,SET    LOGICAL FUNCTION FLAG
EXTERNAL FLAG               .
     :                      .
     :                      .
SET = FLAG          FLAG = ...
                    RETURN
                    END
```

It is considered good programming practice therefore to declare all external subprograms called by a program unit as **EXTERNAL** and all intrinsic functions as **INTRINSIC**.

8.9 Adjustable dimensions

Array names may be passed as arguments to subprograms but the arrays must be dimensioned within the subprogram, e.g.

```
SUBROUTINE SUB(A,B)
REAL A(10),B(100)
```

Two actual arrays X and Y may be passed to this subroutine by

```
CALL SUB(X,Y)
```

However, the subprogram is limited in its application if the arrays (A and B say) are dimensioned with fixed sizes (10 and 100 here). Different invocations of the subprogram may require different sized arrays.

FORTRAN allows arrays in subprograms to be defined with adjustable dimensions, e.g.

```
REAL A(N),B(M,N)
```

Here N and M are integer variables or expressions specifying the dimensions of the arrays in the subprogram. The integer expressions may not contain array or function references.

Values must be assigned to the adjustable dimensions in the calling program and these must be passed as arguments to the subprogram. The arrays must be dimensioned in the calling program with a fixed value and actual values of N and M must not exceed this maximum, e.g.

```
REAL X(500),Y(500,1000)
      . . .
N = 50
M = 100
CALL SUB(X,Y,N,M)
      . . .
      . . .
N = 400
M = 900
      . . .
      . . .
CALL SUB(X,Y,N,M)
```

will call the subroutine

```
SUBROUTINE SUB(A,B,I,J)
INTEGER I,J
REAL A(I),B(I,J)
```

An array in **COMMON** must not be used with adjustable dimensions (Chapter 9).

Note that if a symbolic name is used to dimension an array and the type is not given by the first letter then it must be typed in a statement preceding the declaration statement.

An assumed size array may be created by specifying an asterisk as the upper bound of the last dimension specification. That dimension will take on the upper bound associated with it in the corresponding actual array, e.g. if the main program contains

REAL ARRAY(1:200)
.
.
.

CALL SUB(ARRAY)
.
.
.

Then the subroutine statements

SUBROUTINE SUB(ARR1)
REAL ARR1(*)

will dimension an array **ARR1** in the subprogram with 200 elements **ARR1(1)** to **ARR1(200)**.

Similarly, if the main program contains

REAL ARRAY(1:5, − 3:30,10:500)
.
.
.

CALL SUB(ARRAY)
.
.
.

then the subroutine statements

SUBROUTINE SUB(ARR2)
DIMENSION ARR2(1:5, − 3:30,10:*)

will dimension an array **ARR2** in the subprogram with an upper bound of 500 for the last dimension. Note that because of the way an array is laid out in memory, it is only the *last* dimension which can be specified in this way.

Variable length character strings may be passed to subprograms by declaring the dummy argument to be of length (*), e.g.

SUBROUTINE CHAR(STRING)
CHARACTER*(*) STRING

may be passed actual parameters of differing lengths, e.g.

CHARACTER*4 STRNG1

```
CHARACTER*8 STRNG2
CALL CHAR(STRNG1)
CALL CHAR(STRNG2)
```

Please note the problems that can occur when passing arrays as arguments. Imagine program **BEWARE** which declares a two dimensional array and passes part of this array to **SUBROUTINE PRINTA** as follows:

```
      PROGRAM BEWARE
      INTEGER I,J
      INTEGER A(1:4,1:3)
      DO 20, J = 1,3
          DO 10, I = 1,4
              A(I,J) = I + 1
10        CONTINUE
20    CONTINUE
      CALL PRINTA(A,2,3)
      STOP
      END

      SUBROUTINE PRINTA(A,N,M)
      INTEGER I,J
      INTEGER A(1:N,1:M)
      PRINT *, ((A(I,J),I = 1,N),J = 1,M)
      RETURN
      END
```

Because of the way arrays are laid out in memory, the main program will lay out array A as follows:

```
A(1,1) = 2
A(2,1) = 3
A(3,1) = 4
A(4,1) = 5
A(1,2) = 2
A(2,2) = 3
A(3,2) = 4
A(4,2) = 5
A(1,3) = 2
A(2,3) = 3
A(3,3) = 4
A(4,3) = 5
```

However, the subroutine will access the array elements as follows:

```
A(1,1)
A(2,1)
A(1,2)
```

A(2,2)
A(1,3)
A(2,3)

Thus the **PRINTA** subroutine will print out the following values in order

2 3 4 5 2 3

which are not the values of A(1,1), A(2,1), A(1,2), A(2,2), A(1,3), A(2,3) in
the main program.

8.10 Multiple entry and return points

In our discussion of subprograms so far, we have described only how they
may be entered at the first executable statement and how **RETURN** statements
cause control to be returned to the point in the calling program immediately
following the call. Thus there is only one entry point and only one return
point.

However, multiple entry points are permitted for any function or
subroutine. Each entry point must be specified by a statement of the form

ENTRY *name(list)*

where *name* is the entry point name and *list* is a list of variable, array or
dummy procedure names or an asterisk representing the dummy argument
list for that entry point. For example,

```
SUBROUTINE EXAMPL(I,A,J)
        .
        .
        .
RETURN
ENTRY EX1(I)
        .
        .
        .
RETURN
ENTRY EX2(J)
        .
        .
        .
RETURN
ENTRY EX3(A,J)
        .
        .
        .
RETURN
END
```

This specifies a total of four entry points for the **EXAMPL** subroutine and each entry has different dummy arguments. The statement

CALL EXAMPL(I1,A1,J1)

will enter at the first executable statement of the subprogram in the usual way.

The statement

CALL EX1(I2)

will enter at the first executable statement following the **ENTRY** statement and will pass the actual argument I2 to the dummy argument I. Control proceeds according to the usual rules until the first **RETURN** (or **END**) statement following the entry point is encountered. Similarly,

CALL EX2(J3)

will enter at the entry point **EX2(J)** and

CALL EX3(A4,J4)

will enter at **EX3(A,J)**.

Note that the **ENTRY** statement is a non-executable statement and may appear anywhere within a subprogram (except inside a **DO**-loop or a block-**IF** statement). **ENTRY** statements encountered during execution of a sequence of statements are ignored.

The rules which apply to subroutine and function names and arguments apply to the entry names in the same way. Note that the entry point arguments may differ in order, number and type from the subprogram header statement and other **ENTRY** statements. Entry names for functions may be typed by type declarations in the usual way and need not necessarily be of the same type except that entry names for character functions must all be of type character and of the same length.

In subroutine subprograms only, alternative return paths may be specified by a statement of the form

RETURN e

where e is an integer expression with a value in the range 1 to n and n is the number of asterisks specified in the dummy argument list of the corresponding entry point. The value of e refers to the eth asterisk in that list.

For example,

SUBROUTINE EXAMPL(I,A,J,*,*,*)

    .
    .
    .

RETURN 3

    .

```
        .
        .
RETURN 1
I = 3
J = 2
RETURN I - J
ENTRY EX1(I)
        .
        .
        .
RETURN
ENTRY EX2(J,*,*)
        .
        .
        .
RETURN 1
        .
        .
        .
RETURN 2
ENTRY EX3(A,J,*,*)
        .
        .
        .
RETURN 2
        .
        .
        .
RETURN 1
END
```

Each * in the dummy argument list must have a return specifier associated with it in the corresponding actual argument list of the call. This is of the form

    s

where *s* is the label of an executable statement in the calling program to which control is to be returned.

So in our example the subprogram could be called as follows:

```
CALL EXAMPL(I1,A1,J1,*10,*5,*100)
CALL EX1(I2)
CALL EX2(J3,*50,*25)
CALL EX3(A4,J4,*10,*3)
```

This feature of FORTRAN is not desirable, resulting as it does in a breakdown of program structure. Its use is definitely not recommended.

8.11 Summary

- A FORTRAN program may consist of a main program and one or more subprograms as follows:

PROGRAM *name*

   .
   .
   .

Statements of the main program

   .
   .
   .

END

SUBROUTINE *name(dummy argument list)*

   .
   .
   .

Statements of the subroutine

   .
   .
   .

RETURN
END

FUNCTION *name(dummy argument list)*

   .
   .
   .

Statements of the function

   .
   .
   .

name = expression

   .
   .
   .

RETURN
END

- If a subprogram requires to pass the name of another subprogram as one of its arguments, then this name must be declared in the calling program unit in the **EXTERNAL** statement.
- Arrays in subprograms may be declared with adjustable dimensions. An assumed size array can be declared by specifying an * as the upper bound of the last dimension specification.

- Intrinsic functions called within a subprogram unit can be declared in an **INTRINSIC** statement of the form

    INTRINSIC *list*

    where *list* is a list of intrinsic function names separated by commas.
- Statement functions may be declared within any of the program units by a statement of the form

    name(argument list) = *expression*
- Subroutines are called by the **CALL** statement which is of the form

    CALL *name(argument list)*

    In both functions and subroutines, the **RETURN** statement returns control from the subprogram to the first executable statement immediately following the calling statement in the calling unit.

Exercises 8

1. What is wrong with the following subroutine calls to subroutine CALC? (Assume standard FORTRAN naming conventions.)
    - (a) **CALL CALC(2,5.63,ANSWER)**
    - (b) **CALL CALC(2.,5.63,NUM)**
    - (c) **CALL CALC(2.0∗5.63,VALUE)**
    - (d) **CALL CALC(2.0,5.63,3.7)**

    ```
    SUBROUTINE CALC(X,Y,Z)
    Z = SQRT(X∗X + Y∗Y)
    RETURN
    END
    ```

2. (a) Write a subroutine that takes two one-dimensional integer arrays each of different sizes as specified by integer arguments and produces a result array comprising all the input values in numerical order. The subroutine should also return the size of the output array. It may be assumed that the input arrays are already sorted into numerical order. Note that the output array should not contain the same value twice.
    (b) Show how this subroutine can be called from a main program that reads the two arrays in and prints out the results.
    (c) Show how the subroutine can be used repeatedly with a main program that merges n arrays (where n is read in as data).

3. Write a subroutine which given a line of text as an input argument together with a pointer, will return the next word in the input line (a word being delimited by any character which is not a letter). The subroutine should return a pointer value of -1 when end of line is found.

4. Rewrite Exercise 7.3 as a subroutine with a character string array with adjustable dimensions as its argument, together with a main program which will test it out with arrays of data of different sizes.

5. Write a function subprogram, which given an identifier as an input argument, returns the hashed value of it (the hashed value should be obtained by adding together the internal code values of the characters in the name (sum) and calculating **MOD**(sum,255). Write a main program to test the function and produce a listing of names and corresponding hash values.

9

The organization of store

9.1 Introduction

In Chapter 8 we introduced the concept of program units or subprograms as completely self-contained units which can be independently compiled. In section 8.6 we stated that variables declared and used within a subprogram are local to that subprogram. Thus a variable of a given name in one subprogram refers to a quite different location in memory from a variable of the same name in another subprogram. Suppose that a program contains the following two subroutines:

```
SUBROUTINE SUB1            SUBROUTINE SUB2(Z)
REAL X,Y,Z                 REAL X,Y,Z
X = 10.0                   X = 5.0
Y = 50.0                   Y = 10.0
Z = 100.0                  Z = X + Y
CALL SUB2(Z)               RETURN
WRITE(6,'(3F8.2)')X,Y,Z    END
RETURN
END
```

then the values printed by the **WRITE** statement in **SUB1** will be $X = 10.0$, $Y = 50.0$ and $Z = 15.0$.

So although subroutine **SUB2** sets the two variables X and Y to 5.0 and 10.0 respectively, these statements will not change the values of X and Y in the calling subroutine **SUB1** since these refer to quite different locations. Z however is an argument of **SUB2** and is assigned a value within the body of this subprogram. This value will be returned via the argument list. Its value is obtained by adding the values of the local variables X and Y in **SUB2**, i.e. 15.0. Thus the value of Z (= 100.0) set locally in subroutine **SUB1** is changed by the action of subroutine **SUB2**. The concept of local store can be represented diagrammatically as shown at the top of page 177.

Thus it can be seen that in general a subprogram operates on named memory locations which are private or local to itself, i.e. X and Y in **SUB1** refer to different locations from X and Y in **SUB2**. This is obviously important since it enables one programmer to write a subprogram using names which are independent of any names used in other subprograms by other

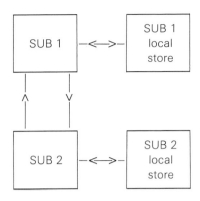

programmers. When a program unit requires to communicate with other program units, then it can do so via its argument list. However, this can prove to
be an irritating restriction in many applications. A FORTRAN program may
develop in such a way that it has many subprograms each with a large number
of arguments, i.e. many program units require to access the same memory
locations. It would be convenient therefore to be able to declare certain
names to be *global* to the whole program so that any subprogram using these
names would be accessing the same memory locations. Thus, if we could in
some way declare X and Y to be global names, then in the preceding example
the **WRITE** statement in **SUB1** would give $X = 5.0$, $Y = 10.0$ and $Z = 15.0$ since
the names X and Y would now refer to the same memory locations in both
subprograms. This can be illustrated diagrammatically as follows:

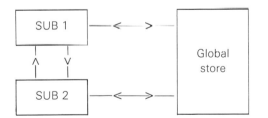

FORTRAN permits the names of variables or arrays of any type to be declared
global to all program units by means of the **COMMON** statement which will be
described in the next section.

It is worth noting in passing that subprogram names also have global scope
within a program, i.e. it is not possible to have two subprograms of the same
name within a program. This applies even when one is a Function and
another is a Subroutine.

9.2 Blank COMMON

The **COMMON** statement is of the general form

COMMON *list*

where *list* is a list of variable or array names or array declarations of any type. This **COMMON** statement must be placed in every program unit which requires to access the same **COMMON** locations.

Suppose the subroutines in the previous example were rewritten thus:

```
SUBROUTINE SUB1          SUBROUTINE SUB2(Z)
REAL X,Y                 REAL X,Y,Z
COMMON X,Y               COMMON X,Y
X = 10.0                 X = 5.0
Y = 50.0                 Y = 10.0
Z = 100.0                Z = X + Y
CALL SUB2(Z)             RETURN
WRITE(6,'(3F8.2)')X,Y,Z  END
RETURN
END
```

This time the values printed by the **WRITE** statement will be $X = 5.0$, $Y = 10.0$ and $Z = 15.0$. This is because X and Y have been declared as **COMMON** in both program units and so the subprogram, **SUB2**, when executed will assign new values (5.0 and 10.0) to the same locations X and Y as used by the calling subprogram.

So this provides an alternative mechanism by which a subprogram may communicate with the external environment. Arguments may be placed in **COMMON** and removed from the argument list. For example, this previous example could equally well be rewritten

```
SUBROUTINE SUB1          SUBROUTINE SUB2
REAL X,Y,Z               REAL X,Y,Z
COMMON X,Y,Z             COMMON X,Y,Z
X = 10.0                 X = 5.0
Y = 50.0                 Y = 10.0
Z = 100.0                Z = X + Y
CALL SUB2                RETURN
WRITE(6,'(3F8.2)')X,Y,Z  END
RETURN
END
```

and the values $X = 5.0$, $Y = 10.0$ and $Z = 15.0$ will be written.

Any subroutine can have access to **COMMON** store, its own local store and its arguments. For example,

```
SUBROUTINE SUB1          SUBROUTINE SUB2(Z)
INTEGER I,J              INTEGER I,J
```

```
REAL X,Y,Z                          REAL X,Y,Z
COMMON X,Y                          COMMON X,Y
I = 1                               I = 100
J = 2                               J = 200
X = 10.0                            X = 5.0
Y = 50.0                            Y = 10.0
Z = 100.0                           Z = X + Y
CALL SUB2(Z)                        WRITE(6,'(3F8.2,2I5)')X,Y,Z,I,J
WRITE(6,'(3F8.2,2I5)')X,Y,Z,I,J     RETURN
RETURN                              END
END
```

In this case the **WRITE** statement of **SUB1** will write the values $I=1$, $J=2$, $X=5.0$, $Y=10.0$, $Z=15.0$. The **WRITE** statement of **SUB2** will write the values $I=100$, $J=200$, $X=5.0$, $Y=10.0$ and $Z=15.0$. So the names I and J are local to each subroutine and therefore access different memory locations; the names X and Y are **COMMON** to the two subroutines and therefore access the same memory locations; the name Z is an argument and so the value is returned by **SUB2** to **SUB1**. This can be represented diagrammatically as follows:

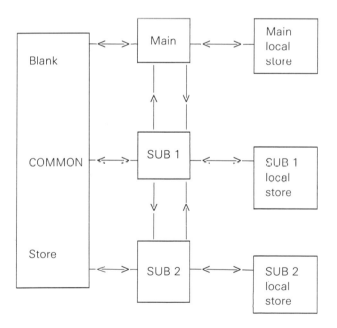

The **COMMON** statement is a non-executable statement and must be placed before any reference is made to names declared in it. Arrays can be declared in **COMMON** and may be dimensioned either in the **COMMON** statement, e.g.

COMMON A(1:10),B(1:50)

or in a type or **DIMENSION** statement preceding the **COMMON** statement, e.g.

REAL A,B
DIMENSION A(1:10),B(1:50)   or   **REAL A(1:10),B(1:50)**
COMMON A,B   **COMMON A,B**

If the arrays A and B are dimensioned in **COMMON** statements, they must not appear in a **DIMENSION** statement as well. All the above statements have the effect of reserving 10 locations for A and 50 locations for B in **COMMON** store. **COMMON** storage may be thought of as a contiguous area of store accessible to all program units. This area of memory is known as blank **COMMON**. The first name declared in **COMMON** will be associated with the first location in this area. Thus

COMMON X,Y,Z

will refer to the first three locations in **COMMON** storage. If this statement appears in two subprograms then references to X, Y and Z in either sub-program will access the first, second or third location in **COMMON** store. However, if one subprogram contains

COMMON X,Y,Z

and the second contains

COMMON P,Q,R

then the first statement causes the first three locations in **COMMON** to be allocated to X, Y, Z and the second statement causes the same three locations to be allocated to P, Q, R. This has the effect of equivalencing X and P, Y and Q, Z and R, i.e. two (or more) distinct FORTRAN names in different sub-programs can refer to the same location. This can be shown diagrammatically as follows:

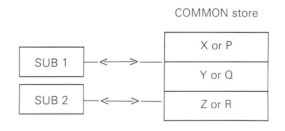

Thus the example earlier in this section could be rewritten

SUBROUTINE SUB1   **SUBROUTINE SUB2**
REAL X,Y,Z   **REAL P,Q,R**

```
COMMON X,Y,Z          COMMON P,Q,R
X = 10.0              P = 5.0
Y = 50.0              Q = 10.0
Z = 100.0            R = P + Q
CALL SUB2            RETURN
WRITE(6,'(3F8.2)')X,Y,Z   END
RETURN
END
```

and the values $X = 5.0$, $Y = 10.0$ and $Z = 15.0$ would be written.

It is also possible to equivalence a two-dimensional array onto a one-dimensional array in a similar way. An array declared in **COMMON** thus

COMMON MARKS(1:3,1:10)

can be accessed in a different subroutine as a one-dimensional array thus

COMMON RESULT(1:30)

The memory locations are mapped as follows:

MARKS(1,1)	RESULT(1)
MARKS(2,1)	RESULT(2)
MARKS(3,1)	RESULT(3)
MARKS(1,2)	RESULT(4)
MARKS(2,2)	RESULT(5)
MARKS(3,2)	RESULT(6)
.	.
.	.
.	.
MARKS(3,10)	RESULT(30)

Blank **COMMON** statements used in different program units do not have to be of the same size, e.g. if subroutine **SUB1** contains

COMMON X,Y,Z,I,A(1:10)

and subroutine **SUB2** contains

COMMON X,Y,Z,I,A(1:3)

then this is perfectly legal but subroutine **SUB2** can only access the first three locations of array A.

However beware of the following mistake

COMMON X,Y,Z,I   COMMON X,Y,I

In this case the first statement assigns real names X, Y, Z to the first three locations of **COMMON**, whereas the second statement refers to these same three locations as real X, Y and integer I.

Note that character variables or character arrays must not be mixed with other types in **COMMON**. These should all be placed together in the same

COMMON block (see next section for a description of named COMMON).

The COMMON statement is a specification statement and must precede any executable statements, but follow any IMPLICIT statement. It is good practice to immediately precede COMMON statements by corresponding type statements which type the names in COMMON.

The subject of equivalencing will be discussed again later.

9.3 Named COMMON

In the previous section we referred only to blank COMMON, i.e. all global names are declared in one unnamed block of COMMON store. An alternative form of the COMMON statement is

COMMON /cb1/list1./cb2/list2. . .

where *cb1*, *cb2* are COMMON block names and *list1*, *list2*, etc. are lists of variables, array names or array declarations as described for blank COMMON. Note that the comma between the list and the next COMMON block name enclosed between slashes is optional.

This form of the statement is known as named or labelled COMMON. The name of the COMMON block is placed between slashes and followed by a list of names which are to be assigned to memory locations in that block. If no block name is given then the names will be allocated space in blank COMMON. In this case the slashes may or may not be present, e.g.

COMMON X,Y,Z
COMMON //X,Y,Z

are equivalent and allocate X, Y and Z to blank COMMON.

The statement:

COMMON //A,B,C,/AREA1/X,Y,Z/AREA2/P,Q,R/COUNTS/C1,C2

allocates A, B and C to blank COMMON, X, Y and Z to named COMMON block AREA1, P, Q, R to block AREA2 and C1, C2 to block COUNTS.

Named COMMON provides a useful way of grouping variables and arrays together in one area and it is often better to organize programs by using this rather than blank COMMON particularly when not all program units require to access all COMMON locations or when it is required to include character types as well as other types in COMMON.

The same block name may be used more than once in the same program unit in which case names will be appended to that block.

For example,

COMMON /VOLTS/V1,V2,V3
COMMON /VOLTS/V4,V5

will allocate V1, V2, V3, V4 and V5 to the first five locations of COMMON block **VOLTS,** However, this practice is not recommended because it leads to errors.

Note that all **COMMON** blocks which have the same name must have the same size, i.e. it is invalid to have the statement

COMMON /AMPS/A1,A2,A3

in one subprogram and the statement

COMMON /AMPS/A1,A2

in another subprogram.

This differs from blank **COMMON** which need not be of the same length in all program units.

Locations in named **COMMON** may be initialized by means of **DATA** statements in a **BLOCK DATA** subprogram (see the next section) but blank **COMMON** may not be initialized.

If character arrays or variables are to be declared in a **COMMON** block then everything in that block must be of type character.

Note that **COMMON** block names cannot exceed six characters and are global to the whole program. A **COMMON** block name must not be the same as the name of any subprogram.

It is good programming practice to ensure that all definitions of the same **COMMON** block in different program units define blocks of the same size. If your system allows it, it is wise to set up all **COMMON** statements in one or more separate files and then insert these files in the program units which require these blocks. Changes to **COMMON** can thus be made easily by amending these files.

For ease of portability, the programmer is advised never to use a **COMMON** block name for any other purpose in the same program unit. Note that although standard FORTRAN allows several named **COMMON** blocks to be declared in one statement it is simpler and safer to avoid this, i.e. write

COMMON /AREA1/A,B,C
COMMON /AREA2/X,Y,Z

rather than:

COMMON /AREA1/A,B,C/AREA2/X,Y,Z

The former case avoids any confusion over the positions of redundant commas which different compilers treat in different ways.

With the exception of the character type, different types may be declared in the same **COMMON** block but it is good practice to ensure that double precision precedes real which precedes integer which in turn precedes logical. If the same **COMMON** block is declared in different program units, it may cause different types to be associated.

The following diagram depicts the way a program consisting of a main program and three subprograms may access blank **COMMON**, named **COMMON** blocks and local variables:

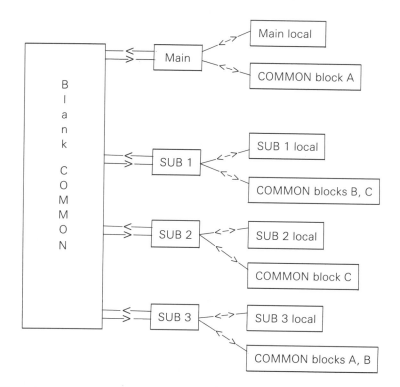

9.4 The BLOCK DATA subprogram

It was described in section 5.9 how **DATA** statements may be used to set initial values in memory locations before program execution begins. This of course only applied to local entities. However, variables and array elements in named **COMMON** blocks may also be assigned initial values in **DATA** statements but the initialization statements must be placed together in a **BLOCK DATA** subprogram.

The **BLOCK DATA** subprogram is of the form

BLOCK DATA *name*

    .
    .
    .

END

where *name* is the **BLOCK DATA** subprogram name and is optional. The subprogram is non-executable and may contain only specification statements, **DATA** statements, comments and an **END** statement.

The use of a **BLOCK DATA** subprogram ensures that **COMMON** storage locations are given initial values only once. It is obviously nonsense to allow a **DATA** statement to initialize global entities in one subprogram and another to give different initial values in another subprogram.

Only one unnamed **BLOCK DATA** subprogram is allowed in any one program but any number of named **BLOCK DATA** subprograms may be used. Compilers do vary in the way they handle **BLOCK DATA**. A safe rule is to use only one unnamed **BLOCK DATA** subprogram and place this immediately before the main program, but this is by no means a universal rule.

The **BLOCK DATA** subprogram name is global and may not be the same as the name of the main program, any subprogram, **COMMON** block or any other **BLOCK DATA** subprogram. Note that it does not contain any executable statements at all and it cannot be called as a subroutine or function can.

The following is an example of an unnamed **BLOCK DATA** subprogram:

```
BLOCK DATA
INTEGER C1,C2,C3
REAL X,Y,Z,A,B
COMMON /COUNT/C1,C2,C3
COMMON /NUM/X,Y,Z,A,B
DATA C1,C2,C3/1,3,5/
DATA X,Y,Z/3.5,4.5,5.1/
END
```

Note that names in blank **COMMON** may not be initialized in this way. Thus any global entities which do require initialization must be placed in a named **COMMON** block. More than one **COMMON** block may be initialized in the same **BLOCK DATA** subprogram. Even if all the entities in a named **COMMON** block are not initialized, they must all be specified.

Comment lines are permitted within **BLOCK DATA** subprograms and the ordering of statements must obey the rules described in section 8.3.

9.5 The SAVE statement

It has been described already how program units may use local variables to hold values which are required only in that program unit. These local variables lose their values when control is returned to the calling program unit. Any subsequent entry to the subprogram cannot assume that these local variables have retained their previous values. For example,

```
SUBROUTINE ADD
DATA I/1/
I = I + 1
RETURN
END
```

cannot be called repeatedly to add 1 to *I* because the value of *I* is lost after the **RETURN** is encountered.

However, FORTRAN provides a **SAVE** statement to enable the programmer to specify that local entities must retain their values between successive calls of a subprogram. It is of the form

SAVE *list*

where *list* is a list of variable or array or **COMMON** block names separated by commas. If a list is not specified then the **SAVE** applies to all variable, array and **COMMON** block names in the subprogram; it does not apply to dummy arguments.

The **SAVE** statement must be placed before all executable statements in the subprogram. A program unit may contain more than one **SAVE** statement.

The above example may be rewritten

```
SUBROUTINE ADD
SAVE I
DATA I/1/
I = I + 1
RETURN
END
```

and can be called repeatedly to add 1 to *I* (from *I* = 1).

The **SAVE** list may contain **COMMON** block names enclosed between slashes, e.g.

SAVE /FLAGS/,/COUNTS/

specifies that all entities in the **COMMON** blocks **FLAGS** and **COUNTS** must have their values saved when the **RETURN** or **END** statement is executed. Variables and arrays in **COMMON** blocks can only be saved by specifying the block name. If a **COMMON** block name is used in a **SAVE** statement it must be specified in every subprogram which uses that **COMMON** block.

One may ask why is it necessary to save **COMMON** blocks since **COMMON** by its very definition is global memory and causes values to be preserved between successive calls of a subprogram? For blank **COMMON** this is always true. However, named **COMMON** blocks which are used in some subprograms but not others, may lose their values (i.e. become undefined) when the subprogram is exited. To illustrate this, consider the structure shown on page 187.

Assume that the main program calls **SUB1**, which in turn calls **SUB2**, which in turn calls **SUB3**. The **RETURN** statements cause control to return back up the hierarchy to the main program.

When **SUB3** is exited, **COMMON** block C becomes undefined since it is not referred to anywhere else. When **SUB2** is exited, **COMMON** block B becomes undefined but A does not because it is referenced in the main program. Similarly when **SUB1** is exited, **COMMON** block D becomes undefined. In

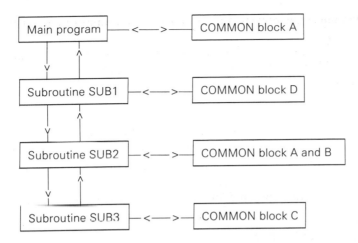

fact, only block A remains defined for the whole program since it is required by the main program. Thus if subroutines **SUB1**, **SUB2** and **SUB3** are re-entered, any values set in common blocks D, B and C will not have been retained.

To ensure that this does not happen, we may use the **SAVE** statement, e.g. in **SUB3** the statement **SAVE /C/** will ensure that block C is available when **SUB3** is called again. Note that if a **SAVE** statement is used for a **COMMON** block then it must be used in every subprogram in which that **COMMON** block is referred to.

The alternative solution to this problem is to declare all **COMMON** blocks in the main program. Blocks declared in the main program do not necessarily all have to be used in that unit.

9.6 The EQUIVALENCE statement

There are occasions in programming when it is more convenient or more efficient to refer to the same physical location in memory by different symbolic names. We have already seen how global names in **COMMON** can be equivalenced in this way. However, in general any names which are to be equivalenced (whether they refer to global or local entities) may be declared in a statement of the form

EQUIVALENCE (*list1*),(*list2*),. . .

where *list1*, *list2*, etc. represent lists of variable, array element, array or character substring names to be equivalenced, e.g.

EQUIVALENCE (X,Y),(A,B,C),(ARRAY1,ARRAY2)

will cause X and Y to refer to the same location, A, B and C to refer to the same location and arrays **ARRAY1** and **ARRAY2** to be the same locations. So the statement

EQUIVALENCE (I1,I2,I3)

followed by

I1 = 2
I2 = I1 ∗ 4
I3 = I1 + I2
WRITE (6,∗)I1,I2,I3

will result in the output 16 16 16.

Entities of different types and length may be equivalenced. For example,

REAL NUM1
DOUBLE PRECISION NUM2
EQUIVALENCE (NUM1,NUM2)

will cause the name **NUM1** to refer to the first real storage location of **NUM2**.

When unsubcripted array names are equivalenced, the effect is as if the first element of each, followed by each successive element in order, is equivalenced. Array elements may be equivalenced but the subscripts must be integer constant expressions.

The effect of equivalencing entities of different lengths is to cause the shorter to be stored in the first bytes of the longer. Thus arrays of different lengths may be equivalenced, e.g.

REAL TAB1(10),TAB2(50)
EQUIVALENCE (TAB1,TAB2)

will cause the first ten elements of **TAB2** to be the same as **TAB1**. Arrays of different dimensions may be equivalenced also, e.g.

REAL VEC1(5),MAT(5,2),VEC2(5)
EQUIVALENCE (VEC1,MAT),(VEC2,MAT(1,2))

will cause **VEC1(1)** to **VEC1(5)** to be the same locations as **MAT(1,1)** to **MAT(5,1)** and **VEC2(1)** to **VEC2(5)** to be the same as **MAT(1,2)** to **MAT(5,2)**. This is illustrated below

VEC1(1)	MAT(1,1)	VEC2(1)	MAT(1,2)
VEC1(2)	MAT(2,1)	VEC2(2)	MAT(2,2)
VEC1(3)	MAT(3,1)	VEC2(3)	MAT(3,2)
VEC1(4)	MAT(4,1)	VEC2(4)	MAT(4,2)
VEC1(5)	MAT(5,1)	VEC2(5)	MAT(5,2)

It is often more efficient to equivalence a one-dimensional array to a multi-dimensional array and perform all operations on the one-dimensional array, e.g.

```
      DO 10 I = 1,5
          VEC1(I) = 0.0
          VEC2(I) = 0.0
  10  CONTINUE
```

would set all elements of the two-dimensional array **MAT** to zero.

Similarly, character arrays can be equivalenced to character variables of the same overall length. For example,

```
  CHARACTER*1 CHAR(10)
  CHARACTER*10 CHAR10
  EQUIVALENCE (CHAR(1),CHAR10)
```

Equivalence statements cannot make self-contradictory demands. Locations which are already defined as separate locations in memory cannot be equivalenced, e.g.

```
  REAL ARRAY(10)
  EQUIVALENCE (ARRAY(1),ARRAY(5))
```

is illegal.

Although entities of different types may be equivalenced, this does not result in type conversion and this should be avoided. An entity of type character may be equivalenced only with other entities of type character.

Data in **COMMON** may be equivalenced but two items in the same **COMMON** block may not be equivalenced nor must a **COMMON** block be equivalenced so that the block will be extended backwards, i.e. before its start.

For example,

```
  REAL ARRAY(10)
  COMMON /AREA1/ARRAY2(5)
  EQUIVALENCE (ARRAY2(1),ARRAY(4))
```

is illegal since **ARRAY(1)** to **ARRAY(3)** would lie before the start of **AREA1**.

A **COMMON** block may however be extended past the end, e.g.

```
  EQUIVALENCE (ARRAY2(4),ARRAY(1))
```

is valid. However, statements of this type are confusing and are best avoided. The use of **EQUIVALENCE** (particularly with optimizing compilers) may cause unexpected results unless you are sure that you know what you are doing.

9.7 Summary

- Data locations in memory may be global to several (or all) program units or local to one program unit.
- The **COMMON** statement allows entities to be declared as global. This

allows different program units to share storage units and access the same data without the use of arguments.

● **COMMON** statements are of the form

   COMMON *list*

where *list* is a list of variables, array names or array declarations to be placed in **COMMON**. This is known as blank **COMMON**.

● An alternative form of **COMMON** statement is named **COMMON** which is of the form

   COMMON /*cb1*/*list1*,/*cb2*/*list2*. . .

where *cb1* and *cb2* are **COMMON** block names and *list1* and *list2* are lists of variables, array names or array declarations to be placed in the named **COMMON** block.

● Locations in named **COMMON** may be initialized in a **BLOCK DATA** subprogram

   BLOCK DATA *name*
   .
   .
   .
   END

where *name* is optional and is the name of the block data subprogram.

● Locations in blank **COMMON** may not be initialized.

● Local entities or **COMMON** blocks may be saved between successive invocations of the subprogram by the **SAVE** statement

   SAVE *list*

where *list* is a list of variables or arrays or **COMMON** block names.

● Symbolic names of variables, array elements, array or character substrings may be equivalenced so that they refer to the same physical locations in memory by the statement

   EQUIVALENCE (*list1*),(*list2*),. . .

where *list1*, *list2*, etc. are lists of the variables, array elements, arrays or character substring names which are to be equivalenced.

Exercises 9

1. What is wrong with the following as the headers of two subroutines which wish to communicate with each other via **COMMON**?

```
SUBROUTINE SUB1                    SUBROUTINE SUB2
REAL A3(1:10,1:5)                  INTEGER I,J,K
INTEGER I,J,K                      REAL X,Y,Z
REAL X,Y,Z,A(10)                   REAL A,B,C
REAL E,F,W,                        CHARACTER*5 CHAR
CHARACTER*5 CHAR                   COMMON X,Z,CHAR,A,A1,A2,K
COMMON X,Y,Z,CHAR,A,A1,A2(5),K     COMMON /B1/A,B,C,D,A3(1:50)
COMMON /B1/D,E,F,E,A3              COMMON /B2/W,I,J,A3(1:40)
COMMON /B2/W,I,J,A3
DOUBLE PRECISION D
DIMENSION A1(20),A2(5)
```

2. What will be the values printed out by the **PRINT** statement in the following main program?

```
PROGRAM EX2                        SUBROUTINE SUB1(ARG1,ARG2)
INTEGER COUNT                      INTEGER COUNT
REAL CV1,CV2,OUT2,ARG1             REAL ARG1,ARG2,CV1,CV2
COMMON CV1,CV2                     COMMON CV1,CV2
COUNT = 10                         COUNT = COUNT + 1
CV1 = 102.2                        CV1 = CV2/10.0
CV2 = 36.9                         ARG2 = ARG1*CV1
CALL SUB1(5.0,OUT2)                RETURN
PRINT *,ARG1,OUT2,CV1,CV2,COUNT    END
STOP
END
```

3. Rewrite Exercise 8.4 using **COMMON** instead of arguments.

4. Rewrite Exercise 4.5 as a main program which reads a date and a subroutine which returns the date of the day N days after this date. Use **COMMON** instead of arguments to pass the information to and from the subroutine. Also modify the program so that it reads and writes the dates in character format dd/mm/yyyy.

5. Three types of aircraft arrive at an airport terminal. Type 1 carries 135 passengers, Type 2 carries 240 passengers and Type 3 carries 412 passengers. Write a subroutine which counts the number of planes and the number of passengers for each type and prints the cumulative totals for these each time the subroutine is entered. Write a main program which reads in an aircraft type and calls this subroutine until an aircraft type number not in the range 1 to 3 is read. At this point the total number of aircraft of all types and the total number of passengers carried should be printed. Use **COMMON** to pass all information to and from the subroutine and initialize **COMMON** data in a **BLOCK DATA** subprogram.

Conclusion

The writing of good FORTRAN programs is an art and, to some extent, what constitutes a good program is a matter of personal taste.

However, during the last ten years, the cost of computer hardware has decreased substantially and the cost of producing computer software has become relatively more expensive. This has led to an increase in awareness of programming standards throughout the computing community.

Computer programs are now often written to last years, to be used by different people, to be run on a variety of machines and to be developed by other programmers over a period of time.

This leads to the requirement that programs should be well structured and well commented so that other programmers can understand and modify the program even if the original programmer is no longer available for consultation. A variety of techniques have been developed to help the programmer to plan the structure of a program before it is written. Jackson's structured programming techniques are now gaining widespread acceptance and the would-be programmer should study *Principles of Program Design* by M. A. Jackson (published by Academic Press) for further guidance on this. In general, programs should be broken down into small parts in which **GOTO** statements are avoided completely if possible. An attempt has been made in this book to encourage the use of structural specifications and diagrams.

In addition to being well structured and documented, programs should be as portable as possible so that the minimum effort is required to produce a working version on a different computer. Comments on portability have been made throughout this text.

Many tips have been given in this book to help the programmer produce good programs. Some of the main points in summary are:

Include explanatory comment in the program text as it is being written, not as an afterthought.

Space out statements with blank comment to improve readability.

Separate subprograms with clear markers such as lines of asterisks.

Used fixed column positions for different statement types, e.g. declarations in column 7 onwards; indent **DO** loops and block-**IF** statements.

Make clear which variables are **COMMON** and which are local. Describe what each one does.

Use meaningful names for variables, subprograms, etc.

Avoid long argument lists. Use **COMMON** instead.

Insert **COMMON** blocks from separate files.

Divide the program into small subprograms each with a well-defined task.

Head each subprogram with a description of what it does.

Write programs to the ANSI standard specification; if your compiler provides an ANSI check option, use it. Clearly mark statements which are liable to be machine dependent.

Avoid mixed mode arithmetic.

For the sake of efficiency:

Avoid using subprograms for too small a task.

Avoid jumping between different parts of the program. Use block-**IF** statements wherever possible.

Use functions in preference to subroutines, and statement functions in preference to functions. This may be more efficient on some systems but not on others.

Optimize frequently used parts of the program. Remember that most programs spend 80% of their time in 20% of the code.

Nest **DO** loops so that the first index varies the fastest.

Remove invariant expressions from inside **DO** loops and avoid multiple evaluations of the same expression. Evaluate the expression once and assign the result to a local variable.

Always use the right type for constants in expressions so that the computer does not have to spend time converting from one type to another.

Appendix A

Intrinsic functions

Generic functions

Each of these functions may take arguments of different types. Unless otherwise stated, the function value returned is of the same type as the argument. For the trigonometrical functions the angles are in radians.

Name	Argument type	Definition
ABS	Integer Real Double Complex	**ABS(a)** returns the absolute value of a.
ACOS	Real Double	**ACOS(a)** returns arccos(a).
AINT	Real Double	**AINT(a)** returns the truncated value of a but the result is the same type as a.
ANINT	Real Double	**ANINT(a)** returns the nearest whole number to a. The result is the same type as a.
ASIN	Real Double	**ASIN(a)** returns the arcsin(a).
ATAN	Real Double	**ATAN(a)** returns the arctan(a).
ATAN2	Real Double	**ATAN2($a1,a2$)** returns arctan($a1/a2$).
COS	Real Double Complex	**COS(a)** returns cosine(a).
COSH	Real Double	**COSH(a)** returns the hyperbolic cosine cosh(a).
DBLE	Integer Real Double Complex	**DBLE(a)** returns the double precision equivalent of a. This obviously returns a double precision result regardless of the argument type.

Name	Argument type	Definition
DIM	Integer Real Double	DIM($a1,a2$) returns the positive difference $a1 - a2$ if $a1 > a2$ otherwise it returns 0.
EXP	Real Double Complex	EXP(a) returns the exponential e**a.
INT	Integer Real Double Complex	INT(a) converts a to integer by truncation. This function always returns an integer type regardless of the type of the argument.
LOG	Real Double	LOG(a) returns the natural logarithm log(a).
LOG10	Real Double	LOG10(a) returns log to the base 10 of a.
MAX	Integer Real Double	MAX($a1,a2,a3,...$) returns the largest value. The function returns a value of the same type as the argument. The specific functions AMAX0 may be used to return a real when the argument is integer and MAX1 to return an integer when the argument is real.
MIN	Integer Real Double	MIN($a1,a2,a3,...$) returns the smallest value. The function returns a value of the same type as the argument. The specific functions AMIN0 may be used to return a real when the argument is integer and MIN1 to return an integer when the argument is real.
MOD	Integer Real Double	MOD($a1,a2$) returns the remainder when $a1$ is divided by $a2$, i.e. $a1 - \text{INT}(a1/a2)*a2$
NINT	Real Double	NINT(a) returns the nearest integer to a. Note that the function value returned is of type integer irrespective of the type of the argument.
REAL	Integer Real Double Complex	REAL(a) converts a to real. This function obviously returns a real result regardless of the argument type.

Name	Argument type	Definition
SIGN	Integer Real Double	SIGN($a1,a2$) returns abs($a1$) if $a2 > 0$ or $a2 = 0$ and $-$abs($a1$) if $a2 < 0$. It effectively transfers the sign of $a2$ to $a1$.
SIN	Real Double Complex	SIN(a) returns sine(a).
SINH	Real Double	SINH(a) returns the hyperbolic sine of a.
SQRT	Real Double Complex	SQRT(a) returns the square root of a.
TAN	Real Double	TAN(a) returns the tangent of a.
TANH	Real Double	TANH(a) returns the hyperbolic tangent of a.

Character handling functions

ICHAR	Character	ICHAR(a) converts the character argument to its integer internal code equivalent.
CHAR	Integer	CHAR(a) converts the integer a to the equivalent character assuming that the integer argument is a valid internal code value.
LEN	Character	LEN(a) gives the length of the character argument. The argument may be a quoted character constant or a variable or array element containing a character string.
INDEX	Character	INDEX($a1,a2$) returns the starting position of the substring $a2$ in the string $a1$. A value of 0 is returned if $a2$ is not in $a1$.
LGE	Character	LGE($a1,a2$) is a logical function which returns the value .TRUE. if $a1 > a2$ or $a1 = a2$ and returns the value .FALSE. otherwise.
LGT	Character	LGT($a1,a2$) is a logical function which returns the value .TRUE. if $a1 > a2$ and returns the value .FALSE. otherwise.

Name	Argument type	Definition
LLT	Character	**LLT(***a*1,*a*2**)** is a logical function which returns the value **.TRUE.** if *a*1 < *a*2 and returns the value **.FALSE.** otherwise.

Functions for complex numbers

ABS	Complex	**ABS(***ca***)** returns **SQRT(REAL(***ca***)****2 + **IMAG(***ca***)****2)
AIMAG	Complex	**AIMAG(***a***)** returns the imaginary part of a complex argument as a real number.
CONJG	Complex	**CONJG(***a***)** returns the complex number which is the conjugate of *a*, i.e. if *a* is *ar,ai* then *ar*, − *ai* is returned.
CMPLX	Integer Real Double Complex	**CMPLX(***a***)** returns the complex equivalent of *a*.

Appendix B

Common character codes

ASCII

32 space	48 0	64 @	80 P	96	112 p
33 !	49 1	65 A	81 Q	97 a	113 q
34 "	50 2	66 B	82 R	98 b	114 r
35 #	51 3	67 C	83 S	99 c	115 s
36 $	52 4	68 D	84 T	100 d	116 t
37 %	53 5	69 E	85 U	101 e	117 u
38 &	54 6	70 F	86 V	102 f	118 v
39 '	55 7	71 G	87 W	103 g	119 w
40 (	56 8	72 H	88 X	104 h	120 x
41)	57 9	73 I	89 Y	105 i	121 y
42 *	58 :	74 J	90 Z	106 j	122 z
43 +	59 ;	75 K	91 [	107 k	123 {
44 ,	60 <	76 L	92 \	108 l	124	
45 –	61 =	77 M	93]	109 m	125 }
46 .	62 >	78 N	94 ^	110 n	126 ~
47 /	63 ?	79 O	95 _	111 o	

EBCDIC

64	space	123	#	145	j	193	A	209	J	226	S
75	.	124	@	146	k	194	B	210	K	227	T
77	(	125	'	147	l	195	C	211	L	228	U
78	+	126	=	148	m	196	D	212	M	229	V
79	|	127	"	149	n	197	E	213	N	230	W
80	&	129	a	150	o	198	F	214	O	231	X
90	!	130	b	151	p	199	G	215	P	232	Y
91	$	131	c	152	q	200	H	216	Q	233	Z
92	*	132	d	153	r	201	I	217	R	240	0
93	)	133	e	161	~					241	1
94	;	134	f	162	s					242	2
96	–	135	g	163	t					243	3
97	/	136	h	164	u					244	4
107	,	137	i	165	v					245	5
108	%			166	w					246	6
109	_			167	x					247	7
110	>			168	y					248	8
111	?			169	z					249	9

Solutions to exercises

Note: Lack of space makes it impossible to fully comment on all of the following programs; similarly full error checking has not been provided nor has a structure diagram or structural specification been given for every one. However, it is hoped that many of these programs can form a basis for producing good production systems and that enough structural specifications have been provided to illustrate the point.

Exercises 1

1. The following are correct integer constants:

   ```
   2225   -25   -97612   10000   0   005326
   ```

   The following are correct real constants:

   ```
   .137   2E-7   1.562   -.137   +0162.2E-02   +258.   3.6E-22
   ```

   The following are not valid:

E-10	(exponent alone not allowed; this must be written 1.E − 10)
101.2E+2.	(exponent not an integer)
2,360	(comma not allowed)

2. The following are correct integer variable names:

   ```
   NUMBER   I123   ITER   IP   L1369P
   ```

   The following are correct real variable names:

   ```
   PI   AMPS   FRED   ZETA   Q   COUNTS   POWER
   ```

   The following are not correct:

2X13	(does not begin with a letter)
M63-2	(contains a character other than a letter or a digit)
BSQUARED	(contains more than six characters)
X+Y	(contains a character other than a letter or a digit)
K(2)	(contains a character other than a letter or a digit)
INC*	(contains a character other than a letter or a digit)
NUMBER1	(contains more than six characters)

I.3.6   (contains a character other than a letter or a digit)
JIM'S   (contains a character other than a letter or a digit)

3. The decimal equivalents are

   3   5   57   255

   The binary representations are

   100000   100000001   1010   11011

4. The structural specification should read as follows:

   Read the number to be found *M*
   Read the number of numbers in the list *N*
   Repeat the following *N* times:
     Read a number
     If the number is the same as the required value then
         Increment the number of occurrences counter
         Print the position of the number in the list
     end if
   End repeat
   Print the number of occurrences of *M* in the list

5. The algorithm should read as follows:

   Read *a, b* and *c*
   Compute $s = 0.5*(a + b + c)$
   Compute area $= (s * (s - a) * (s - b) * (s - c))^{\frac{1}{2}}$
   Compute number of tins $=$ area/10
   If the remainder of this division is not zero
         Add 1 to the number of tins
   end if
   Print the number of tins of paint required

Exercises 2

1.1 `A = (3.0*X*Y**2* (Z + 1.0) + 0.5*Y*Z) / (1.0 + X + X**3)`

1.2 `B = 1.5*X* (X - 1.0) * SQRT(7.0*Y - LOG(COS(X)))`

1.3 `I = INT((REAL(K) / REAL(J)) * (X*100.0 - (REAL(K)**2`
    `    / (3.0*REAL(J)))))`

    `I = INT(REAL(K/J) * (100.0*X - (REAL(K**2/J)/3.0)))`

1.4 `Z = 5.0*X**2*SQRT((COS(X**2 - Y**2))**3 + ATAN(X*COS(X)))`
    `    / (EXP(X + 1.0) * EXP(Y + 1.0) + 1.0)`

   In 1.3, when $J = 3$, $K = 7$ and $X = 0.5$ then $I = 103$ and $I = 89$ for the two cases.

2.   I = 8, J = 7, X = -4.75, Y = -9.75, Z = 5.0

         P = -224.75, Q = -24.75, R = 20.0

3.
```
PROGRAM PAINT
PRINT *,'Enter A in metres: '
READ *,A
PRINT *,'Enter B in metres: '
READ *,B
PRINT *,'Enter C in metres: '
READ *,C
S    = 0.5*(A+B+C)
AREA = SQRT(S*(S-A) * (S-B) * (S-C))
NTINS = INT(AREA/10.0 + 0.999999))
PRINT *,'The number of tins of paint required is ',NTINS
STOP
END
```

4.
```
PROGRAM FTOC
PRINT *,'Enter the temperature in degrees Fahrenheit: '
READ *,F
C = (F-32.0) * 5.0/9.0
PRINT *,'The corresponding temperature in degrees Centigrade is ',
1         C
STOP
END
```

5.
```
PROGRAM INTRST
PRINT *,'Enter the sum invested in the form Pounds.pence: '
READ *,SUM
PRINT *,'Enter the rate of interest: '
READ *,RATE
PRINT *,'Enter the total number of years: '
READ *,N
TOTINT = SUM*(1.0 + RATE/100.0)**N -SUM
DOLLRS = 1.8*TOTINT
PRINT *,'The total interest in pounds  and pence is ',TOTINT
PRINT *,'The total interest in dollars and cents is ',DOLLRS
STOP
END
```

Exercises 3

1. (a) True
   (b) False
   (c) True

2.
```
PROGRAM FUNCS
PRINT *,'Enter a value for X1: '
READ *,X1
PRINT *,'Enter a value for X2: '
READ *,X2
PRINT *,'Enter function number in the range 1 to 4: '
READ *,NOFUN
IF (NOFUN .EQ. 1) THEN
    FX = (X1 - X2**2)**2 + (1.0 - X2)**2
ELSE IF (NOFUN .EQ. 2) THEN
    FX = 100.0*(X2 - X1**2)**2 + (1.0 - X1)**2
```

```
      ELSE IF (NOFUN .EQ. 3) THEN
         FX = 100.0*(X1 - X2**3)**2 + (1.0 - X2)**2
      ELSE IF (NOFUN .EQ. 4) THEN
         FX = (X1 + 2.0 * X2 - 7.0)**2 + (2.0*X1 + X2 - 5.0)**2
      ELSE
         PRINT *,'***Error - function number ',NOFUN,' out of range'
         STOP
      ENDIF
      PRINT *,'The value of function ',NOFUN,' is ',FX
      STOP
      END
```

3.

```
      PROGRAM SEARCH
      PRINT *,'Enter the integer value to be searched for: '
      READ *,M
      PRINT *,'Enter the length of the list to be searched: '
      READ *,N
      I    = 1
      IOCC = 0
      PRINT *,'Enter this number of integers one per line: '
   10 IF (I .GT. N) GOTO 20
      READ *,NUM
      IF (NUM .EQ. M)THEN
         IOCC = IOCC + 1
         PRINT *,'This number occurs at position ',I,' in the list'
      ENDIF
      I = I + 1
      GOTO 10
   20 PRINT *,'There are ',IOCC,' occurrences of ',M,' in the list'
      STOP
      END
```

4.

```
      PROGRAM ROOT
      PRINT *,'Enter the number for which you require the square root: '
      READ *,X
      A = X/2.0
   10 B -(X/A + A)/2.0
      C = B - A
      IF (C .LT. 0.0)C = -C
      IF (C .LT. 1.0E-6)GOTO 20
      A = B
      GOTO 10
   20 PRINT *,'the square root of ',X,' is ',B
      STOP
      END
```

5.

```
      PROGRAM LEAPYR
   10 PRINT *,'Enter the year (or 0 to terminate the program): '
      READ *,IYEAR
      IF (IYEAR .EQ. 0)STOP
      IF (MOD(IYEAR,400) .EQ. 0 .OR.
    1    MOD(IYEAR,4) .EQ. 0 .AND. MOD(IYEAR,100) .NE. 0)THEN
         PRINT *,'The year ',IYEAR,' is a leap year'
      ELSE
         PRINT *,'The year ',IYEAR,' is not a leap year'
      ENDIF
      GOTO 10
      END
```

Exercises 4

1. (a) There is no type statement (or **DIMENSION** statement) to dimension the arrays, e.g.

    ```
    INTEGER NO(500)
    REAL    X(500)
    ```

   (b) **NSMODD** is not initialized to zero, i.e. there should be a statement **NSMODD** = 0 placed somewhere before this variable is used at line 7.

   (c) At line 15 a subscript of zero will be generated for NO(I − 1) when I = 1. To correct this, the first element of X (X(1)) must be computed outside the loop as is the last element. Thus, line 15 should be replaced by

    ```
    DO 40, I = 2,N-1
    ```

   and an extra line

    ```
    X(1) = NO(1)/2
    ```

   should be inserted after line 17.

   (d) The integer division at line 15 will give a truncated result which is not what is required here. The arithmetic mean of two integers (e.g. 2 and 3) will in general be a real number (i.e. 2.5) and not the truncated value (i.e. 2). Thus the expression should be replaced by

    ```
    X(I) = REAL(NO(I-1) + NO(I+1))/2.0
    ```

   (e) It would be better to replace

    ```
    X(1) = NO(1)/2
    X(I) = NO(I)/2
    ```

   by

    ```
    X(1) = REAL(NO(1)/2)
    X(N) = REAL(NO(N)/2)
    ```

   although neither of these changes is essential since (a) the integer value will be converted to real before the assignment and (b) I has the value N on exit from the loop.

2.

```
PROGRAM ARRSUM
INTEGER N1(5,3),N2(5,3),N3(5,3),N4(3,5)
PRINT *,'Enter the elements for N1 and N2 two per line: '
DO 20, J = 1,3
   DO 10, I = 1,5
      READ *,N1(I,J),N2(I,J)
      N3(I,J) = N1(I,J) + N2(I,J)
      N4(J,I) = N3(I,J)
10    CONTINUE
20 CONTINUE
```

```
        DO 40, J = 1,3
           DO 30, I = 1,5
              PRINT *,N1(I,J),N2(I,J),N3(I,J),N4(J,I)
30         CONTINUE
40      CONTINUE
        STOP
        END
```

3.

```
        PROGRAM RNUMS
        REAL X(1000)
        PRINT *,'Enter the number of real numbers: '
        READ *,N
        IF (N .GT. 1000)STOP
        SUM = 0.0
        SQDIFF = 0.0
        XMIN    = 10.0E10
        XMAX    = 0.0
        PRINT *,'Enter ',N,' real numbers one per line: '
        DO 10, I = 1,N
           READ *,X(I)
           SUM = SUM + X(I)
           IF (X(I) .GT. XMAX)XMAX = X(I)
           IF (X(I) .LT. XMIN)XMIN = X(I)
10      CONTINUE
        XMEAN = SUM/REAL(N)
        DO 20, I = 1,N
           SQDIFF = SQDIFF + (X(I) - XMEAN)**2
20      CONTINUE
        STDEV = SQRT(SQDIFF/REAL(N))
        PRINT *,'The maximum number is    : ',XMAX
        PRINT *,'The minimum number is    : ',XMIN
        PRINT *,'The mean is              : ',XMEAN
        PRINT *,'The standard deviation is: ',STDEV
        STOP
        END
```

4. A structural specification for this program might read as follows:

Read the number of marks
Read the marks into a two-dimensional array
Do for each row of the array
    Do for each column
        If mark > 70 then
            Increment grade A counter for this subject
        else if mark is between 60 and 70
            Increment grade B counter for this subject
        else if mark is between 50 and 60 then
            Increment grade C counter for this subject
        else if mark is between 40 and 50
            Increment grade D counter for this subject
        else if mark < 40
            Increment fail counter for this subject
        else
            error — invalid entry
        endif
    End do for each column

End do for each row
Print the number of grade A, grade B, grade C, grade D and fail
marks for each subject
Stop
End

This might be implemented as follows

```
      PROGRAM EMARKS
      INTEGER I,J,MARK
      INTEGER MARKS(500,4),ACOUNT(4),BCOUNT(4)
      INTEGER CCOUNT(4),DCOUNT(4),FCOUNT(4)
      PRINT *,'Enter the number of marks: '
      READ *,N
      PRINT *,'Enter ',N,' marks for each subject one per line: '
      DO 20, J = 1,N
         DO 10, I = 1,4
            READ *,MARKS(I,J)
   10    CONTINUE
   20 CONTINUE
      DO 40, J = 1,N
         DO 30, I = 1,4
            MARK = MARKS(I,J)
            IF (MARK .GT. 70) THEN
               ACOUNT(I) = ACOUNT(I) + 1
            ELSE IF (MARK .GE. 60 .AND. MARK .LE. 70) THEN
               BCOUNT(I) = BCOUNT(I) + 1
            ELSE IF (MARK .GE. 50 .AND. MARK .LE. 60) THEN
               CCOUNT(I) = CCOUNT(I) + 1
            ELSE IF (MARK .GE. 40 .AND. MARK .LE. 50) THEN
               DCOUNT(I) = DCOUNT(I)
            ELSE IF (MARK .LT. 40) THEN
               FCOUNT(I) = FCOUNT(I) + 1
            ELSE
               PRINT *,'***Error - invalid entry ',MARK,
     1            ' at row ',I,' for subject ',J
            ENDIF
   30    CONTINUE
   40 CONTINUE
      DO 50, I = 1,4
         PRINT *,'The number of Grade A marks for subject ',
     1         I,' are ',ACOUNT(I)
         PRINT *,'The number of Grade B marks for subject ',
     1         I,' are ',BCOUNT(I)
         PRINT *,'The number of Grade C marks for subject ',
     1         I,' are ',CCOUNT(I)
         PRINT *,'The number of Grade D marks for subject ',
     1         I,' are ',DCOUNT(I)
         PRINT *,'The number of fails for subject            ',
     1         I,' are ',FCOUNT(I)
         PRINT *,' '
   50 CONTINUE
      STOP
      END
```

5. A structural specification for this might read as follows:

Set the number of days for every month in the year
Read the day, month and year
If the year is a leap year then

       Set the number of days in February to 29
else
       Set the number of days in February to 28
endif
Divide the year into two integers − century and year
Add 14 to day
If days is > the number of days in the specified month then
       Set new value of day = day − (number of days in
                             the specified month)
      If the month is December then
         Set the month to January
         If the year is 99 then
             Increment the century
             Set year to 0
         else
             Increment the year
         endif
      else
         Increment the month
      endif
Reassemble the century and year
Print the new date
Stop
End

This might be implemented as follows:

```
      PROGRAM DATES
*
* A program to compute the date which is 14 days after a given date
*
      INTEGER DAYS(12)
*
* Set up the number of days in each month
*
      DO 10, I = 1,12
         DAYS(I) = 31
  10  CONTINUE
      DAYS(4) = 30
      DAYS(6) = 30
      DAYS(9) = 30
      DAYS(11)= 30
*
* Read the required date
*
      PRINT *,'Enter day(dd)  : '
      READ *,IDAY
      PRINT *,'Enter month(mm): '
      READ *,IMONTH
      PRINT *,'Enter year(yyyy): '
      READ *,IYEAR
*
```

```
* Determine whether the year is a leap year
*
      IF (MOD(IYEAR,400) .EQ. 0 .OR.
     1    MOD(IYEAR,4) .EQ. 0 .AND. MOD(IYEAR,100) .NE. 0) THEN
          DAYS(2) = 29
      ELSE
          DAYS(2) = 28
      ENDIF
*
* Compute the century and year
*
      ICENT = IYEAR/100
      NYEAR = IYEAR - (ICENT*100)
*
* Compute the day 14 days hence
*
      IDAY = IDAY + 14
*
* Check if this crosses a month boundary
*
      IF (IDAY .GT. DAYS(IMONTH)) THEN
          IDAY = IDAY - DAYS(IMONTH)
*
* Check if this crosses a year boundary
*
          IF (IMONTH .EQ. 12) THEN
              IMONTH = 1
*
* Check if this crosses a century boundary
*
              IF (NYEAR .EQ. 99) THEN
                  ICENT = ICENT + 1
                  NYEAR = 0
              ELSE
                  NYEAR = NYEAR + 1
              ENDIF
          ELSE
              IMONTH = IMONTH + 1
          ENDIF
      ENDIF
*
* Print the resulting data
*
      IYEAR = ICENT * 100 + NYEAR
      PRINT *,'The day which is 14 days after this date is: '
      PRINT *,'Day:    ',IDAY
      PRINT *,'Month:  ',IMONTH
      PRINT *,'Year:   ',IYEAR
      STOP
      END
```

Exercises 5

1. (a) The following are valid FORTRAN constants:

```
'TODAY''S DATE IS 15:10:81' (length 24)
2.35675D2
.TRUE.
(3.65,2E5)
```

(b) The following are not valid constants:

```
'ALL'S WELL THAT ENDS WELL'   (this should be ALL'S)
'THE VALUE OF X =             (closing quote is missing)
(5.3 2.1)                     (the separating comma is missing)
.F.                           (this should be .FALSE.)
```

2.

```
C1 = 'duty'
C2 = 'do this'
C3 = 'Englishmen'
C4 = 'Englishmen do their duty'
```

3.

```
CHARACTER*45 SAYING
CHARACTER*39 NEW
SAYING = 'before tomorrow note the questions that arise'
NEW(1:3) = SAYING(8:9)
NEW(4:6) - SAYING(1:2)
NEW(7:9) = SAYING(4:5)
NEW(10:13) = SAYING(17:19)
NEW(14:19) = NEW(1:6)
NEW(20:24) = SAYING(36:40)
NEW(25:26) = SAYING(43:44)
NEW(28:39) = SAYING(22:33)
```

4.

```
      PROGRAM CRYPTIC
*
* A program to encode or decode text according to the rules of
* Caesar's cipher.
*
      INTEGER CHNUM
      CHARACTER*1 TAB(1:26)
      INTEGER BUFPTR,L
      LOGICAL ENCODE
      CHARACTER*80 IPREC,OPREC
      DATA TAB/'A','B','C','D','E','F','G','H',
     1         'I','J','K','L','M','N','O','P',
     2         'Q','R','S','T','U','V','W','X','Y','Z'/
      READ *,IPREC
*
* Check whether Encode or Decode is required
*
      IF (IPREC(1:6) .EQ. 'ENCODE') THEN
         ENCODE - .TRUE.
      ELSE IF (IPREC(1:6) .EQ. 'DECODE') THEN
         ENCODE = .FALSE.
      ELSE
         PRINT *,'Invalid input. The first line should be ENCODE or '
     1          //'DECODE and not: ',IPREC
         STOP
      ENDIF
*
* Read lines of text
*
      DO 20, I = 1,10000
         READ *,IPREC
         IF (IPREC(1:4) .EQ. '****') THEN
            STOP
         ELSE
            DO 10, L = 1,80
*
* Copy non alphabetic characters unchanged
```

```
*
                IF (IPREC(L:L) .LT. 'A' .OR. IPREC(L:L) .GT. 'Z') THEN
                   OPREC(L:L) = IPREC(L:L)
                ELSE
*
* Encode or Decode alphabetic characters as required
*
                   CHNUM = ICHAR(IPREC(L:L)) - ICHAR('A') + 1
                   IF (ENCODE) THEN
                      CHNUM = CHNUM - 3
                      IF (CHNUM .LE. 0)CHNUM = CHNUM + 26
                   ELSE
                      CHNUM = CHNUM + 3
                      IF (CHNUM .GT. 26)CHNUM = CHNUM - 26
                   ENDIF
                   OPREC(L:L) = TAB(CHNUM)
                ENDIF
  10         CONTINUE
*
* Print the converted line of text
*
          PRINT *,OPREC
          ENDIF
  20      CONTINUE
          PRINT *,'***Error - too many input records'
          STOP
          END
```

5.

```
          PROGRAM SORT
          INTEGER I,N,J
          INTEGER INTVAL,COUNT
          CHARACTER*80 NAMES(1000),TEMP
          PRINT *,'Enter the number of names to be sorted: '
          READ *,N
          PRINT *,'Enter these names, one per line: '
          DO 10, I = 1,N
             READ *,NAMES(I)
  10      CONTINUE
          INTVAL = N/2
          DO 40, COUNT = 1,1000
             IF (INTVAL .LE. 0)GOTO 50
             DO 30, I = INTVAL,N-1
                DO 20, J = I - INTVAL+1,1,-INTVAL
                   IF (NAMES(J) .GT. NAMES(J+INTVAL))THEN
                      TEMP = NAMES(J)
                      NAMES(J) = NAMES(J+INTVAL)
                      NAMES(J+INTVAL) = TEMP
                   ENDIF
  20            CONTINUE
  30         CONTINUE
             INTVAL = INTVAL/2
  40      CONTINUE
  50      PRINT *,'The names sorted into ascending order are: '
          DO 60, I = 1,N
             PRINT *,NAMES(I)
  60      CONTINUE
          STOP
          END
```

Exercises 6

1.

```
        PROGRAM FTOC
        INTEGER I,J
        REAL C(100)
        DO 10, I = 1,100
            C(I) = (REAL(I) - 32.0)*5.0/9.0
   10   CONTINUE
        WRITE(*,'(12X,''TABLE OF DEGREES FAHRENHEIT AND CENTIGRADE''//)')
        WRITE(*,'(5(''    F      C''))')
        DO 20, I = 1,20
            WRITE(*,'(5(I5,F7.2))')(I+J,C(I+J),J = 0,80,20)
   20   CONTINUE
        STOP
        END
```

. 2. A structural specification for this program might read as follows:

```
Initialize data
Repeat until end of data
    Read record
        if sex is female then
            if units/week < 8
                increment female light drinker count
            else if units/week is between 8 and 14
                increment female moderate drinker count
            else if units/week > 14
                increment female heavy drinker count
                set heavy drinker to TRUE
            else
                error — Invalid number of units per week
            endif
            if cigarettes/day < 8
                increment female light smoker count
            else if cigarettes/day is between 8 and 14
                increment female moderate smoker count
            else if cigarettes/day > 14
                increment female heavy smoker count
                if heavy drinker is TRUE then print details
            else
                error — Invalid number of cigarettes/day
            endif
        else if sex is male then
            if units/week < 11
                increment male light drinker count
            else if units/week is between 11 and 20
                increment male moderate drinker count
            else if units/week > 20
```

```
                        increment male heavy drinker count
                        set heavy drinker to TRUE
                   else
                        error − Invalid number of units/week
                   endif
                   if cigarettes/day < 11
                        increment male light smoker count
                   else if cigarettes/day is between 11 and 20
                        increment male moderate smoker count
                   else if cigarettes/day > 20
                        increment male heavy smoker count
                        if heavy drinker is TRUE then print details
                   else
                        error − Invalid number of cigarettes/day
                   endif
              else
                   error − Invalid sex
              endif
     End of data
     Print table of results
     Stop
```

This program implemented in FORTRAN 77 using formatted I/O statements reads as follows:

```
        PROGRAM SURVEY
*
* A program to analyse people's smoking and drinking habits.
*
        INTEGER AGE,UNITS,CIGS,I,FLDCNT,FMDCNT,FHDCNT
        INTEGER FLSCNT,FMSCNT,FHSCNT,MLDCNT,MMDCNT,MHDCNT
        INTEGER MLSCNT,MMSCNT,MHSCNT
        CHARACTER NAME*20,SEX*1,ADDRES*25,STATUS*7
        LOGICAL HDRINK
        DATA FLDCNT,FMDCNT,FHDCNT,FLSCNT,FMSCNT,FHSCNT/6*0/
        DATA MLDCNT,MMDCNT,MHDCNT,MLSCNT,MMSCNT,MHSCNT/6*0/
        DATA HDRINK/.FALSE./
        DO 10, I = 1,10000
*
* Read a data record
*
        READ(5,'(A20,1X,I2,1X,A1,1X,A25,1X,A7,1X,I4,1X,I3)')
     1        NAME,AGE,SEX,ADDRES,STATUS,UNITS,CIGS
        IF (NAME .NE. '999')THEN
*
* Analyse female data
*
            IF (SEX .EQ. 'F')THEN
*
* Check female drinkers
*
                IF (UNITS .LT. 8)THEN
                    FLDCNT = FLDCNT + 1
                ELSE IF (UNITS .GE. 8 .AND. UNITS .LE. 14)THEN
                    FMDCNT = FMDCNT + 1
```

```
                  ELSE IF (UNITS .GT. 14)THEN
                     FHDCNT = FHDCNT + 1
                     HDRINK = .TRUE.
                  ELSE
                     PRINT *,'***Error - invalid number of units/week'
                     PRINT *,'The following record has been ignored:'
                     WRITE(*,'(A20,1X,I2,1X,A1,1X,A25,1X,A7,1X,I4,1X,I3)')
     1                      NAME,AGE,SEX,ADDRES,STATUS,UNITS,CIGS
                  ENDIF
*
* Check female smokers
*
                  IF (CIGS .LT. 8)THEN
                     FLSCNT = FLSCNT + 1
                  ELSE IF (CIGS .GE. 8 .AND. CIGS .LE. 14)THEN
                     FMSCNT = FMSCNT + 1
                  ELSE IF (CIGS .GT. 14)THEN
                     FHSCNT = FHSCNT + 1
*
* Print out details of those females who are both heavy drinkers
* and heavy smokers
*
                  IF (HDRINK) THEN
                     PRINT *,' This female is both a heavy drinker'
     1                   //' and a heavy smoker: '
                     WRITE(*,'(/A20,1X,I2,1X,A1,1X,A25,1X,A7,1X,I4,1X,I3
     1                   /)')NAME,AGE,SEX,ADDRES,STATUS,UNITS,CIGS
                  ENDIF
               ELSE
                  PRINT *,'***Error - invalid number of cigarettes/day'
                  PRINT *,'The following record has been ignored:'
                  WRITE(*,'(A20,1X,I2,1X,A1,1X,A25,1X,A7,1X,I4,1X,I3)')
     1                   NAME,AGE,SEX,ADDRES,STATUS,UNITS,CIGS
               ENDIF
*
* Analyse male data
*
            ELSE IF (SEX .EQ. 'M')THEN
*
* Check male drinkers
*
               IF (UNITS .LT. 11)THEN
                  MLDCNT = MLDCNT + 1
               ELSE IF (UNITS .GE. 11 .AND. UNITS .LE. 20)THEN
                  MMDCNT = MMDCNT + 1
               ELSE IF (UNITS .GT. 20)THEN
                  MHDCNT = MHDCNT + 1
                  HDRINK = .TRUE.
               ELSE
                  PRINT *,'***Error - invalid number of units/week'
                  PRINT *,'The following record has been ignored:'
                  WRITE(*,'(A20,1X,I2,1X,A1,1X,A25,1X,A7,1X,I4,1X,I3)')
     1                   NAME,AGE,SEX,ADDRES,STATUS,UNITS,CIGS
               ENDIF
*
* Check male smokers
*
               IF (CIGS .LT. 11)THEN
                  MLSCNT = MLSCNT + 1
               ELSE IF (CIGS .GE. 11 .AND. CIGS .LE. 20)THEN
                  MMSCNT = MMSCNT + 1
               ELSE IF (CIGS .GT. 20)THEN
                  MHSCNT = MHSCNT + 1
*
* Print out details of those males who are both heavy drinkers
* and heavy smokers
```

```
      *
                          IF (HDRINK) THEN
                             PRINT *,' This male is both a heavy drinker'
          1                        //' and a heavy smoker: '
                             WRITE(*,'(/A20,1X,I2,1X,A1,1X,A25,1X,A7,1X,I4,1X,I3
          1                        /)')NAME,AGE,SEX,ADDRES,STATUS,UNITS,CIGS
                          ENDIF
                       ELSE
                          PRINT *,'***Error - invalid number of cigarettes/day'
                          PRINT *,'The following record has been ignored:'
                          WRITE(*,'(A20,1X,I2,1X,A1,1X,A25,1X,A7,1X,I4,1X,I3)')
          1                    NAME,AGE,SEX,ADDRES,STATUS,UNITS,CIGS
                       ENDIF
                    ELSE
                       PRINT *,'***Error - Invalid sex ',SEX
                       PRINT *,'The following record has been ignored:'
                       WRITE(*,'(A20,1X,I2,1X,A1,1X,A25,1X,A7,1X,I4,1X,I3)')
          1                 NAME,AGE,SEX,ADDRES,STATUS,UNITS,CIGS
                    ENDIF
                 ELSE
      *
      * Print table of results
      *
                 WRITE(*,'('' FEMALE DRINKERS:''/)')
                 WRITE(*,'(''           LIGHT       '',I5)')FLDCNT
                 WRITE(*,'(''           MODERATE    '',I5)')FMDCNT
                 WRITE(*,'(''           HEAVY       '',I5)')FHDCNT
                 WRITE(*,'(/'' FEMALE SMOKERS:''/)')
                 WRITE(*,'(''           LIGHT       '',I5)')FLSCNT
                 WRITE(*,'(''           MODERATE    '',I5)')FMSCNT
                 WRITE(*,'(''           HEAVY       '',I5)')FHSCNT
                 WRITE(*,'(/'' MALE DRINKERS:''/)')
                 WRITE(*,'(''           LIGHT       '',I5)')MLDCNT
                 WRITE(*,'(''           MODERATE    '',I5)')MMDCNT
                 WRITE(*,'(''           HEAVY       '',I5)')MHDCNT
                 WRITE(*,'(/'' MALE SMOKERS:''/)')
                 WRITE(*,'(''           LIGHT       '',I5)')MLSCNT
                 WRITE(*,'(''           MODERATE    '',I5)')MMSCNT
                 WRITE(*,'(''           HEAVY       '',I5)')MHSCNT
                 STOP
              ENDIF
       10     CONTINUE
              PRINT *,'***Error - Too many data records for program'
              STOP
              END
```

3.

```
              PROGRAM PLOT
              INTEGER I,J,M,NOSP
              REAL X
              CHARACTER CH(120),AST,BL
              DATA AST,BL/'*',' '/
              J = 10
      *
      * Print Graph Title and mark ordinates
      *
              WRITE(7,'(''1''/'' COSINE GRAPH ''//10X,''-1'',22X,''-0.5'',23X,
          1          ''0'',23X,''0.5'',23X,''1''/11X,''!'',4(24X,''!''))')
              DO 20, I = 1,41
      *
      * Set up 0.05 increments for X
      *
                 X = REAL(I-1)*0.05
                 IF (J .NE. 10)THEN
      *
      * Draw the axis
```

```
*
              J = J+1
              WRITE(7,'(61X,''¦'')')
         ELSE
*
* Mark the 0, pi/2, pi etc. axes
*
              J = 1
              WRITE(7,'(11X,''+'',2(24X,''+''),F4.2,20X,''+'',24X,''+''
    1                )')X
         ENDIF
*
* Set character array to spaces
*
         DO 10, M = 1,120
              CH(M) = BL
  10     CONTINUE
*
* Compute COS(X) and calculate the number of spaces required to
* print this value at the correct position
*
         NOSP = 61.5 + 50.0*COS(X)
         CH(NOSP) = AST
*
* Overprint this on the current line
*
         WRITE(7,'(''+'',120A1)')CH
  20     CONTINUE
         STOP
         END
```

4. The structure plan for this might read as follows:

Initialize integer part, fractional part and exponent to 0
Read and ignore leading spaces
If sign is present then
        save it
else
        set sign to plus
endif
Do until decimal point
        Read a digit or space
        Convert to its numeric equivalent
        Multiply the current value of integer part by 10
        Add the current number
End do until decimal point
Ignore the decimal point
Do until end of line or until E or e found
        Read a digit or space
        Increment digit counter
        Convert to its numeric equivalent
        Multiply the current value of fractional part by 10
        Add the current number
End do until end of line or until E or e found

If E or e found then
    Ignore E
    If sign present then
        save exponent sign
    else
        set exponent sign to plus
    endif
    Do until end of line
        Read a digit or space
        Convert to its numeric equivalent
        Multiply the current value of the exponent by 10
        Add the current number
    End do until end of line
endif
Compute the value of the floating point number
Print it

This might be implemented as follows

```
      PROGRAM CONVRT
*
* A program which converts a character representation of a floating
* point number to its equivalent numeric value
*
      INTEGER INTPT,FRACPT,EXPON,FCOUNT,SIGN,ESIGN,I,J
      CHARACTER*80 IPLINE
      CHARACTER*1 CHAR
      REAL REALN
      LOGICAL START
      DATA INTPT,FRACPT,EXPON,FCOUNT/4*0/START/.FALSE./ESIGN/1/
      PRINT *,'Enter a floating point number: '
      READ *,IPLINE
      DO 10, I = 1,80
          CHAR = IPLINE(I:I)
*
* Error if input line is blank
*
          IF (IPLINE(I:80) .EQ. ' ')GOTO 70
*
* Ignore leading spaces and search for sign or first digit
*
          IF (.NOT.START)THEN
            IF (CHAR .EQ. ' ')THEN
                GOTO 10
            ELSE IF (CHAR .EQ. '-')THEN
                SIGN = -1
            ELSE IF (CHAR .EQ. '+')THEN
                SIGN = 1
            ELSE IF (CHAR .GE. '0' .AND. CHAR .LE. '9')THEN
                SIGN = 1
                INTPT = INTPT*10 + ICHAR(CHAR)-ICHAR('0')
            ELSE
                GOTO 70
            ENDIF
            START = .TRUE.
            GOTO 10
```

```
*
* Once the start of the number has been found, assemble the integer part
*
          ELSE IF (CHAR .GE. '0' .AND. CHAR .LE. '9')THEN
              INTPT = INTPT*10 + ICHAR(CHAR)-ICHAR('0')
          ELSE IF (CHAR .EQ. ' ') THEN
              INTPT = INTPT*10
          ELSE IF (CHAR .EQ. '.') THEN
            START = .FALSE.
            GOTO 20
          ELSE
            GOTO 70
          ENDIF
   10   CONTINUE
        GOTO 70
*
* Now assemble the fractional part
*
   20   DO 30, J = I+1,80
          CHAR = IPLINE(J:J)
          IF (IPLINE(J:80) .EQ. ' ')THEN
            GOTO 60
          ELSE IF (CHAR .EQ. 'E' .OR. CHAR .EQ. 'e')THEN
            GOTO 40
          ELSE IF (CHAR .GE. '0' .AND. CHAR .LE. '9')THEN
            FRACPT = FRACPT*10 + ICHAR(CHAR)-ICHAR('0')
            FCOUNT = FCOUNT + 1
          ELSE IF (CHAR .EQ. ' ')THEN
            FRACPT = FRACPT*10
            FCOUNT = FCOUNT + 1
          ELSE
            GOTO 70
          ENDIF
   30   CONTINUE
        GOTO 70
*
* Now assemble the exponent
*
   40   DO 50, I = J+1,80
          CHAR = IPLINE(I:I)
          IF (IPLINE(I:80) .EQ. ' ')GOTO 60
          IF (.NOT.START)THEN
              IF (CHAR .EQ. ' ')THEN
                  GOTO 50
              ELSE IF (CHAR .EQ. '-')THEN
                  ESIGN = -1
              ELSE IF (CHAR .EQ. '+')THEN
                  ESIGN = 1
              ELSE IF (CHAR .GE. '0' .AND. CHAR .LE. '9')THEN
                  ESIGN = 1
                  EXPON = EXPON*10 + ICHAR(CHAR)-ICHAR('0')
              ELSE
                  GOTO 70
              ENDIF
              START = .TRUE.
              GOTO 50
          ELSE IF (CHAR .GE. '0' .AND. CHAR .LE. '9')THEN
              EXPON = EXPON*10 + ICHAR(CHAR)-ICHAR('0')
          ELSE IF (CHAR .EQ. ' ')THEN
              EXPON = EXPON*10
          ELSE
              GOTO 70
          ENDIF
   50   CONTINUE
*
* Print the resulting numeric value
*
```

```
60    REALN = SIGN*REAL(INTPT*10**FCOUNT + FRACPT)/(10.0**FCOUNT)
      REALN = REALN*10.0**(ESIGN*EXPON)
      WRITE(*,'('' The real number is: '',E14.4)')REALN
      STOP
70    PRINT *,'***Error - Invalid format: ',IPLINE
      STOP
      END
```

5.

```
      PROGRAM SATLIT
*
* A program to calculate the orbital speed of an artificial satellite
*
      INTEGER I
      REAL SPEED(250),DAYS(250),HEIGHT(250),RADIUS(250)
      DO 10, I = 1,250
         HEIGHT(I) = REAL(I)*1000.0
         RADIUS(I) = HEIGHT(I) + 3960.0
         SPEED(I)  = SQRT(1.44E12/RADIUS(I))
         DAYS(I)   = (2.0*3.1416*RADIUS(I)/SPEED(I))/24.0
10    CONTINUE
      WRITE(*,'(5X,''HEIGHT'',14X,''SPEED'',4X,''ORBIT TIME''/
     1         4X,''(MILES)'',4X,''(MILES PER HOUR)'',6X,''(DAYS)''/
     2         (F11.3,8X,F11.3,3X,F11.3))')
     3         (HEIGHT(I),SPEED(I),DAYS(I),I = 1,250)
      STOP
      END
```

Exercises 7

1. The invalid I/O statements are:
   (a) The Unit and Format specifiers must be prefixed with **UNIT**= and **FMT**= if they are not the first and second specifiers of the **READ** or **WRITE** statement.
   (c) **INQUIRE** cannot be used to inquire by name and by unit at the same time.
   (d) The **RECL** specifier must only be used when a file is connected for direct access otherwise it must be omitted.

2. This program will write its results to a sequential access file on unit 6:

```
      PROGRAM FTOC
      INTEGER I,J,ERR
      REAL C(100)
      DO 10, I = 1,100
         C(I) = (REAL(I) - 32.0)*5.0/9.0
10    CONTINUE
      OPEN(UNIT=6,FILE='DEGTAB',ERR=30,IOSTAT=ERR)
      WRITE(6,'(12X,''TABLE OF DEGREES FAHRENHEIT AND CENTIGRADE''//)')
      WRITE(6,'(5(''    F      C''))')
      DO 20, I = 1,20
            WRITE(6,'(5(I5,F7.2))')(I+J,C(I+J),J = 0,80,20)
20    CONTINUE
      CLOSE(6)
      STOP
30    PRINT *,'***OPEN Error ',ERR,' on unit 6'
      STOP
      END
```

3.

```
      PROGRAM SORT
      INTEGER I,N,COUNT,J
      INTEGER INTVAL,ERR1
      CHARACTER*80 NAMES(1000),TEMP
      OPEN(UNIT=5,FILE='UNSORTED',ERR=100,IOSTAT=ERR1)
      OPEN(UNIT=6,FILE='SORTED',ERR=110,IOSTAT=ERR1)
      READ (UNIT=5,FMT='(I5)',ERR=120,IOSTAT=ERR1)N
      DO 10, I = 1,N
          READ (UNIT=5,FMT='(A80)',ERR=120,IOSTAT=ERR1)NAMES(I)
10    CONTINUE
      INTVAL = N/2
      DO 40, COUNT = 1,1000
         IF (INTVAL .LE. 0)GOTO 50
         DO 30, I = INTVAL,N-1
            DO 20, J = I - INTVAL+1,1,-INTVAL
               IF (NAMES(J) .GT. NAMES(J+INTVAL))THEN
                  TEMP = NAMES(J)
                  NAMES(J) = NAMES(J+INTVAL)
                  NAMES(J+INTVAL) = TEMP
               ENDIF
20          CONTINUE
30       CONTINUE
         INTVAL = INTVAL/2
40    CONTINUE
50    DO 60, I = 1,N
         WRITE(UNIT=6,FMT='(A80)',ERR=130,IOSTAT=ERR1)NAMES(I)
60    CONTINUE
      CLOSE(5)
      CLOSE(6)
      STOP
100   PRINT *,'***OPEN Error ',ERR1,' on unit 5'
      STOP
110   PRINT *,'***OPEN Error ',ERR1,' on unit 6'
      STOP
120   PRINT *,'***READ Error ',ERR1,' on unit 5'
      STOP
130   PRINT *,'***WRITE Error ',ERR1,' on unit 6'
      STOP
      END
```

4. The structural specification for this program might read as follows:

Open the weekly payroll file
Open the master file
Open the pay slip file
Do until end of weekly payroll file
    Read a record
    Calculate the gross pay for this week
    Search the master file for a record with the same employee
        number
    Calculate tax
    Calculate net pay
    Update the master file with net pay and number of hours
        worked
    Print the pay slip for this week
End do until end of weekly payroll file

Close all files
Stop
End

File handling is the area in which individual compilers are most likely to depart from the ANSI standard. The above program has been implemented in the following way on one particular machine:

```
      PROGRAM PAYROL
*
* A program to read weekly pay data from a file on unit 5, to
  update a master file on unit 6 and to print weekly payslips
* on unit 7.
*
      INTEGER EMPNO,MEMPNO,N,I,J,ERR1
      REAL RATE,WKHRS,WKGROS
      REAL TOTHRS,GROSS,TOTNET,ALLOW,WKALL
      REAL TAX,TAXINC,WKNET
      CHARACTER*20 EMPNAM
      OPEN(UNIT=5,FILE='WEEKLY',ERR=100,IOSTAT=ERR1)
      OPEN(UNIT=6,FILE='MASTER',ERR=110,IOSTAT=ERR1,
     1     ACCESS='DIRECT',FORM='FORMATTED',RECL=80)
      OPEN(UNIT=7,FILE='PAY',ERR=120,IOSTAT=ERR1)
      N = 10000
      DO 30, I = 1,N
*
* Read employee number and number of hours worked this week
*
      READ(5,'(I5,F6.2)',END=40,ERR=130,IOSTAT=ERR1)EMPNO,WKHRS
      DO 10, J = 1,N
*
* Locate the record for this employee in the master file
*
          READ(6,'(I5,A20,5F8.2)',REC=J,ERR=25,IOSTAT=ERR1)
     1          MEMPNO,EMPNAM,ALLOW,RATE,GROSS,TOTNET,TOTHRS
          IF (MEMPNO .EQ. EMPNO)GOTO 20
 10   CONTINUE
*
* Calculate the gross pay for this week
*
 20       IF (WKHRS .GT. 40.0)THEN
              WKGROS = RATE*40.0 + (WKHRS-40.0)*RATE*1.5
          ELSE
              WKGROS = WKHRS*RATE
          ENDIF
*
* Compute the net pay for this week
*
      WKALL = ALLOW/52.0
      TAXINC = WKGROS - WKALL
      TAX = 30.0*TAXINC/100.0
      WKNET = WKGROS-TAX
*
* Print the pay slip
*
      WRITE(7,'(I5,A20,4F8.2)',ERR=150,IOSTAT=ERR1)
     1          EMPNO,EMPNAM,WKHRS,TAX,WKGROS,WKNET
      GROSS = GROSS + WKGROS
      TOTNET = TOTNET + WKNET
      TOTHRS = TOTHRS + WKHRS
*
* Update the master file
*
```

```
         WRITE(6,'(I5,A20,5F8.2)',REC=J,ERR=160,IOSTAT=ERR1)
      1          EMPNO,EMPNAM,ALLOW,RATE,GROSS,TOTNET,TOTHRS
         GOTO 30
25       IF (ERR1 .GE. 0)GOTO 140
         PRINT *,'***No entry in Master file for this employee'
         PRINT *,'Record ignored for employee: ',EMPNO
30       CONTINUE
40       CLOSE(UNIT=5)
         CLOSE(UNIT=6)
         CLOSE(UNIT=7)
         STOP
100      PRINT *,'***OPEN error ',ERR1,' on unit5, file WEEKLY'
         STOP
110      PRINT *,'***OPEN error ',ERR1,' on unit6, file MASTER'
         STOP
120      PRINT *,'***OPEN error ',ERR1,' on unit7, file PAY'
         STOP
130      PRINT *,'***READ error ',ERR1,' on unit5, file WEEKLY'
         PRINT *,'Trying to read Employee number and Hours worked'
         STOP
140      PRINT *,'***READ error ',ERR1,' on unit6, file MASTER'
         PRINT *,'Trying to read the complete record'
         STOP
150      PRINT *,'***WRITE error ',ERR1,' on unit7, file PAY'
         PRINT *,'Trying to write the complete record'
         STOP
160      PRINT *,'***WRITE error ',ERR1,' on unit6, file MASTER'
         PRINT *,'Trying to write the complete record'
         STOP
         END
```

5. The structural specification for this program might read as follows:

```
Open Customer file
Open Bank account file
Do until end of Bank account file
    Read a record
    If balance < 0 then
        Do until end of customer file
            Read a record
            If customer numbers are equal then
                Read permitted overdraft
                If balance > permitted overdraft then
                    Print name and address of customer
                Endif
            Endif
        End do until end of customer file
    Endif
End do until end of Bank account file
Close all files
Stop
End
```

The program for this might be implemented as follows:

```
      PROGRAM BANK
*
* A program to identify customers whose bank account balance
* has exceeded their permitted overdraft.
*
      INTEGER ACNUM,CUSNO1,CUSNO2,I,J,N,ERR1
      REAL BAL,OVER
      CHARACTER*20 CUSNAM
      CHARACTER*30 CUSADD
      OPEN(UNIT=5,FILE='BALNCE',ERR=100,IOSTAT=ERR1)
      OPEN(UNIT=6,FILE='CUSTOM',ERR=110,IOSTAT=ERR1)
      OPEN(UNIT=7,FILE='EXCEED',ERR=120,IOSTAT=ERR1)
      N = 10000
      DO 20, I = 1,N
*
* Read a customer account record
*
         READ(5,'(I5,F8.2)',END=30,ERR=130,IOSTAT=ERR1)CUSNO1,BAL
         IF (BAL .LT. 0)THEN
            DO 10, J = 1,N
*
* If the balance is negative, read the customer record
*
               READ(6,'(I5,A20,A30,F8.2)',ERR=15,IOSTAT=ERR1)
     1               CUSNO2,CUSNAM,CUSADD,OVER
               IF (CUSNO1 .EQ. CUSNO2)THEN
*
* Check if the customer has exceeded the permitted overdraft
*
                  IF (-BAL .GT. OVER)THEN
*
* If so, write out this customer's record
*
                     WRITE(7,'(I5,A20,A30,2F9.2)',ERR=150,IOSTAT=ERR1)
     1                     CUSNO1,CUSNAM,CUSADD,BAL,OVER
                  ENDIF
                  REWIND(6)
                  GOTO 20
               ENDIF
10          CONTINUE
15          IF (ERR1 .GE. 0)GOTO 140
            PRINT *,'***No record for customer: ',CUSNO1
         ENDIF
20    CONTINUE
30    PRINT *,'***Processing complete'
      STOP
*
* Error messages
*
100   PRINT *,'***OPEN error ',ERR1,' on unit5 file BALNCE'
      STOP
110   PRINT *,'***OPEN error ',ERR1,' on unit6 file CUSTOM'
      STOP
120   PRINT *,'***OPEN error ',ERR1,' on unit7 file EXCEED'
      STOP
130   PRINT *,'***READ error ',ERR1,' on unit5 file BALNCE'
      PRINT *,'Trying to read Customer number and Balance'
      STOP
140   PRINT *,'***READ error ',ERR1,' on unit6 file CUSTOM'
      PRINT *,'Trying to read Customer number, name, address'
     1        //' and permitted overdraft'
      STOP
150   PRINT *,'***WRITE error ',ERR1,' on unit7 file EXCEED'
      PRINT *,'Trying to read the complete record'
      STOP
      END
```

Exercises 8

1. The subroutine requires two real arguments for input and a real argument for output.

    (a) The first argument is an integer.

    (b) The last argument is an integer.

    (c) Only two arguments are provided.

    (d) A constant is used as an actual output argument.

2. (a)

```
      SUBROUTINE MERGE(IN1,IN2,N1,N2,NOUT,OUT)
      INTEGER IN1(N1),IN2(N2),OUT(*)
      INTEGER IP0,IP1,IP2,NOUT
      IP0 = 1
      IP1 = 1
      IP2 = 1
10    IF (IP2 .GT. N2 .OR. IN1(P1) .LT. IN2(P2)) THEN
         OUT(IP0) = IN1(IP1)
         IP1 = IP1 + 1
      ELSE IF (IP1 .GT. N1 .OR. IN1(IP1) .GT. IN2(IP2)) THEN
         OUT(IP0) = IN2(IP2)
         IP2 = IP2 + 1
      ELSE IF (IN1(IP1) .EQ. IN2(IP2)) THEN
         OUT(IP0) = IN2(IP2)
         IP1 = IP1 + 1
         IP2 = IP2 + 1
      END IF
      IF (IP0 .EQ. 1 .OR. OUT(IP0) .GT. OUT(IP0-1)) THEN
         IP0 = IP0 + 1
      END IF
      IF (IP1 .LT. N1 .OR. IP2 .LT. N2) GOTO 10
      NOUT = IP0 - 1
      RETURN
      END
```

    (b)

```
      PROGRAM FMERGE
      INTEGER IN1(100),N1,IN2(100),IN2,OUT(200),NO,I
      READ *,N1,(IN1(I),I=1,N1),N2,(IN2(I),I=1,N2)
      CALL MERGE(IN1,IN2,N1,N2,NO,OUT)
      PRINT *,NO,(OUT(I),I = 1,NO)
      STOP
      END
```

    (c)

```
      PROGRAM FMERGE
      INTEGER MAIN(500),NEXT(100),SPARE(500),NMAIN,NNEXT,NSPARE
      INTEGER N,I,J
      READ *,N
      READ *,NMAIN,(MAIN(I), I = 1,NMAIN)
      J = 2
10    READ *,NNEXT,(NEXT(I), I = 1,NNEXT)
      CALL MERGE(MAIN,NEXT,NMAIN,NNEXT,NSPARE,SPARE)
      DO 20, I = 1,NSPARE
         MAIN(I) = SPARE(I)
20    CONTINUE
      NMAIN = NSPARE
      J    = J + 1
      IF (J .LE. N) GOTO 10
      PRINT *,NMAIN,(MAIN(I), I = 1,NMAIN)
      STOP
      END
```

3.

```
      SUBROUTINE GETWD(IPLINE,PTR,WORD)
      INTEGER PTR,I,J
      CHARACTER*80 IPLINE,CHAR,WORD
      LOGICAL WORDST
      WORDST = .FALSE.
      J = 1
      WORD = ' '
      DO 10, I = PTR,80
         IF (IPLINE(I:80) .EQ. ' ')THEN
            PTR = -1
            RETURN
         ENDIF
         CHAR = IPLINE(I:I)
         IF (CHAR .GE. 'A' .AND. CHAR .LE. 'Z' .OR.
     1      CHAR .GE. 'a' .AND. CHAR .LE. 'z') THEN
            IF (WORDST) THEN
               GETWD(J:J) = CHAR
               J = J + 1
            ELSE
               WORDST = .TRUE.
               WORD(J:J) = CHAR
               J = J + 1
            ENDIF
         ELSE IF (WORDST) THEN
            GOTO 20
         ENDIF
10    CONTINUE
20    PTR = I
      RETURN
      END
```

4.

```
      PROGRAM SORT2
      INTEGER I,N,J
      INTEGER ERR1
      CHARACTER*80 NAMES(1000),TEMP
      OPEN(UNIT=5,FILE='UNSORTED',ERR=100,IOSTAT=ERR1)
      OPEN(UNIT=6,FILE='SORTED',ERR=110,IOSTAT=ERR1)
      READ (UNIT=5,FMT='(I5)',ERR=120,IOSTAT=ERR1)N
      DO 10, I = 1,N
         READ (UNIT=5,FMT='(A80)',ERR=120,IOSTAT=ERR1)NAMES(I)
10    CONTINUE
      CALL SORT(NAMES,N)
      DO 20, I = 1,N
         WRITE(UNIT=6,FMT='(A80)',ERR=130,IOSTAT=ERR1)NAMES(I)
20    CONTINUE
      CLOSE(5)
      CLOSE(6)
      STOP
100   PRINT *,'***OPEN Error ',ERR1,' on unit 5'
      STOP
110   PRINT *,'***OPEN Error ',ERR1,' on unit 6'
      STOP
120   PRINT *,'***READ Error ',ERR1,' on unit 5'
      STOP
130   PRINT *,'***WRITE Error ',ERR1,' on unit 6'
      STOP
      END

      SUBROUTINE SORT(ARRAY,N)
      INTEGER N,I,J
      CHARACTER*80 ARRAY(N),TEMP
      INTEGER INTVAL,COUNT
      INTVAL = N/2
```

```
        DO 30, COUNT = 1,N
           IF (INTVAL .LE. 0)RETURN
           DO 20, I = INTVAL,N-1
              DO 10, J = I - INTVAL+1,1,-INTVAL
                 IF (ARRAY(J) .GT. ARRAY(J+INTVAL))THEN
                    TEMP = ARRAY(J)
                    ARRAY(J) = ARRAY(J+INTVAL)
                    ARRAY(J+INTVAL) = TEMP
                 ENDIF
10            CONTINUE
20         CONTINUE
           INTVAL = INTVAL/2
30      CONTINUE
        RETURN
        END
```

5.

```
        PROGRAM HASHIT
        CHARACTER* 80 NAME
        INTEGER HASHVL,I
        DO 10, I = 1,1000
           PRINT *,'Enter name to be hashed(or 999 to stop): '
           READ (*,'(A80)')NAME
           IF (NAME .EQ. '999')STOP
           HASHVL = HASH(NAME)
           PRINT *,'The hashed value of ',NAME,' is ',HASHVL
10      CONTINUE
        STOP
        END

        INTEGER FUNCTION HASH(NAME)
        CHARACTER*(*) NAME
        INTEGER I
        HASH = 0
        DO 10, I = 1,80
           IF (NAME(I:I) .EQ. ' ')GOTO 20
           HASH = HASH + ICHAR(NAME(I:I))
10      CONTINUE
20      HASH = MOD(HASH,255)
        RETURN
        END
```

Exercises 9

1. In Subroutine SUB1:
   (a) The character variable **CHAR** should not be mixed with other types in blank **COMMON**.
   (b) The declaration for D should be placed before the **COMMON** statement and not after it.
   (c) The **DIMENSION** statement should be placed before the **COMMON** statement and not after it.
   (d) The array A2 should not be dimensioned in both a **COMMON** statement and a **DIMENSION** statement.

   In Subroutine SUB2:
   (a) The real variable Y is not declared in blank **COMMON**.
   (b) The character variable **CHAR** should not be mixed with other types in blank **COMMON**.

(c) The array A2 is not typed or dimensioned.

(d) The variable D is not declared to be Double Precision.

(e) The **COMMON** block B2 is of a different size from the same block in SUB1.

2. The values printed by the **PRINT** statement will be as follows:

   ????   18.45   3.69   36.9   10

   Since the variable **ARG1** is local to **SUB1**, it will have no known value in the main program. This will either cause an error or will result in some random value being printed out (represented by ???? in the statement above); this may be 0 on machines that clear memory before execution.

3.

```
      PROGRAM SORT 2
      INTEGER I,N,J
      INTEGER ERR1
      CHARACTER*80 NAMES,TEMP
      COMMON N,/B1/NAMES(1000)
      OPEN(UNIT=5,FILE='UNSORTED',ERR=100,IOSTAT=ERR1)
      OPEN(UNIT=6,FILE='SORTED',ERR=110,IOSTAT=ERR1)
      READ (UNIT=5,FMT='(I5)',ERR=120,IOSTAT=ERR1)N
      DO 10, I = 1,N
         READ (UNIT=5,FMT='(A80)',ERR=120,IOSTAT=ERR1)NAMES(I)
10    CONTINUE
      CALL SORT
      DO 20, I = 1,N
         WRITE(UNIT=6,FMT='(A80)',ERR=130,IOSTAT=ERR1)NAMES(I)
20    CONTINUE
      CLOSE(5)
      CLOSE(6)
      STOP
100   PRINT *,'***OPEN Error ',ERR1,' on unit 5'
      STOP
110   PRINT *,'***OPEN Error ',ERR1,' on unit 6'
      STOP
120   PRINT *,'***READ Error ',ERR1,' on unit 5'
      STOP
130   PRINT *,'***WRITE Error ',ERR1,' on unit 6'
      STOP
      END

      SUBROUTINE SORT
      INTEGER N,I,J
      CHARACTER*80 ARRAY(1000),TEMP
      INTEGER INTVAL,COUNT
      COMMON N,/B1/ARRAY
      INTVAL = N/2
      DO 30, COUNT = 1,N
         IF (INTVAL .LE. 0)RETURN
         DO 20, I = INTVAL,N-1
            DO 10, J = I - INTVAL+1,1,-INTVAL
               IF (ARRAY(J) .GT. ARRAY(J+INTVAL))THEN
                  TEMP = ARRAY(J)
                  ARRAY(J) = ARRAY(J+INTVAL)
                  ARRAY(J+INTVAL) = TEMP
               ENDIF
10          CONTINUE
20       CONTINUE
         INTVAL = INTVAL/2
```

```
 30     CONTINUE
        RETURN
        END
```

4.

```
        PROGRAM DATES
*
* A program to compute the date which is N days after a given day
*
        INTEGER DAYS(12),I,DAY,MONTH,YEAR,N,ZERO
        CHARACTER*10 DATE1,DATE2
        COMMON DAY,MONTH,YEAR,DAYS,N,ZERO
        COMMON/C1/DATE2
*
* Set up the number of days in each month
*
        DO 10, I = 1,12
           DAYS(I) = 31
 10     CONTINUE
        DAYS(4) = 30
        DAYS(6) = 30
        DAYS(9) = 30
        DAYS(11)= 30 *
* Read the required date
*
        PRINT *,'Enter the date (dd/mm/yyyy): '
        READ (*,'(A10)')DATE1
        PRINT *,'Enter the number of days: '
        READ *,N
        ZERO = ICHAR('0')
        DAY   = (ICHAR(DATE1(1:1))-ZERO)*10+(ICHAR(DATE1(2:2))-ZERO)
        MONTH = (ICHAR(DATE1(4:4))-ZERO)*10+(ICHAR(DATE1(5:5))-ZERO)
        YEAR  = (ICHAR(DATE1(7:7))-ZERO)*10+(ICHAR(DATE1(8:8))-ZERO)
        YEAR  = YEAR*10 + (ICHAR(DATE1(9:9))-ZERO)
        YEAR  = YEAR*10 + (ICHAR(DATE1(10:10))-ZERO)
        CALL DATE
        WRITE(*,'('' The day which is '',I4,'' days after this date is: ''
       1         ,A10)')N,DATE2
        STOP
        END


        SUBROUTINE DATE
*
* A subroutine which computes the date which is N days after a
* given date. All data are passed via COMMON.
*
        INTEGER DAY,MONTH,YEAR,DAYS(12),CENT,NYEAR,N,ZERO
        CHARACTER*10 DATE2
        COMMON DAY,MONTH,YEAR,DAYS,N,ZERO
*       COMMON/C1/DATE2
* First determine whether the year is a leap year
*
        IF (MOD(YEAR,400) .EQ. 0 .OR.
       1    MOD(YEAR,4) .EQ. 0 .AND. MOD(YEAR,100) .NE. 0) THEN
           DAYS(2) = 29
        ELSE
           DAYS(2) = 28
        ENDIF
*
* Compute the century and year
*
        CENT  = YEAR/100
        NYEAR = YEAR - (CENT*100)
*
```

```
* Compute the day N days hence
*
      DAY = DAY + N
*
* Check if this crosses a month boundary
*
      IF (DAY .GT. DAYS(MONTH)) THEN
          DAY = DAY - DAYS(MONTH)
*
* Check if this crosses a year boundary
*
          IF (MONTH .EQ. 12) THEN
              MONTH = 1
*
* Check if this crosses a century boundary
*
              IF (NYEAR .EQ. 99) THEN
                  CENT  = CENT + 1
                  NYEAR = 0
              ELSE
                  NYEAR = NYEAR + 1
              ENDIF
          ELSE
              MONTH = MONTH + 1
          ENDIF
      ENDIF
*
* Now re-assemble the date
*
      DATE2 = CHAR(DAY/10+ZERO)//
     1        CHAR(MOD(DAY,10)+ZERO)//'/'//
     2        CHAR(MONTH/10+ZERO)//
     3        CHAR(MOD(MONTH,10)+ZERO)//'/'//
     4        CHAR(CENT/10+ZERO)//
     5        CHAR(MOD(CENT,10)+ZERO)//
     6        CHAR(NYEAR/10+ZERO)//
     7        CHAR(MOD(NYEAR,10)+ZERO)
      RETURN
      END
```

5.

```
      PROGRAM AIRPRT
      INTEGER N1,N2,N3,PASS1,PASS2,PASS3,TYPE,NPLANE,NPASS
      COMMON/B1/ N1,N2,N3,PASS1,PASS2,PASS3,TYPE
   10 PRINT *,'Enter aircraft type 1, 2 or 3 (0 to end): '
      READ *,TYPE
      IF (TYPE .LT. 0 .OR. TYPE .GT. 3)THEN
          PRINT *,'***Error invalid aircraft type: ',TYPE
      ELSE IF (TYPE .EQ. 0)THEN
          NPLANE = N1 + N2 + N3
          NPASS  = PASS1 + PASS2 + PASS3
          WRITE(*,'('' Total Number of Aircraft: '',I5)')NPLANE
          WRITE(*,'('' Total Number of Passengers: '',I5)')NPASS
          STOP
      ELSE
          CALL COUNT
      ENDIF
      GOTO 10
      END



      SUBROUTINE COUNT
      INTEGER N1,N2,N3,PASS1,PASS2,PASS3,TYPE
      COMMON/B1/ N1,N2,N3,PASS1,PASS2,PASS3,TYPE
```

```
      IF (TYPE .EQ. 1)THEN
         N1 = N1 + 1
         PASS1 = PASS1 + 135
         WRITE(*,'('' Type: '',I5,'' Aircraft: '',I5,'' Passengers: '',
     1          I5/)')TYPE,N1,PASS1
      ELSE IF (TYPE .EQ. 2)THEN
         N2 = N2 + 1
         PASS2 = PASS2 + 240
         WRITE(*,'('' Type: '',I5,'' Aircraft: '',I5,'' Passengers: '',
     1          I5/)')TYPE,N2,PASS2
      ELSE IF (TYPE .EQ. 3)THEN
         N3 = N3 + 1
         PASS3 = PASS3 + 412
         WRITE(*,'('' Type: '',I5,'' Aircraft: '',I5,'' Passengers: '',
     1          I5/)')TYPE,N3,PASS3
      ENDIF
      RETURN
      END
      BLOCK DATA
      INTEGER N1,N2,N3,PASS1,PASS2,PASS3
      COMMON/B1/N1,N2,N3,PASS1,PASS2,PASS3
      DATA N1,N2,N3,PASS1,PASS2,PASS3/6*0/
      END
```

Index

ACCESS = 37–40, 149
Accumulator 3
Accuracy 20, 90
Actual Argument 156, 164
Address 2
Adjustable dimensions 167, 173
A format 122
Algorithm 3–5
Alphabet 13
Alphanumeric Character 13
Alternate Entry 170
Alternate Return 171
American National Standards Institute
   (ANSI) 9
AND 47
Apostropha 13, 82, 121
Argument
  actual 156, 164
  dummy 156, 164
Arithmetic
  assignment 33, 40
  constant 15
  expression 29, 40
  operand 29
  operator 29, 40
Arithmetic IF 54
Arithmetic unit 3
Array
  adjustable 167
  assumed size 168
  declarator 70, 76, 81
  dimensions 70, 78
  element 71
  names 70
  storage sequence 74
ASCII 21, 84, 198
ASSIGN 56

Assigned GOTO 56
Assignment statement
  arithmetic 33, 40
  character 83
  logical 93
  statement label 56
Assumed size array 168
Asterisk
  as array bound 168
  as character string length 81, 83, 168
  as default I/O unit 25, 104
  as dummy argument 171
  in list-directed I/O 25, 112

Backing store 3
BACKSPACE 146, 149
Binary 19
BLANK = 137, 149
Blank COMMON 178–82, 190
Block DATA subprogram 184, 190
Block IF 43–7, 57
BN format 120
Bound, upper and lower of array 70,
  73, 76, 77
Byte 2, 82
BZ format 120

CALL statement 162–5, 171, 174
Carriage control characters 124
Central memory 1–3
Central processing unit 3
Character
  alphanumeric 13
  assignment 83
  comparison 86
  constant 82
  expression 85

function 87, 160, 196
I/O 121–24
length 85
operator 85
relational expression 86
set 13
string 82, 86
substring 86
type 82–90
variable 83
CHARACTER declaration 83, 101
CLOSE 138
Collating sequence 85
Colon editing 126
Columns 10
Comment 11, 22
COMMON
blank 178–82, 190
initialization 184
named 182, 190
Comparison of real values 50
Compiler 8
Complex constants 92
COMPLEX declaration 92, 101
Computed GOTO 55
Constants
arithmetic 17
character 82
complex 92
double precision 90
Hollerith 123
integer 17
logical 93
real 17
symbolic name of 96
Connection 136
CONTINUE 64, 77
Continuation line 10, 22
Control list 105
Control statement 43, 51, 56
Control variable of a DO loop 61
Currency symbol 13

Data record 109–12
DATA statement 97, 102
Debug 37
Declarations 80, 153
Device, input/output 3, 25, 104

D format 120
DIMENSION statement 76, 78
Direct access I/O 133, 137, 148
DIRECT = 137, 149
DO
implied 115
loop 60, 77
statement 60, 77
DOUBLE PRECISION
constants 90
declaration 91, 101
Dummy argument 156, 164, 173

EBCDIC 21, 84, 199
E format 118
Element of array 71
ELSE statement 44, 57
ELSE IF statement 45, 57
END 14, 22, 173
END = 135, 148
ENDFILE 145, 149
END IF statement 44, 57
ENTRY 170
Entry point 163, 170
EQ 47
EQV 47
EQUIVALENCE 187, 190
ERR = 134, 148, 149
Execution of program 9
Executable statement 14
EXIST = 140, 149
Exponant 17
Exponentiation 29
Expression
arithmetic 29, 40
character 85
logical 93
mixed 99
relational 43, 47
EXTERNAL statement 165, 173

F format 118
Field width 117–26
File 133, 148
FILE = 136, 149
File pointer 134
Floating point 18
FMT = 105, 130

FORM = 137, 140, 149
FORMAT statement 108, 130
Format specifications
  A 122
  BN 120
  BZ 120
  colon 126
  D 120
  E 118
  F 118
  G 119
  H 123
  I 117
  L 125
  P 127
  S 120
  SP 120
  SS 120
  slash 125
  T 126
  TL 126
  TR 126
  X 121
FORMATED = 140, 149
Formatted
  I/O statements 104–28, 130
  READ 105, 130
  WRITE 106, 130
FORTRAN
  development 9
  standards 9
Function reference 37, 160
FUNCTION subprogram 157–61, 173

GE 47
Generic functions 157
G format 119
Global variables 177, 189
GOTO
  assigned 56
  computed 55
  unconditional 51–54, 57
GT 47

Hexadecimal constants 101
H format 123
Hollerith 123

I format 117
IF
  arithmetic 54
  block 43–7
  logical 51, 57
IMPLICIT 95, 101
Implied DO 115, 116, 130
Incrementation parameter of a DO 60
Initialization 34, 97, 184
Initial parameter of a DO 60
Input device 3
INQUIRE 139, 149
INTEGER declaration 80, 101
Integer
  constant 17
  variable 18, 80
Internal files 142, 148
INTRINSIC 154, 173
Intrinsic function 37, 154
IOSTAT = 134, 148, 149
I/O
  list 25, 109
  unit 25, 105

Label 10, 22, 56
Labelled COMMON 182
Layout of FORTRAN programs 10, 22
LE 47
L format 125
Lineprinter 31, 124
List-directed 25, 39, 104, 112, 130
Local variables 160, 176, 189
Logical
  assignments 93
  constants 93
  declarations 80, 101
  expressions 47, 93
  IF 51, 57
  operators 47, 93
  variables 93
LOGICAL 93, 101
Loop
  DO 60, 77
  variable 60, 77
LT 47

Machine language 8
Main program 152

Mixed mode arithmetic 101
Module mode 52
Multi-dimensioned arrays 73, 78
Multiple entry points 170
Multiple return 170

NAME = 140, 149
Named COMMON 182, 190
Named file 136, 140
NAMED = 140, 149
Name, symbolic 14, 22
NE 47
NEQV 47
Nested
  loops 66
  IF 46
NEXTREC = 140, 149
Normalized 20
NOT 47
NUMBER = 140, 149

Octal constant 101
Operand 29
Operators
  arithmetic 29, 40
  logical 47, 93
  priority of 21, 40, 49
  relational 47
  usary 30
OPEN 136, 149
OPENED = 140, 149
OR 47
Order of evaluation 31, 49
Order of statements 153
Output device 3

PARAMETER 96, 102
Parameters of a DO loop 60
PAUSE 128
Portability 9
Preconnected 134, 136
PRINT 27, 39, 106, 130
Priority of operators 31, 40, 49
PROGRAM 13, 22, 152, 173
Program
  object 37
  source 37
  unit 151

P scale factor 127

Random access 133
READ statement 39, 130
  formatted 105, 107, 130
  unformatted 107
REAL declaration 80, 101
Real
  constant 17
  variable 18, 80
Record 133, 148
REC = 134, 148
RECL = 137, 140, 149
Recursion 163
Relational
  expressions 43, 47
  operators 47
Repetition factor 113
Rescan 109, 113, 126
RETURN statement 157, 170, 173
REWIND 146, 149
Run-time formats 128

SAVE 185, 190
Scale factors 127
Scan 108, 113, 126
Sequential access 133, 148
SEQUENTIAL = 140, 149
S format 120
SP format 120
SS format 120
Slash 125
Sorting 76
Statement function 155, 174
Statement numbers 10
Statement order 153
STATUS = 136, 139, 149
STOP statement 36, 40, 179
String 82, 86
Structured programming 6
Subprogram 151
SUBROUTINE statement 161, 173
Subroutine subprogram 161
Subscripted variables 69
Subscripts 69
Substring 86
Symbolic names 14, 22

Terminal parameter of a DO 60
T format 126
TL format 126
TR format 126
THEN 43–7, 57
Transfer of control 43
Translator 8
Type
  conversion 34, 38, 99–101, 154, 194, 195
  statements 80, 101

Unary operator 30
Unconditional GOTO 51–4
UNFORMATTED – 140, 149
Unformatted I/O
  READ 107, 130

WRITE 107, 130
Unit 25, 105
UNIT = 105, 130, 149

Variable dimensions 167
Variables
  subscripted 69
  symbolic name 14

Word 2
WRITE statement
  formatted 106, 130
  unformatted 107, 130

X format 121

Zero blank significance 137